Connecting Math Concepts

Siegfried Engelmann
Bernadette Kelly
Douglas Carnine

LEVEL F

TEXTBOOK

Copyright © 1996 SRA/McGraw-Hill. All rights reserved. Except as permitted under the United States Copyright Act, no part of this publication may be reproduced or distributed in any form or by any means, or stored in a database or retrieval system, without the prior written permission of the publisher.

Printed in the United States of America.

Send all inquiries to:
SRA/McGraw-Hill
250 Old Wilson Bridge Road
Suite 310
Worthington, OH 43085

ISBN: 0-574-15674-7

2 3 4 5 6 7 8 9 10   RRC   99 98 97 96

Connecting Math Concepts
Level F

Connecting Math Concepts will teach you a great deal about doing mathematics. When something new is introduced, your teacher will show you how to work the problems. Later, you'll work the problems on your own, without help.

Remember, everything that is introduced is important. It is knowledge you will need to work difficult problems that will be introduced later.

You must follow your teacher's directions. Your teacher sometimes will direct you to work **part** of a problem, sometimes a **whole** problem, and sometimes a group of problems.

Listen very carefully to the directions. Work quickly and accurately. Most important of all, work hard. You'll be rewarded with math skills that will surprise you.

Lesson 1

Part 1

- Here's how to change mixed numbers into fractions:

✔ Start with the denominator.

$5\frac{2}{3} = \boxed{}$

✔ Multiply that value by the **whole number**.
✔ Then add the numerator of the fraction.

$5\frac{2}{3} = \frac{15 + 2}{3}$

- So the fraction that equals $5\frac{2}{3}$ is $\frac{17}{3}$.

$5\frac{2}{3} = \frac{17}{3}$

Part 2

Copy and complete each equation. Write the fraction that equals each mixed number.

Sample problem
$5\frac{1}{4} = \boxed{}$

a. $2\frac{5}{6} = \boxed{}$

b. $7\frac{5}{9} = \boxed{}$

c. $1\frac{7}{8} = \boxed{}$

d. $10\frac{2}{5} = \boxed{}$

Part 3

Copy and complete each equation. Write the decimal value that equals each fraction.

a. $\frac{24}{100} = \boxed{}$

b. $\frac{3}{100} = \boxed{}$

c. $\frac{4}{10} = \boxed{}$

d. $\frac{80}{100} = \boxed{}$

e. $\frac{95}{1000} = \boxed{}$

Part 4

- Every operation has an opposite operation that can be used to "undo" the original operation. The undoing operation is called the inverse operation.
- Here is each operation and its inverse:

Operation	Inverse Operation
addition (+) →	← subtraction (−)
subtraction (−) →	← addition (+)
multiplication (×) →	← division (÷)
division (÷) →	← multiplication (×)

Part 5 For each item, write the undoing problem and the answer.

Sample problems
1. ■ × 3 = 42   2. ■ − 10 = 85

a. ■ + 14 = 100   b. ■ ÷ 2 = 51   c. ■ × 5 = 95

d. ■ ÷ 7 = 49   e. ■ − 28 = 71

Part 6

- You're going to work mixed number problems with fractions that are **too large**.

$$3\frac{70}{60} = \boxed{}$$

$$\frac{70}{60} = \frac{60}{60} + \frac{10}{60} = 1\frac{10}{60}$$

$$3 + 1\frac{10}{60} = 4\frac{10}{60}$$

$$3\frac{70}{60} = 4\frac{10}{60}$$

- Remember:
  ✔ Change the fraction into a mixed number.
  ✔ Add that mixed number to the original whole number.
  ✔ Write the answer as the new mixed number.

Part 7 Copy and complete each equation. Figure out the proper mixed number for each item.

Sample problem 1   *Sample problem 2*

$$7\frac{5}{4} = \boxed{} \qquad 2\frac{9}{5} = \boxed{}$$

a. $2\frac{13}{9} = \boxed{}$ b. $6\frac{5}{3} = \boxed{}$ c. $4\frac{17}{10} = \boxed{}$

d. $3\frac{22}{12} = \boxed{}$ e. $9\frac{8}{7} = \boxed{}$

Part 8

- You've learned that if the decimal part of a number is **hundredths,** it ends two places after the decimal point.
- If the decimal part is **thousandths,** it ends three places after the decimal point.
- To write those values, you may need zeros **before** the last digit.
- There's a big difference between decimal numbers and whole numbers. If you make zeros **after** the whole number 7, you make numbers that are bigger.
- But if you make zeros after a decimal number, the number **does not get bigger.**
- All these decimal numbers show exactly the same value. They all equal 4.7.
- Remember, zeros after the last digit of a decimal number do not change the value.

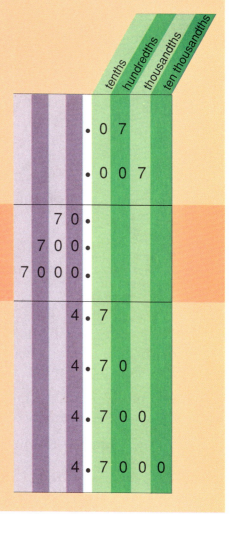

Part 9 Write each equation to show the simplified decimal number.

a. 5.400 = ▬

b. 21.50 = ▬

c. 8.4700 = ▬

d. 2.04000 = ▬

Lesson 1 5

Part 10

- The area of a figure is the number of squares inside the figure.

- You can use the equation for the area of a rectangle to find the area of any square, any rectangle, or any other parallelogram.

  - The equation is: **Area = base x height**

    or

    base x height = Area

- The area is always square units.

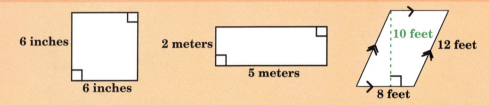

- Notice that the parallelogram has a dotted line that shows the **height.** You cannot use the length of a side for the height of that figure. You must use **10 feet.**

- Remember, you find the area of any of these figures with the equation: **b x h = A**

- The unit name is not just **inches** or **feet,** but **square inches** or **square feet.**

Part 11 Find the area of each figure. Use the equation: **b x h = A.**

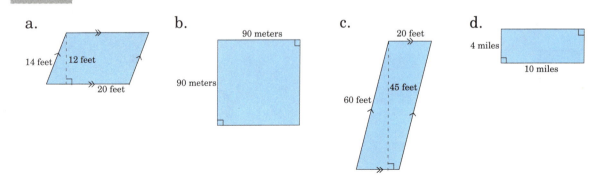

6   Lesson 1

Independent Work

Part 12 Copy and work each problem. Show each answer as a fraction.

a. $\frac{4}{3} + \frac{12}{5} =$

b. $\frac{13}{20} - \frac{11}{20} =$

c. $\frac{11}{17} + \frac{0}{17} =$

d. $\frac{7}{9} \times \frac{1}{3} =$

e. $\frac{2}{5} \times \frac{7}{5} =$

f. $5 \times \frac{1}{9} =$

Part 13 Copy and work each problem. Show the answer as a whole number or a mixed number.

a. $7\overline{)271}$

b. $9\overline{)271}$

c. $3\overline{)271}$

d. $20\overline{)58}$

Part 14 Use inverse operations to solve each problem. Write the undoing problem and the answer.

a. ■ − 8 = 190

b. ■ + 27 = 200

c. ■ ÷ 3 = 60

Not **those** kind of square feet.

Lesson 1

Lesson 2

Part 1 Copy and complete each equation. Show the decimal value that equals each fraction.

> **Rules**
> ✔ First write the **digits** that are in the **numerator**.
> ✔ Then look at the **denominator** to see how many decimal places you need.

Sample problem
$$\frac{342}{100} = \blacksquare$$

a. $\frac{152}{10} = \blacksquare$ b. $\frac{1321}{1000} = \blacksquare$ c. $\frac{2001}{100} = \blacksquare$ d. $\frac{80}{10} = \blacksquare$

Part 2 For each item, write the undoing problem and the answer.

a. ■ x 4 = 60 b. ■ + 17 = 55 c. ■ + 20 = 48

d. ■ ÷ 5 = 25 e. ■ x 8 = 40

Part 3 For each item, write an equation to show the mixed number and the fraction it equals.

a. $2\frac{3}{4} = \blacksquare$ b. $7\frac{1}{3} = \blacksquare$ c. $6\frac{9}{10} = \blacksquare$ d. $1\frac{5}{9} = \blacksquare$

Part 4 For each value that can be simplified, write the simplified value.

a. 14.07 b. 8.20 c. 6.001 d. 5.090 e. 12.400

Part 5

Write an equation that shows the proper mixed number for each mixed number shown.

a. $4\frac{15}{8} =$ ▮   b. $5\frac{9}{7} =$ ▮   c. $1\frac{10}{6} =$ ▮

d. $3\frac{14}{9} =$ ▮   e. $9\frac{11}{8} =$ ▮

Part 6

- You're going to add and subtract decimal values. The decimal points must be lined up.
- Here are three values to be added: $4.2 + 9.079 + 243.53$
- Here they are written with the decimal points lined up:

$$\begin{array}{r} 4.2 \\ 9.079 \\ + \ 243.53 \\ \hline \end{array}$$

- Before you add, you make zeros so that all the values have digits to the thousandths.
- Remember, adding zeros **after** the last digit of a decimal value does not change the value.

$$\begin{array}{r} 4.200 \\ 9.079 \\ + \ 243.530 \\ \hline \boxed{256.809} \end{array}$$

- Remember:
  ✔ Line up the decimal points.
  ✔ Make zeros so that all the numbers end at the same decimal place.
  ✔ Add.

Part 7

Rewrite each problem in columns, then work it.

a. $16.42 + 11.205 + .6$
b. $130.02 + 6.005 + 90.2$
c. $12.1 + .9 + .36$

Part 8 Find the area of each figure.

a.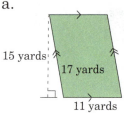

b.

Part 9 Find the perimeter of each figure.

a.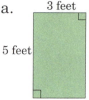

b.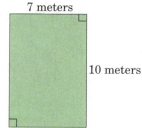

c.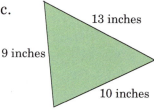

Independent Work

Part 10 For each problem, make the ratio equation. Answer the question the problem asks. The answer must have a number and a unit name.

  a. If it takes a runner 11 seconds to run 30 feet, how many feet would the runner travel in 55 seconds?

  b. 4 tires cost $200. How much do 12 tires cost?

  c. If 9 identical drapes weigh 99 ounces, how much do 54 drapes weigh?

Part 11 Use inverse operations to solve each problem. Write the undoing problem and the answer.

  a. ■ + 100 = 113
  b. ■ x 6 = 300
  c. ■ − 45 = 0

Part 12 Copy and complete each equation to show the fraction and the decimal value.

  a. $\frac{2}{100}$ = ■
  b. $\frac{12}{100}$ = ■
  c. $\frac{7}{10}$ = ■
  d. $\frac{14}{1000}$ = ■

Part 13 Use the inequality sign (> or <) to write the complete statement for each item.

  a. $\frac{2}{5}$ ■ 1
  b. $\frac{7}{8}$ ■ $\frac{8}{7}$
  c. $\frac{12}{13}$ ■ $\frac{11}{13}$

Lesson 3

Part 1 For each item, write an equation. Show the fraction and the decimal value it equals.

a. $\dfrac{1508}{1000} = \blacksquare$ b. $\dfrac{115}{10} = \blacksquare$ c. $\dfrac{627}{100} = \blacksquare$ d. $\dfrac{768}{10} = \blacksquare$

Part 2 Write each problem in columns and work it.

a. 25.8 − 8.94 b. 8.44 − 3.27 c. 20.002 − 16.1

Part 3 Copy and complete the table.

Sample 1 $4\dfrac{7}{10}$
Sample 2 $6\dfrac{15}{1000}$

	Mixed number	Decimal
a.	$4\dfrac{3}{100}$	
b.		11.041
c.		8.12
d.	$3\dfrac{5}{10}$	

Part 4 Copy each item. Figure out the mystery number.

Sample problem $\blacksquare - 11 = \overset{?}{\blacksquare}$
$\blacksquare \times 2 = 8$

a. $\blacksquare \times 4 = \overset{?}{\blacksquare}$
   $\blacksquare - 12 = 48$

b. $\blacksquare + 17 = \overset{?}{\blacksquare}$
   $\blacksquare \div 5 = 11$

c. $\blacksquare \times 2 = \overset{?}{\blacksquare}$
   $\blacksquare \div 7 = 6$

d. $\blacksquare - 8 = \overset{?}{\blacksquare}$
   $\blacksquare + 3 = 20$

Part 5
Write an equation that shows the proper mixed number for each mixed number shown.

a. $3\frac{8}{5} = $ ▮   b. $1\frac{11}{6} = $ ▮   c. $7\frac{10}{7} = $ ▮

d. $8\frac{15}{10} = $ ▮   e. $10\frac{17}{9} = $ ▮

Part 6
For each item, write an equation to show the mixed number and the fraction it equals.

a. $2\frac{7}{8} = $ ▮   b. $8\frac{1}{4} = $ ▮   c. $3\frac{2}{5} = $ ▮   d. $4\frac{5}{7} = $ ▮

Part 7
Find the area of each figure. Find the perimeter of each figure.

a.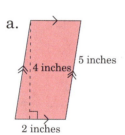

b.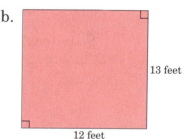

Independent Work

Part 8
For each item, write the complete equation. Use an inequality sign or the equal sign.

a. $\frac{5}{5}$ ▮ 1 b. $\frac{13}{12}$ ▮ $\frac{12}{12}$

c. $\frac{3}{10}$ ▮ $\frac{4}{10}$ d. $\frac{4}{10}$ ▮ $.4$

Part 9
Use inverse operations to solve each problem.

a. ▮ $\div 13 = 26$ b. ▮ $+ 17 = 30$

c. ▮ $- 70 = 80$ d. ▮ $\times 5 = 100$

Part 10 For each problem, make the ratio equation. Answer the question the problem asks. The answer must have a number and a unit name.

a. A machine makes 5 buttons every 6 seconds. How many buttons would the machine make in 54 seconds?

b. There are 18 edges on 2 identical prisms. How many identical prisms would have 198 edges?

c. The ratio of used cars to new cars is 7 to 5. If there are 714 used cars, how many new cars are there?

Part 11 Copy and work each problem.

a. $7 \times \frac{2}{3} = \blacksquare$

b. $\frac{2}{9} \times \frac{10}{9} = \blacksquare$

c. $\frac{1}{2} \times \frac{5}{8} = \blacksquare$

d. $\frac{7}{3} + \frac{11}{3} = \blacksquare$

e. $\frac{17}{8} - \frac{9}{8} = \blacksquare$

Part 12 For each value that can be simplified, write the simplified value.

a. 4.05

b. 10.600

c. 1.050

d. 100.58

Lesson 3   13

Lesson 4

Part 1

- You can express any fraction that is more than 1 as a mixed number or a whole number by working a division problem.

  Here's: $\dfrac{56}{9}$

- You can figure out what it equals by working the problem: $9\overline{)56}$

  The answer is: $9\overline{)56} \rightarrow 6\dfrac{2}{9}$

- Remember, if the fraction is more than 1, you can work a division problem to figure out the mixed number or a whole number it equals.

Part 2   For each fraction that is more than 1, figure out the mixed number it equals.

a. $\dfrac{50}{3}$ b. $\dfrac{30}{50}$ c. $\dfrac{7}{2}$ d. $\dfrac{28}{5}$ e. $\dfrac{16}{20}$ f. $\dfrac{200}{6}$ g. $\dfrac{8}{90}$

Part 3   Write each problem in columns and work it.

a. 110.4 − 8.972   b. 4.02 − 3.096   c. 3.468 + 12.123

Part 4 Copy and complete the table.

	Mixed number	Fraction
a.		$\frac{26}{3}$
b.	$5\frac{1}{4}$	
c.		$\frac{19}{7}$
d.		$\frac{62}{9}$
e.	$10\frac{5}{6}$	
f.	$3\frac{10}{11}$	

Part 5 Copy each problem. Figure out the mystery number.

a. ?
   ■ − 7 = ■
       ■ x 2 = ■
           ■ + 10 = 16

b. ?
   ■ ÷ 3 = ■
       ■ + 18 = ■
           ■ x 2 = 76

c. ?
   ■ x 7 = ■
       ■ − 10 = ■
           ■ ÷ 2 = 23

d. ?
   ■ + 15 = ■
       ■ + 20 = ■
           ■ ÷ 10 = 10

Part 6 Copy and complete the table.

	Fraction	Decimal	Mixed number
a.	$\frac{789}{10}$		
b.	$\frac{105}{100}$		
c.	$\frac{1949}{100}$		
d.	$\frac{2018}{1000}$		
e.	$\frac{86}{10}$		

Lesson 4

Independent Work

Part 7 Write an equation that shows the proper mixed number for each mixed number shown.

a. $2\frac{7}{5} = $ ■   b. $5\frac{11}{7} = $ ■   c. $8\frac{15}{10} = $ ■   d. $1\frac{25}{24} = $ ■

Part 8 Find the perimeter of each figure.

a. rectangle: 5 feet by 8 feet

b. triangle: 4 inches, 11 inches, 7 inches

c. pentagon: 5 feet, 8 feet, 6 feet, 9 feet, 10 feet

Part 9 Copy and complete each problem. Use inverse operations to find each mystery number.

a. ?
■ x 3 = ■
■ − 5 = 40

b. ?
■ − 265 = ■
■ ÷ 2 = 20

c. ?
■ x 2 = ■
■ − 56 = 4

Part 10 For each item, write the complete equation. Use an inequality sign or the equal sign.

a. $\frac{50}{100}$ ■ $.42$ b. $\frac{40}{100}$ ■ $.32$ c. 1.6 ■ $1\frac{6}{10}$

Part 11 For each problem, make the ratio equation. Answer the question the problem asks. The answer must have a number and a unit name.

a. If 3 tires cost $75, how many tires could a person buy for $150?

b. 4 identical bugs weigh 3 grams. How much do 12 identical bugs weigh?

c. Rhonda saves $3,000 every 3 years. How long will it take her to save $15,000?

16 Lesson 4

Lesson 5

Part 1

- You've changed improper mixed numbers into proper mixed numbers.

    $8\frac{7}{5} =$ ▮

- You did that by changing the fraction into a mixed number.

    $8 + 1\frac{2}{5} = 9\frac{2}{5}$

    So: $8\frac{7}{5} = 9\frac{2}{5}$

- You can also work any of those items by writing the fraction as a division problem.

    - Here's: $3\frac{9}{7} =$ ▮

- You can write the fraction as a divison problem: 9 divided by 7. The answer is $1\frac{2}{7}$.

- You add $1\frac{2}{7}$ to 3 and you have the proper mixed number: $4\frac{2}{7}$.

    $3 + 1\frac{2}{7} = 4\frac{2}{7}$

    So: $3\frac{9}{7} = 4\frac{2}{7}$

- When you work the fraction as a division problem, you can deal with any improper fraction, even those that are much larger than 1.

    - Here's: $3\frac{47}{5} =$ ▮

- The fraction is 47 divided by 5. That's $9\frac{2}{5}$.

- You add $9\frac{2}{5}$ to 3. That gives the proper mixed number: $12\frac{2}{5}$.

    $3 + 9\frac{2}{5} = 12\frac{2}{5}$

    So: $3\frac{47}{5} = 12\frac{2}{5}$

- Remember, write the fraction as a division problem. Add the answer to the whole number in the original mixed number.

Part 2 For each improper mixed number, write an equation to show the proper mixed number it equals.

a. $5\frac{11}{12}$ b. $4\frac{38}{5}$ c. $7\frac{3}{20}$ d. $4\frac{15}{9}$

e. $2\frac{96}{10}$ f. $1\frac{45}{6}$ g. $8\frac{52}{100}$ h. $3\frac{13}{8}$

Part 3

- You've treated fractions as division problems. You can also treat division problems as fractions.

  - Here's: $3\overline{)46}$

- You can show that problem as the fraction: $\frac{46}{3}$

  - Here's: $2\overline{)11}$

- You can show that problem as the fraction: $\frac{11}{2}$

- For some items, you can show a fraction instead of working a division problem.

  - Here's a problem: $\blacksquare \times 7 = 9$

- The first number is missing. You can figure out the missing number by working a division problem: $7\overline{)9}$

- You can also show the missing value as the fraction: $\frac{9}{7}$

  - Here's the complete equation: $\boxed{\frac{9}{7}} \times 7 = 9$

Part 4 For each item, write the complete equation. Show the missing value as a fraction.

a. ■ x 4 = 3   b. ■ x 8 = 5

c. ■ x 16 = 8   d. ■ x 10 = 7

Part 5 Here are the steps on your calculator to check problem **a** in part 4.

a. $\frac{3}{4}$ x 4 = 3

[3] [÷] [4] [X] [4] [=]

Part 6 Figure out the mystery number for each item.

> *Sample problem*
> You start with some number and add 14.   ■ + 14 = ?■
> You divide by 3 and end up with 5.   ■ ÷ 3 = 5
> What's the mystery number?

a. You start with some number and divide by 6. You add 9 and end up with 12. What's the mystery number?

b. You start with some number and multiply by 7. You divide by 2 and end up with 21. What's the mystery number?

c. You start with some number and divide by 4. Then you add 15. You end up with 20. What's the mystery number?

d. You start with a number and multiply by 8. Then you subtract 50. You end up with 38. What's the mystery number?

Lesson 5   19

Part 7

- Your calculator shows all whole numbers with a decimal point after them. `354.` `10.` `180.`
- That's because you can add a decimal point to the end of any whole number without changing the value of the number. You can also add zeros **after the decimal point** without changing the value.
- You can write 45 as 45 with a decimal point, 45 with a decimal point and 1 zero or 45 with a decimal point and 4 zeros. They all equal 45.

  45.
  45.0
  45.0000

- You can use your calculator to show that 45.00 equals 45.
- Remember, a decimal point and zeros at the end of a whole number don't change the value.

Part 8 Write each problem in columns and work it.

a. 120 + .2 + 3.34   b. 11.34 − 7   c. 93 − 51.41

Part 9 Copy and complete the table.

	Fraction	Decimal	Mixed number
a.	$\frac{403}{10}$		
b.	$\frac{5008}{1000}$		
c.	$\frac{115}{100}$		
d.	$\frac{61}{10}$		

Independent Work

Part 10 Write an equation that shows the proper mixed number for each mixed number shown.

a. $3\frac{9}{5}$ = ▇

b. $2\frac{26}{20}$ = ▇

c. $9\frac{5}{4}$ = ▇

Part 11 Copy and complete the table.

	Mixed number	Fraction
a.		$\frac{11}{3}$
b.		$\frac{12}{10}$
c.	$4\frac{1}{8}$	
d.	$6\frac{4}{9}$	

Part 12 Copy each problem. Use inverse operations to figure out each mystery number.

a. ▇ − 300 = ?
   ▇ × 4 = 400

b. ▇ + 175 = ?
   ▇ ÷ 2 = 100

c. ▇ × 8 = ?
   ▇ − 40 = 56

Part 13 For each problem, make the ratio equation. Answer the question the problem asks. The answer must have a number and a unit name.

a. There are 24 square inches in every 4 tiles. If there are 960 square inches, how many tiles are there?

b. The ratio of girls to boys at Gregory School is 11 to 10. There are 140 boys in the school. How many girls are in the school?

c. A recipe calls for 3 onions for every 7 potatoes. If a military cook uses 42 onions, how many potatoes are needed?

Part 14 Write each problem in columns and work it.

a. .421 − .06

b. 56.3 + 5.63

Lesson 5

Lesson 6

Part 1 For each improper mixed number, write an equation to show the proper mixed number it equals.

a. $5\frac{61}{30}$ b. $2\frac{17}{20}$ c. $1\frac{14}{10}$ d. $8\frac{3}{5}$

e. $5\frac{17}{4}$ f. $3\frac{28}{30}$ g. $9\frac{23}{5}$

Part 2 Write the equation to show the fraction that equals each decimal value.

a. 3.05 = ▮   b. 11.4 = ▮   c. 4.058 = ▮

d. 11.28 = ▮   e. 2.8 = ▮

Part 3

- You've learned that you can write a division problem as a fraction.
- The missing fraction is the same for both these problems: ▮ x 8 = 3   8 x ▮ = 3
- For both problems, the missing value is 3 ÷ 8. That's the same as $\frac{3}{8}$. $\frac{3}{8}$ x 8 = 3   8 x $\frac{3}{8}$ = 3

Part 4 For each item, write the complete equation. Show the missing value as a fraction.

a. 10 x ▮ = 6   b. 5 x ▮ = 4   c. ▮ x 8 = 15

d. 20 x ▮ = 38   e. ▮ x 11 = 52

Part 5

- You're going to write equations for word problems. Some of the problems refer to **doubling, tripling** or making something **twice as large.**
- To **double** any number, you multiply by 2. ■ x 2 = ■
- To **triple** any number, you multiply by 3. ■ x 3 = ■
- To make a number **twice as large,** you multiply by 2. ■ x 2 = ■

Part 6

Write an equation for each item.

a. She started out with some money and then tripled it.

b. The elephant calf was twice as heavy at the end of the month as it was at the beginning of the month.

c. The shop started out with some shoes. After the delivery, the number of shoes had tripled.

d. Sam doubled the number of baseball cards he had.

Part 7

Figure out the mystery number for each item.

a. You start with a number and subtract 20. You multiply by 8 and end up with 64. What's the mystery number?

b. You start with a number and divide by 10. Then you subtract 5. You end up with 3. What's the mystery number?

c. You start with a number and multiply by 7. Then you divide by 9. The answer is 14. What's the mystery number?

d. You start with a number and add 17. Then you add 38. You end up with 55. What's the mystery number?

Lesson 6

Part 8

- You've learned to write fractions as whole numbers or mixed numbers. You read the fraction as a division problem and work it.

- That procedure works with any fraction:

$$\frac{29}{4} \qquad 4\overline{)29} = 7\frac{1}{4}$$

$$\frac{37}{10} \qquad 10\overline{)37} = 3\frac{7}{10}$$

- But for some fractions, you don't have to work the division. Those are fractions that have denominators of 10, 100 or 1,000.

$$\frac{\blacksquare}{10} \quad \frac{\blacksquare}{100} \quad \frac{\blacksquare}{1000}$$

- For those fractions, you can write a decimal value, then write the mixed number for that decimal value.

$$\frac{125}{100} = 1.25 = 1\frac{25}{100}$$

- For some of these fractions, you divide. For others, you write the decimal number, then the mixed number for that decimal value.

$$\frac{13}{4} \qquad \frac{237}{100} \qquad \frac{15}{10} \qquad \frac{26}{20} \qquad \frac{1002}{1000}$$

Part 9

Copy each fraction. Show the mixed number it equals.

a. $\frac{258}{10} = \blacksquare$

b. $\frac{10}{4} = \blacksquare$

c. $\frac{17}{15} = \blacksquare$

d. $\frac{4201}{1000} = \blacksquare$

e. $\frac{600}{100} = \blacksquare$

Independent Work

Part 10 Write each problem in columns and work it.

a. 5 − 3.15
b. 10 − 2.6
c. 11.305 + 8 + 3.9
d. 10.3 + 246.21

Part 11 Copy and complete each equation. Write the missing value as a fraction.

a. ■ × 5 = 3
b. ■ × 4 = 7
c. ■ × 100 = 1
d. ■ × 9 = 2

Part 12 Figure out the mystery number for each item.

a. ?
  ■ × 7 = ■
  ■ − 10 = ■
  ■ × 3 = 75

b. ?
  ■ ÷ 3 = ■
  ■ + 25 = ■
  ■ − 35 = 0

Part 13 For each problem, make the ratio equation. Answer the question the problem asks. The answer must have a number and a unit name.

a. The ratio of fish to alligators in Dino Pond is 8 to 5. If there are 40 alligators in the pond, how many fish are there?

b. A train travels at a steady rate of 58 miles per hour. How long does it take for the train to travel 232 miles?

c. If 4 identical stamps cost 52¢, how much do 5 stamps cost?

Part 14 Find the area of each figure. Find the perimeter of each figure.

a.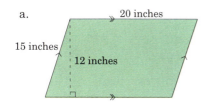
20 inches, 15 inches, 12 inches

b.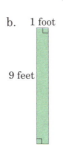
1 foot, 9 feet

Part 15 Copy and complete the table.

	Mixed number	Fraction
a.	$3\frac{2}{10}$	
b.		$\frac{91}{20}$
c.		$\frac{201}{100}$
d.	$36\frac{1}{2}$	
e.	$5\frac{3}{5}$	

Lesson 7

Part 1 Copy and complete each fraction number family.

> Here are the rules for these families:
> ✔ Each family has three fractions.
> ✔ The value at the end of the arrow is 1.
> ✔ The other values are less than 1.
> ✔ All the values are shown as fractions.
> ✔ All fractions have the same denominator.

Sample $\frac{11}{15}$ ➡ ▮ ▮

a. ▮ $\frac{7}{19}$➡ ▮

b. $\frac{1}{45}$ ➡ ▮ ▮

c. ▮ $\frac{3}{7}$➡ ▮

d. $\frac{9}{50}$ ➡ ▮ ▮

Part 2

- You know that the denominator of a fraction tells the number of parts in each whole unit.
- The numerator tells the number of parts you use or have.
- If there are 4 parts in each unit and you use 3 parts, the fraction is $\frac{3}{4}$.
- Here's the number line:

- If there are 12 parts in each unit and you use 15 parts, the fraction is $\frac{15}{12}$.
- Here's the number line:

Part 2 continued

- Related units, like **inches** and **feet,** can be shown as fractions. The **denominator** of the fraction tells how many parts are in each whole unit. The parts are inches. The whole unit is a foot.
- There are 12 inches in each foot. So the denominator is 12: $\frac{\blacksquare}{12}$
- The fraction for 6 inches is: $\frac{6}{12}$
- That tells you that there are 12 parts in each whole unit and you use 6 parts.
- The fraction for 17 inches is: $\frac{17}{12}$
- That's more than 1 whole unit. There are 12 parts in each unit. You use 17 parts.
- Remember, the smaller units are the parts. The denominator shows the number of parts in each whole unit.

Part 3 For each item, write the correct denominator.

There are 4 seasons in	1 year.
There are 12 months in	1 year.
There are 365 days in	1 year.
There are 3 feet in	1 yard.
There are 36 inches in	1 yard.
There are 24 hours in	1 day.
There are 60 minutes in	1 hour.
There are 60 seconds in	1 minute.

a. years and months
b. feet and yards
c. inches and yards
d. hours and minutes

Lesson 7

Part 4 Write fractions for each item.

a. There are 4 **seasons** in each **year.**

   1) What fraction shows 1 year?
   2) What fraction shows 9 seasons?
   3) What fraction shows 1 season?

b. There are 12 **months** in a **year.**

   1) What fraction shows 5 months?
   2) What fraction shows 1 year?
   3) What fraction shows 1 month?

c. There are 24 **hours** in a **day.**

   1) What fraction shows 36 hours?
   2) What fraction shows 1 hour?
   3) What fraction shows 1 day?

d. There are 100 **cents** in each **dollar.**

   1) What fraction shows 1 dollar?
   2) What fraction shows 1 cent?
   3) What fraction shows 75 cents?

Part 5 Write a complete equation for each item.

a.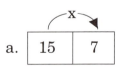

c.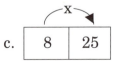

b. 3 × 19 (arrow)

Part 6 Copy and complete the table.

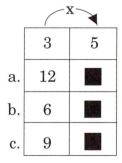

Part 7 Write the complete equation to show the whole number or mixed number for each fraction.

a. $\dfrac{521}{100} = \blacksquare$ b. $\dfrac{640}{10} = \blacksquare$ c. $\dfrac{11}{5} = \blacksquare$ d. $\dfrac{68}{10} = \blacksquare$

Part 8 For each item, make two equations and figure out the mystery number.

a. Sam had some money in the bank. Then he took $28 from his account. Then he put $20 into his account. His account ended up with $90. How much money did Sam have in his account to begin with?

b. A train started out with some people in it. After the first stop, there were twice as many people in the train. After 38 people got off at the second stop, there were 120 people on the train. How many people were in the train at the start of the journey?

c. A delivery truck set out with some bicycles in it. In the morning it delivered 35 bicycles. After a visit to the warehouse, the number of bicycles in the truck tripled. There were now 60 bicycles in the truck. How many bicycles were in the truck to begin with?

Independent Work

Part 9 Write each problem in columns and work it.

  a. 3.26 − 1.79   b. 13 − 4.07   c. 26.3 + 8.906   d. 15.1 + .26 + 1.08

Part 10 Figure out the mystery number for each item.

a. ?
■ − 26 = ■
■ × 3 = ■
■ + 200 = 200

b. ?
■ × 4 = ■
■ − 25 = ■
■ ÷ 5 = 75

Part 11 Copy and complete the table.

	Fraction	Decimal	Mixed number
a.	$\frac{426}{100}$		
b.		3.8	
c.			$144\frac{6}{10}$
d.	$\frac{365}{100}$		

Part 12 For each problem, make the ratio equation. Answer the question the problem asks. The answer must have a number and a unit name.

a. In Franklin Park, the ratio of sparrows to worms is 3 to 11. There are 600 sparrows in Franklin Park. How many worms are there?

b. It takes a machine 36 minutes to make 3 patterns. How many patterns could the machine make in 720 minutes?

c. A truck travels 56 miles each hour. How long would it take for the truck to travel 168 miles?

Part 13 Copy and complete each equation. Write the missing value as a fraction.

  a. ■ × 620 = 500   b. ■ × 13 = 600   c. ■ × 4 = 7   d. ■ × 7 = 4

Lesson 8

Part 1 For each item, refer to the table to find the right denominator. Then answer the questions.

There are 4 seasons in	1 year.
There are 12 months in	1 year.
There are 52 weeks in	1 year.
There are 365 days in	1 year.
There are 3 feet in	1 yard.
There are 36 inches in	1 yard.

a. For this item, the parts of a **year** are **weeks.**

   1) What fraction shows 83 weeks?

   2) What fraction shows 1 week?

   3) What fraction shows 1 year?

b. For this item, the parts of a **year** are **months.**

   1) What fraction shows 1 year?

   2) What fraction shows 3 months?

   3) What fraction shows 9 months?

c. For this item, the parts of a **yard** are **inches.**

   1) What fraction shows 1 inch?

   2) What fraction shows 72 inches?

   3) What fraction shows 1 yard?

Part 2

- When you **multiply decimal values,** you don't have to line up the decimal points.

- Here's how you work the problems:
    - ✓ First, multiply and write the digits in the answer.
    - ✓ Then count all the decimal places in the values that are multiplied.
    - ✓ Show the same number of decimal places in the answer.

```
  .95
x  .4
  380
```

```
  .95  ⎤
x  .4  ⎦ 3 places
 .380
 3 places
```

Part 3   Write each item as a column problem and work it.

> **Sample problem**   1.38 x .2

a. 2.6 x .05   b. 8.08 x .51   c. 9.02 x .6   d. 8.5 x 1.4

Part 4   Use inverse operations to solve each problem.

a. Sam weighed too much so he went on a diet. He lost 13 pounds during the summer. In the fall, he lost 11 more pounds. He ended up weighing 185 pounds. What was his starting weight?

b. A large elevator started out with many people in it. After it stopped at the second floor, the number of people in the elevator had been divided by 3. On the fifth floor, 12 people got in the elevator. The number of people in the elevator was now 25. How many people were in the elevator when it started out?

c. A delivery truck started out with packages in it. After it picked up more packages, the number of packages in it doubled. At the next stop, the truck unloaded 79 packages. There were still 67 packages on the truck. How many packages were in the truck to begin with?

d. A company was worth some money. After a good year, the value of the company tripled. During the next year, the company's value dropped by $40,000. The company was now worth $920,000. How much was the company worth to begin with?

Part 5 Copy and complete each table. Write the answers as whole numbers or mixed numbers.

Table 1 (× from 3 → 10)

	in	out
a.	7	■
b.	6	■
c.	4	■
d.	$\frac{3}{10}$	■

Table 2 (× from 9 → 8)

	in	out
a.	$\frac{10}{3}$	■
b.	$\frac{11}{5}$	■
c.	$\frac{9}{8}$	■
d.	18	■

Part 6 Copy and complete the number family. Box the fraction that answers the question.

$$\xrightarrow{\quad\text{green}\quad\text{other}\quad\text{bottles}\quad} \quad \frac{3}{11}$$

a. What's the fraction for the other bottles?

$$\xrightarrow{\quad\text{men}\quad\text{women}\quad\text{employees}\quad} \quad \frac{62}{84}$$

b. What's the fraction for all the employees?

$$\xrightarrow{\quad\text{good}\quad\text{defective}\quad\text{products}\quad} \quad \frac{97}{100}$$

c. What's the fraction for defective products?

$$\xrightarrow{\quad\text{wet}\quad\text{dry}\quad\text{umbrellas}\quad} \quad \frac{14}{25}$$

d. What's the fraction for wet umbrellas?

Lesson 8

Independent Work

Part 7 Copy and work each item. Write each answer as a whole number or mixed number.

a. $\frac{3}{5} \times 4 = \blacksquare$
b. $\frac{12}{5} - \frac{3}{5} = \blacksquare$
c. $\frac{1}{8} + \frac{7}{8} = \blacksquare$
d. $\frac{5}{8} \times \frac{11}{3} = \blacksquare$

Part 8 For each item, write an equation to show the proper mixed number.

a. $3\frac{26}{5}$
b. $7\frac{11}{9}$
c. $2\frac{80}{6}$
d. $1\frac{23}{3}$

Part 9 Find the area and perimeter of each figure.

a.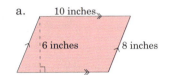
  10 inches, 6 inches, 8 inches

b. 20 miles, 28 miles

Part 10 Figure out the mystery number for each item.

a. $\blacksquare \div 12 = \overset{?}{\blacksquare}$
   $\blacksquare + 6 = 18$

b. $\blacksquare - 240 = \overset{?}{\blacksquare}$
   $\blacksquare \div 2 = 1$

Part 11 Copy and complete each equation. Write the missing value as a fraction.

a. $\blacksquare \times 6 = 7$
b. $\blacksquare \times 14 = 9$
c. $\blacksquare \times 120 = 205$

Part 12 Copy each equation and write the mixed number for each fraction.

a. $\frac{15}{4} = \blacksquare$
b. $\frac{525}{10} = \blacksquare$
c. $\frac{26}{10} = \blacksquare$
d. $\frac{444}{8} = \blacksquare$

Lesson 9

Part 1 For each item, answer the questions. Refer to the *Table of Weights and Measures* in the back of your textbook if you need to.

a. For this item, the parts of a **week** are **days**.

1) What fraction shows 3 days?
2) What fraction shows 7 days?
3) What fraction shows 48 days?

b. For this item, the parts of a **year** are **seasons**.

1) What fraction shows 7 seasons?
2) What fraction shows 4 seasons?
3) What fraction shows 1 year?

c. For this item, the parts of a **gallon** are **pints**.

1) What fraction shows 1 pint?
2) What fraction shows 1 gallon?
3) What fraction shows 45 pints?

d. For this item, the parts of a **gallon** are **quarts**.

1) What fraction shows 1 quart?
2) What fraction shows 4 quarts?
3) What fraction shows 6 quarts?

Part 2 Copy and complete each table.

a.

	x →
5	■
7	42
total ■	72

b.

	x →
15	■
■	2
total 25	■

c.

	x →
6	■
3	■
total ■	3

Part 3

- If problems add mixed numbers with the same denominator, you can work the problems by first adding the fractions, then adding the whole numbers.

- Here's: $3\frac{2}{7}$
  $+ 6\frac{1}{7}$

- The fractions have the same denominator, so you can add them: $\frac{3}{7}$

- Then you add the whole numbers:

  $3\frac{2}{7}$
  $+ 6\frac{1}{7}$
  $9\frac{3}{7}$

- The answer to the problem is $9\frac{3}{7}$.

- Remember, first work the fractions. Then work the whole numbers.

Part 4 Copy and work each item.

a. $11\frac{5}{8}$
    $- 8\frac{4}{8}$

b. $12\frac{5}{9}$
    $- 1\frac{2}{9}$

c. $\frac{2}{15}$
    $+ 7\frac{9}{15}$

d. $28\frac{1}{5}$
    $+ 2\frac{3}{5}$

Part 5

- Some problems that **add** or **subtract** have the middle number missing.

  $88 - \square = 14$

  $14 + \square = 88$

- You can always figure out the missing middle number by subtracting.

- To find the missing value in both the problems that are shown, you work the problem:

  $$\begin{array}{r} 88 \\ -14 \\ \hline 74 \end{array}$$

  $88 - \boxed{74} = 14$

- The missing value is **74**.

  $14 + \boxed{74} = 88$

- Remember, for addition problems or subtraction problems, you can find a missing middle value by subtracting.

Part 6

For each problem, make equations. Figure out the answer to the question the problem asks.

> **Sample** A car had 15 liters of gas in the tank. At the gas station, 20 more liters were put in the tank. The car used up some of the gas on a trip. At the end of the trip, the car had 4 liters in the tank. How many liters were used up on the trip?

a. A truck had 185 gallons of fuel. On a trip, it used up 96 gallons. The tank was filled after the trip. The tank now has 190 gallons in it. How much gas was put in the tank after the trip?

b. Dan started out with $24. Then he tripled that amount. Dan spent some money and ended up with $31. How much money did Dan spend?

c. Dolly had $500. A year later she had twice as much. The following year, the amount she had was multiplied by a different number. She ended up with $20,000. During the second year, the amount she had increased by how many times?

Lesson 9

Part 7 Copy and complete each number family. Box the fraction that answers the question.

```
    sick    well  animals
             78
            ——— ▶
             89
```

a. What's the fraction for sick animals?

```
    boys   girls  children
     9
    ——— ▶
    27
```

b. What's the fraction for the girls?

```
  cracked  uncracked  plates
    45
   ——— ▶
    55
```

c. What's the fraction for all the plates?

```
   odd    even   numbers
    7
   ——— ▶
    12
```

d. What's the fraction for the odd numbers?

I made a picture of $\frac{45}{55}$ of a plate.

No, Jim. The problem referred to $\frac{45}{55}$ of the **plates**.

38 Lesson 9

Independent Work

Part 8 Copy and complete the table.

	Fraction	Mixed number
a.	$\frac{23}{5}$	
b.		$2\frac{5}{7}$
c.		$13\frac{1}{10}$
d.	$\frac{56}{6}$	

Part 9 For each problem, write two equations. Figure out the mystery number and answer the question.

a. Mary started out with some money. She tripled the amount that she had. Then she spent $200. She ended up with $40. How much money did she start out with?

b. A train left the station with lots of passengers on board. At the first stop, 35 people got off the train and 82 got in the train. The train now had 212 passengers. How many passengers did the train have when it started out?

Part 10 Copy and complete each equation. Write the missing value as a fraction.

a. ■ x 7 = 10

b. 36 x ■ = 224

c. 12 (■) = 1

d. ■ x 50 = 86

Part 11 Copy and complete the table.

	Fraction	Decimal	Mixed number
a.			$3\frac{1}{10}$
b.		5.05	
c.	$\frac{311}{10}$		
d.			$8\frac{7}{100}$
e.			$1\frac{3}{10}$

Part 12 Write the complete equation that shows the proper mixed number for each improper mixed number.

a. $5\frac{17}{4}$

b. $1\frac{28}{23}$

Part 13 For each problem, make the ratio equation. Answer the question the problem asks. The answer must have a number and a unit name.

a. Every butterfly has 6 legs. In Mary's collection, there are 144 legs. How many butterflies are in her collection?

b. The ratio of old trees to saplings in Gregory Park is 2 to 15. There are 120 old trees in Gregory Park. How many saplings are in the park?

c. Jim spends $7 for every $3 he saves. Last year, Jim saved $900. How much did he spend?

Lesson 9

Lesson 10

Part 1 Copy and complete each number family and ratio table.

a.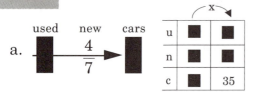

b.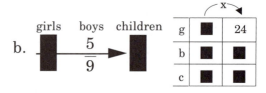

c.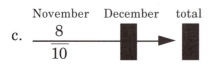

Part 2 Write each item as a column problem and work it.

a. .24 x 2.1   b. 11.5 x .7   c. 28.2 x .04   d. .65 x .21

Part 3 Copy and work each item.

a. $15\frac{4}{9}$
   $+20\frac{3}{9}$

b. $6\frac{3}{10}$
   $+12\frac{6}{10}$

c. $35\frac{8}{17}$
   $-1\frac{2}{17}$

Test 1

Part 1 Write a complete equation for each item. Show the proper mixed number for each improper mixed number.

a. $3\frac{12}{5}$ b. $12\frac{9}{2}$ c. $4\frac{16}{10}$

Part 2 Write each problem in columns and work it.

a. 4 + 2.76 + .8 b. 5.309 − 1.2

Part 3 Copy and complete the table.

	Fraction	Decimal	Mixed number
a.		3.26	
b.	$\frac{14}{10}$		
c.			$6\frac{3}{1000}$

Part 4 For each item, use inverse operations to figure out the mystery number.

a.
?
■ ÷ 5 = ■
■ + 200 = ■
■ × 3 = 618

b.
?
■ × 20 = ■
■ − 25 = 35

Part 5 For each item, make two equations. Figure out the mystery number and answer the question.

a. A store started out with some running shoes. The number of shoes in the store was doubled after a delivery. Then 42 pairs of those shoes were sold. The store now had 4 pairs left. How many pairs did the store start out with?

b. In the morning, a bin had lots of corn in it. By noon, the original amount had been divided by 3. In the afternoon, 36 tons of corn were added to the bin. Now the bin had 60 tons of corn in it. How much corn did the bin have to begin with?

Part 6
Copy and complete the table.

Mixed number	Fraction
a. $7\frac{5}{8}$	
b.	$\frac{45}{7}$
c. $10\frac{4}{5}$	

Part 7
Make the complete number family for each item.

a. girls boys children
   ⊢——$\frac{3}{8}$——▶

b. women men employees
   $\frac{330}{400}$

c. used new cars
   $\frac{84}{130}$

Part 8
Copy and complete each equation. Show the missing value as a fraction.

a. ■ x 6 = 212   b. 36 x ■ = 13   c. ■ x 84 = 2   d. 24 x ■ = 25

Part 9
Write the fractions.

> The units are **months** and **years**.

a. What fraction shows 1 month?
b. What fraction shows 1 year?
c. What fraction shows 36 months?

Lesson 11

Part 1 For each item, make a fraction number family and a ratio table. Answer the questions.

a. $\frac{2}{5}$ of the children were hungry. There were 33 children who were not hungry.

   1) How many children were hungry?
   2) How many children were there in all?

b. $\frac{3}{4}$ of the cars on the lot had good tires. There were 60 cars on the lot.

   1) How many had good tires?
   2) How many did not have good tires?

c. $\frac{11}{12}$ of the cartons were fresh. The rest were stale. There were 5 stale cartons.

   1) How many fresh cartons were there?
   2) How many cartons were there in all?

How can you find the stale cartons with those clothespins on your noses?

Part 2

- Here's an equivalent fraction problem:
- The **denominator** of the last fraction is missing.

$$\frac{4}{10}\left(\frac{}{}\right) = \frac{5}{\blacksquare}$$

- The fractions are equivalent. So you must multiply the first fraction by 1.

- To work the problem, you figure out what you multiply 4 by to get 5. The answer is $\frac{5}{4}$.

$$\frac{4}{10}\left(\frac{\frac{5}{4}}{}\right) = \frac{5}{\blacksquare}$$

- So the fraction that equals 1 is $\dfrac{\frac{5}{4}}{\frac{5}{4}}$.

$$\frac{4}{10}\left(\frac{\frac{5}{4}}{\frac{5}{4}}\right) = \frac{5}{\blacksquare}$$

- Now you just multiply on the bottom and write the missing value as a fraction. That's $\frac{50}{4}$.
- Then you rewrite the fraction as a mixed number. That's $12\frac{2}{4}$.

$$\frac{4}{10}\left(\frac{\frac{5}{4}}{\frac{5}{4}}\right) = \boxed{\frac{50}{4}} \quad \boxed{12\frac{2}{4}}$$

- Remember these steps:
  - ✔ Work the problem either on the top or on the bottom.
  - ✔ Show the fraction that equals 1 as a **fraction over the same fraction.**
  - ✔ Then multiply to find the value that goes in the box.

Part 3 Copy and complete each equation. Rewrite each answer as a whole number or a mixed number.

a. $\frac{3}{5} \left(\boxed{} \right) = \frac{\boxed{}}{7} \boxed{}$

b. $\frac{7}{9} \left(\boxed{} \right) = \frac{3}{\boxed{}} \boxed{}$

c. $\frac{3}{8} \left(\boxed{} \right) = \frac{5}{\boxed{}} \boxed{}$

d. $\frac{2}{10} \left(\boxed{} \right) = \frac{\boxed{}}{5} \boxed{}$

Part 4 Write the unit name for each item.

Each item tells about parts of a year.

a. $\frac{1}{52}$ of a year is 1 ▬▬▬.

b. $\frac{1}{12}$ of a year is 1 ▬▬▬.

c. $\frac{1}{4}$ of a year is 1 ▬▬▬.

d. $\frac{1}{365}$ of a year is 1 ▬▬▬.

Part 5 Write the unit name for each item.

Each item tells about parts of a gallon.

a. $\frac{1}{8}$ of a gallon is 1 ▬▬▬.

b. $\frac{1}{4}$ of a gallon is 1 ▬▬▬.

c. $\frac{1}{16}$ of a gallon is 1 ▬▬▬.

d. $\frac{1}{128}$ of a gallon is 1 ▬▬▬.

Part 6

- You've made fraction number families from sentences that tell about a fraction. You can make fraction number families from sentences that tell about a percent or a decimal value. You just show the percent or decimal value as a fraction.

  Sample sentence 1   .4 of the students wore white socks.

- Here's the number family with .4 shown as a fraction:

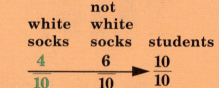

  Sample sentence 2   80% of the days were hot.

- Here's the number family with **80%** shown as a fraction:

  $$\frac{80}{100} \quad \frac{20}{100} \longrightarrow \frac{20}{100}$$
  hot   not hot   days

Part 7   Make a fraction number family for each sentence.

a. 3% of the adults owned sailboats.

b. .29 of the fish were bass.

c. 78% of the students graduated.

d. The bus was late on 30% of the days.

e. .02 of the products were defective.

Part 8   Write each item as a column problem and work it.

a. 1.7 x .008   b. 4.001 x 2.3   c. 2.5 x .03

Independent Work

Part 9 Find the area and perimeter of each figure.

a, b.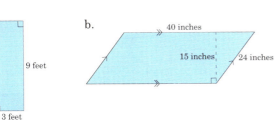

Part 10 Copy and complete each equation. Write each missing value as a fraction.

a. ■ x 7 = 6
b. 3 x ■ = 29
c. 3 x ■ = 4
d. 3 x ■ = 1
e. ■ x 261 = 1

Part 11 Copy and complete each number family.

a.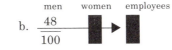
b.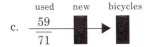
c. used / new / bicycles — $\frac{59}{71}$ ■ ■

Part 12 Copy and complete each equation. Show the proper mixed number for each improper mixed number.

a. $3\frac{11}{4}$ = ■
b. $7\frac{26}{25}$ = ■
c. $2\frac{80}{3}$ = ■

Part 13 Write each item in columns and work it.

a. 4.36 + .8 + 32
b. 26.54 − 19.006
c. 821.3 + 4.17

Part 14 Figure out the mystery number for each item and answer the question.

a. You start with the mystery number and subtract 14. Then you multiply by 3. You end up with 24. What's the mystery number?

b. A train started out with some passengers. At the first stop, 56 people got in the train. Then 14 people got off. There were 103 people left in the train. How many people were on the train to begin with?

Lesson 11 47

Lesson 12

Part 1 For each item, write the number and the unit name.

> **Sample**
> $\frac{1}{365}$ of a year is ▬▬▬.

a. $\frac{1}{4}$ of a year is ▬▬▬.
b. $\frac{1}{8}$ of a gallon is ▬▬▬.
c. $\frac{1}{3}$ of a yard is ▬▬▬.
d. $\frac{1}{12}$ of a year is ▬▬▬.

Part 2 For each item, write the number and the unit name.

a. $\frac{5}{12}$ of a year is ▬▬▬.
b. $\frac{5}{7}$ of a week is ▬▬▬.
c. $\frac{7}{4}$ years is ▬▬▬.
d. $\frac{2}{3}$ of a yard is ▬▬▬.
e. $\frac{9}{4}$ gallons is ▬▬▬.

Part 3 For each problem make two equations. Answer each question.

a. A sandbox had some sand in it. After children played in the sandbox, 15 pounds of sand had been removed from the sandbox. Later that day, the amount of sand in the box was doubled. The sandbox ended up with 470 pounds of sand in it. How much sand was in the box to begin with?

b. A log started out being 268 inches long. A section that was 42 inches long was sawed off. Later, another section was sawed off. The log was now 180 inches long. What was the length of the second section that was sawed off?

c. Ginger started out with 90 beads. She tripled the number of beads she had. Then she purchased some more beads and ended up with 300 beads. How many did she purchase?

d. Jan had some ribbon. At the end of the week, the amount she started out with had been divided by 5. She bought another 56 yards of ribbon. She now had 76 yards. How much ribbon did she have to begin with?

Part 4 Copy and complete each equation. Rewrite each answer as a whole number or a mixed number.

a. $\dfrac{3}{8}\left(\dfrac{\blacksquare}{\blacksquare}\right) = \dfrac{10}{\blacksquare} \blacksquare$

b. $\dfrac{4}{3}\left(\dfrac{\blacksquare}{\blacksquare}\right) = \dfrac{\blacksquare}{2} \blacksquare$

c. $\dfrac{20}{9}\left(\dfrac{\blacksquare}{\blacksquare}\right) = \dfrac{\blacksquare}{1} \blacksquare$

d. $\dfrac{20}{15}\left(\dfrac{\blacksquare}{\blacksquare}\right) = \dfrac{\blacksquare}{3} \blacksquare$

I know I have 76 yards of ribbon, but I don't know how much I started out with, ...

... and I don't know why I wanted so much ribbon.

Lesson 12

Part 5 For each item, make a fraction number family and a ratio table. Answer the questions.

a. 65% of the coins were pennies. There were 175 coins that were not pennies. How many coins were there in all? How many pennies were there?

b. 20% of the buildings were less than 5 years old. 60 buildings were less than 5 years old. How many buildings were at least 5 years old? How many buildings were there in all?

c. .7 of the cartons were empty. There were 21 empty cartons. How many cartons were there? How many cartons were not empty?

d. .08 of the trees were old. The rest were young. If there were 112 old trees, how many young trees were there? How many trees were there in all?

Part 6

- Sometimes a problem does not refer to the amount a person started out with. It tells about what the person did next.
- Here's a sentence:
    Sam spent $15 on Tuesday.
- We can write an equation for that sentence. The equation shows that he started out with some money. We know that he must have had some money or he wouldn't have been able to spend it.
- Here's the equation: ☐ − 15 = ☐
- Here's another sentence:
    Tom doubled the amount of money he had.
- We know he started out with some money.
- Here's the equation: ☐ × 2 = ☐

Part 7 Write an equation for each sentence.

a. A truck delivered 58 packages.

b. Bill had twice as much as he had before.

c. Sally gained 25 pounds.

Part 8 Write the equations for each problem. Answer the questions.

a. Triple my age. Then add 11 and you'll get 83. How old am I?

b. After a trip, the amount of gas in a tank had been divided by 8. After 18 gallons were added to the tank, there were 21 gallons in the tank. How much gas was in the tank before the trip?

Independent Work

Remember to work the problems in part 3 and part 8 and answer each question. Use abbreviations if you can.

Part 9 Write each item as a column problem and work it.

a. 62 x .04   b. 4.2 x .009   c. .12 x .04

Part 10 Copy and complete the table.

	Fraction	Decimal	Mixed number
a.	$\frac{463}{100}$		
b.		2.9	
c.			$34\frac{5}{100}$

Part 11 For each problem, make a fraction number family and a ratio table. Answer the questions the problem asks.

a. $\frac{3}{7}$ of the students owned hiking shoes. There were 28 students who did not own hiking shoes. How many students were there in all? How many owned hiking shoes?

b. There were 244 rose bushes in the garden. $\frac{1}{4}$ of the rose bushes died during the winter. How many died during the winter? How many survived?

Part 12 Write the fractions for each item.

a. The units are **days** and **weeks**.
1) What fraction shows 1 day?
2) What fraction shows 11 days?
3) What fraction shows 1 week?

b. The units are **years** and **seasons**.
1) What fraction shows 1 year?
2) What fraction shows 9 seasons?
3) What fraction shows 1 season?

Lesson 13

Part 1 For each item, make a ratio equation and answer the question.

> **Sample** The ratio of whales to seals was 7 to 17. There were 102 seals. How many whales were there?

a. In a mixture, there were 7 parts of sand for every 4 parts of gravel. There were 200 parts of sand. How many parts of gravel were there?

b. A tractor used 3 gallons of fuel every 2 hours it worked. The tractor worked 11 hours. How many gallons of fuel did it use?

c. A soup recipe called for 3 onions for every 8 pints of water. The cook used 5 onions. How many pints of water did the cook use?

Part 2 Write the answer to each item as a number and a unit name.

a. What is $\frac{5}{365}$ of a year?

b. What is $\frac{15}{60}$ of an hour?

c. What is $\frac{2}{7}$ of a week?

d. What is $\frac{1}{12}$ of a year?

e. What is $\frac{5}{36}$ of a yard?

f. What is $\frac{1}{2}$ of a quart?

g. What is $\frac{3}{4}$ of a gallon?

h. What is $\frac{12}{52}$ of a year?

Part 3

- Some problems that add or subtract have a whole number **and** a mixed number. When you work **addition** problems, you just copy the fraction in the answer. Then you add the whole numbers.

- Here's:
$$34$$
$$+\ 13\tfrac{5}{7}$$

- You're adding nothing to $\tfrac{5}{7}$, so you just copy the fraction in the answer.
$$34$$
$$+\ 13\tfrac{5}{7}$$

- Then you add 34 and 13. The total is $47\tfrac{5}{7}$.
$$47\tfrac{5}{7}$$

- Here's:
$$75\tfrac{12}{57}$$
$$+\ 18$$

- The fraction is $\tfrac{12}{57}$. You copy that fraction in the answer. Then you add the whole numbers: 75 and 18.
$$75\tfrac{12}{57}$$
$$+\ 18$$

- The answer to the whole problem is $93\tfrac{12}{57}$.
$$93\tfrac{12}{57}$$

- Some **subtraction** problems work the same way. If the **top number** in the problem is the mixed number, you just copy the fraction in the answer.

- Here's a problem with $25\tfrac{17}{19}$ on top:
$$25\tfrac{17}{19}$$
$$-\ 9$$

- The fraction is $\tfrac{17}{19}$. You're subtracting nothing from $\tfrac{17}{19}$, so the fraction part of the answer is $\tfrac{17}{19}$.

- For the rest of the problem, you subtract 9 from 25. The answer to the whole problem is $16\tfrac{17}{19}$.
$$25\tfrac{17}{19}$$
$$-\ 9$$
$$16\tfrac{17}{19}$$

Lesson 13

Part 4 Copy and work each item.

a. $27\frac{25}{38}$
    $+20$
    ───

b. $45\frac{7}{11}$
    -13
    ───

c. 25
    $+7\frac{10}{19}$
    ───

Part 5 For each item, make a fraction number family and a ratio table. Answer the questions.

a. 25% of the items in a store were on sale. There were 525 items on sale. How many items were not on sale? How many items were in the store?

b. .8 of the optometrist's clients wear glasses. The rest wear contact lenses. The optometrist has 450 clients. How many of his clients wear glasses? How many of his clients wear contact lenses?

Part 6 For each problem, make two equations. Answer the question.

a. The store started out with 126 coins and doubled that amount. Then the store sold some coins and ended up with 87 coins. How many coins did the store sell?

b. Triple Mary's age. Then add 14 to that number. You end up with 80. What's Mary's age?

c. A store sold 118 coins on Monday. On Tuesday, the number of coins in the store was divided by 4. The store ended up with 20 coins. How many coins did the store have on Monday morning?

Independent Work

Remember to complete the problems in part 6.

Part 7 Copy and work each item.

a. $15\frac{7}{8}$
   $-\ 3\frac{5}{8}$
   ___

b. $29\frac{3}{19}$
   -26
   ___

c. $12\frac{3}{11}$
   $\ \ \ \ 4$
   $+\ 2\frac{7}{11}$
   ___

Part 8 Copy and complete each equation. Write the proper mixed number

a. $2\frac{24}{7} = \blacksquare$

b. $15\frac{5}{3} = \blacksquare$

c. $1\frac{96}{5} = \blacksquare$

Part 9 Copy and complete each item. Figure out the mystery number.

a. $\overset{?}{\blacksquare} \times 4 = \blacksquare$
   $\blacksquare - 79 = 1$

b. $\overset{?}{\blacksquare} \div 25 = \blacksquare$
   $\blacksquare + 100 = 300$

Part 10 For each problem, make the ratio equation. Answer the question the problem asks. The answer must have a number and a unit name.

a. The ratio of roosters to hens is 3 to 11. If there are 121 hens, how many roosters are there?

b. A train traveling at a steady rate goes 126 miles every 3 hours. How far does the train travel in 15 hours?

c. There are 6 bottles in each carton. If there are 96 bottles, how many cartons are there?

Part 11 Write the fractions for each item.

a. The units are **days** and **years**.
   1) What's the fraction for 21 days?
   2) What's the fraction for 1 year?
   3) What's the fraction for 1 day?

b. The units are **gallons** and **quarts**.
   1) What's the fraction for 4 quarts?
   2) What's the fraction for 1 quart?
   3) What's the fraction for 1 gallon?

Lesson 14

Part 1 For each item, write the number and the unit name.

a. What is $\frac{20}{60}$ of an hour?

b. What is $\frac{7}{7}$ of a week?

c. What is $\frac{9}{24}$ of a day?

d. What is $\frac{1}{60}$ of a minute?

e. What is $\frac{50}{52}$ of a year?

f. What is $\frac{15}{2000}$ of a ton?

g. What is $\frac{10}{36}$ of a yard?

Part 2 Copy and work each item.

a. $17 - 4\frac{3}{5}$

b. $23 - 10\frac{1}{4}$

c. $10 - \frac{5}{11}$

Part 3 For each item, write equations. Answer the questions.

a. 56 plants were removed from the garden. The number of plants that were left was tripled when new plants were planted. The garden ended up with 108 plants. How many plants did the garden start out with?

b. A truck started out with 88 bales. Then it picked up another 94 bales. It delivered some bales and ended up with 33 bales. How many bales did it deliver?

c. The amount of money in Jill's bank account increased by $135. Then she took out $64. She ended up with $90. How much was in her account to begin with?

Part 4 For each item, make a ratio equation and answer the question.

a. A pie factory uses 9 apples for every 2 pies made. How many apples are needed for 3 pies?

b. At a picnic, the ratio of children to adults is 12 to 8. There are 120 adults. How many children are there?

c. A conveyer belt moves at the rate of 10 yards every 7 seconds. How far does the conveyer belt move in 15 seconds?

Part 5

- Not all fractions of a whole unit show **related units.**
- Here are different fractions of a year:

  $\frac{3}{5}$ of a year $\qquad$ $\frac{2}{3}$ of a year $\qquad$ $\frac{5}{8}$ of a year

- None of those fractions shows related units because none of those fractions has a **denominator** that shows the number of **days** in a year, the number of **weeks** in a year, the number of **months** in a year or the number of **seasons** in a year.
- These fractions **do** show related units:

  $\frac{5}{12}$ of a year $\qquad$ $\frac{3}{4}$ of a year $\qquad$ $\frac{6}{365}$ of a year

- Remember, if the **denominator** shows a number for related units, the **numerator** also has a unit name.

Part 6 Some fractions show related units. Write the answer to those items as a number and a unit name.

a. $\frac{5}{9}$ of a week $\qquad$ b. $\frac{1}{12}$ of a week $\qquad$ c. $\frac{5}{7}$ of a week

d. $\frac{3}{4}$ of a week $\qquad$ e. $\frac{3}{4}$ of a year $\qquad$ f. $\frac{4}{24}$ of a year

Lesson 14   57

Part 7 For each item, make a fraction number family and a ratio table. Answer the questions.

a. 35% of the mixture is sand. The sand in the mixture weighs 2 pounds. How much does the entire mixture weigh? What's the weight of the material that is not sand?

b. The steak has a fat content of 30%. 5 ounces of the meat is not fat. How many ounces of fat are in the steak? How much does the entire steak weigh?

Part 8 Find the area of each triangle.

Equations: $\dfrac{b \times h}{2} = A \qquad A = \dfrac{b \times h}{2}$

a.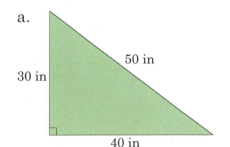

b.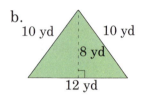

Independent Work

Remember to complete the problems in part 3.

Part 9 Write the fractions for each item.

a. The units are **ounces** and **pounds.**
1) What's the fraction for 56 ounces?
2) What's the fraction for 1 pound?
3) What's the fraction for 1 ounce?

b. The units are **hours** and **days.**
1) What's the fraction for 1 day?
2) What's the fraction for 1 hour?
3) What's the fraction for 12 hours?

Part 10 Copy and complete each equation.

a. ◼ × 56 = 55
b. 2 × ◼ = 1
c. 13 × ◼ = 1
d. 2 × ◼ = 13
e. ◼ × 11 = 12
f. ◼ × 2 = 26

Part 11 Work each item. Show the complete work.

a. $\frac{1}{9}$ of the tires in a garage were worn out. The rest were good. There were 225 tires in the garage. How many were worn out? How many were good?

b. $\frac{12}{57}$ of the workers were sick. There were 36 sick workers. How many workers were not sick? How many workers were there in all?

c. John started out with some money in his account. He added another $126 on Monday. On Wednesday, he took $200 from his account. On Friday, he tripled the amount he had in his account. The account now had $600 in it. How much was in the account to begin with?

Part J

a. 20 min
b. 7 d
c. 9 hr
d. 1 sec
e. 50 wk
f. 15 lb
g. 10 in

Everybody told me I couldn't get 225 tires in this garage, but I guess I showed them.

Lesson 14

Lesson 15

Part 1 For each item, write the number and the unit name.

a. What is $\frac{12}{24}$ of a day?

b. What is $\frac{5}{2}$ quarts?

c. What is $\frac{4}{12}$ of a year?

d. What is $\frac{60}{60}$ of an hour?

e. What is $\frac{5}{4}$ years?

f. What is $\frac{10}{8}$ gallons?

g. What is $\frac{1}{4}$ of a gallon?

h. What is $\frac{28}{60}$ of a minute?

i. What is $\frac{12}{36}$ of a yard?

j. What is $\frac{88}{365}$ of a year?

k. What is $\frac{88}{3}$ yards?

Part 2 For each item, make a fraction number family and a ratio table. Answer the questions.

a. A truck started out with a full tank of fuel. .4 of the fuel was used up. If 7 gallons of fuel were used up, how much fuel remains in the tank? How much fuel does the tank hold?

b. 20% of the wool is dyed. 9 pounds of the wool is not dyed. How much wool is dyed? How much wool is there in all?

Part 3 Copy and work each problem.

a. $12 - 10\frac{5}{8}$

b. $16 - 4\frac{7}{20}$

c. $17 - 15\frac{1}{3}$

d. $108 - 100\frac{9}{16}$

Part 4 For each item, write equations and answer the question.

a. The truck used up 21 gallons of fuel on Tuesday. On Wednesday morning, 85 gallons were put in the tank. The truck used up 89 gallons. There were now 11 gallons in the tank. How many gallons were in the tank on Tuesday morning?

b. Robert had some money in the bank. On Monday, he added $30 to his account. On Tuesday, he put in enough money to triple the amount he had. On Wednesday, he took out $130. He ended up with $80. How much did he have in his account to begin with?

c. A tank had 280 liters of water in it. The original amount was divided by 2. Then 50 liters were added to the tank. Then the tank sprung a leak. Water leaked out until the tank had only 5 liters in it. How many liters leaked out?

Part 5 Some items tell about related names. Write the answer to those items as a number and a unit name.

a. $\frac{3}{8}$ of an hour
b. $\frac{9}{4}$ gallons
c. $\frac{8}{365}$ of a year
d. $\frac{9}{24}$ of a year
e. $\frac{3}{9}$ of a gallon
f. $\frac{2}{5}$ of a yard
g. $\frac{8}{60}$ of an hour
h. $\frac{5}{9}$ of a dollar
i. $\frac{13}{100}$ of a dollar

Part 6 Find the area of each figure.

a.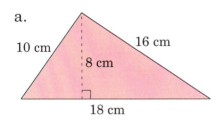

b.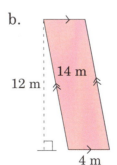

c.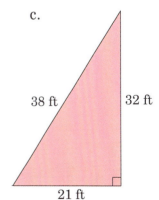

Independent Work

Part 7 Write the complete unit name for each statement.

a. $\frac{1}{12}$ of a year is 1 ▬▬▬. b. $\frac{1}{4}$ of a year is 1 ▬▬▬.

c. $\frac{1}{365}$ of a year is 1 ▬▬▬. d. $\frac{1}{16}$ of a pound is 1 ▬▬▬.

Part 8 Copy and complete each equation.

a. ■ x 4 = 3 b. 6 x ■ = 1 c. ■ x 18 = 28

d. 3 x ■ = 90 e. 50 x ■ = 3

Part 9 Copy and complete the table.

	Fraction	Mixed number
a.	$\frac{56}{17}$	
b.		$2\frac{5}{9}$
c.		$20\frac{2}{11}$
d.	$\frac{108}{5}$	

Part 10 Write each item as a column problem and work it.

a. .3 x 50

b. .02 x 13.4

c. .45 x .051

Part 11 Write the fractions for each item.

a. The units are **meters** and **centimeters**.
1) What's the fraction for 1 meter?
2) What's the fraction for 1 centimeter?
3) What's the fraction for 45 centimeters?

b. The units are **pounds** and **tons**.
1) What's the fraction for 1 ton?
2) What's the fraction for 1 pound?
3) What's the fraction for 6,489 pounds?

Part 12 For each item, make a ratio equation and answer the question.

a. In a forest, there were 4 old-growth trees for every 9 young trees. If there were 810 young trees in the forest, how many old-growth trees were there?

b. The ratio of gasoline engines to diesel engines was 9 to 2. There were 56 diesel engines. How many gasoline engines were there?

Part J

a. 12 hr e. 5 seasons i. 12 in
b. 5 pt f. 10 pt j. 88 d
c. 4 mo g. 1 qt k. 88 ft
d. 60 min h. 28 sec

Lesson 16

Part 1   For each item, write equations and answer the question.

a. A train in a switchyard went forward and backward. It started out 650 feet from the station. It went forward 460 feet. That's going farther from the station. Then the train went backward. It ended up 40 feet from the station. How far did the train go backward? ②

b. A train started out 600 feet from the station. Then it moved forward and doubled its distance from the station. Then it backed up 110 feet. Then it moved forward until it was 1,100 feet from the station. How far did the train move forward the last time it moved? ③

c. A passenger train had people in it. After the first stop, the number of people in the train had been divided by 3. At the second stop, the number of people in the train increased by 45. At the third stop, 77 people got off the train and the train was empty. How many people were in the train to begin with? ③

Part 2

- You can simplify fractions if both the numerator and denominator end in one or more zeros.
- You just cross out the same number of zeros in the numerator and the denominator.
- If you cross out one zero in the numerator and denominator, you're crossing out $\frac{10}{10}$.

$$\frac{380\cancel{0}}{45\cancel{0}} = \frac{380 \times \cancel{10}}{45 \times \cancel{10}}$$

- If you cross out two zeros in the numerator and denominator, you're crossing out $\frac{100}{100}$.

$$\frac{4\cancel{00}}{1\cancel{00}} = \frac{4 \times \cancel{100}}{1 \times \cancel{100}}$$

- Here's: $\frac{45\cancel{0}}{360\cancel{0}}$
- One zero is crossed out in the numerator and denominator. The simplified fraction is $\frac{45}{360}$.

$$\frac{450}{3600} = \frac{45}{360}$$

- Here's: $\frac{2\cancel{00}}{65\cancel{00}}$
- Two zeros are crossed out in both the numerator and denominator. The simplified fraction is $\frac{2}{65}$.

$$\frac{200}{6500} = \frac{2}{65}$$

- Remember, you cross out as many zeros as you can, but you must cross out the same number in both the numerator and denominator. And the zeros must be at the end of the numbers.

Part 3 Copy and complete each equation. Cross out zeros in the numerator and denominator. Write the simplified fraction.

a. $\frac{24000}{32700} = $ ▓   b. $\frac{100}{8000} = $ ▓   c. $\frac{2070}{400} = $ ▓   d. $\frac{60000}{20040} = $ ▓

Part 4 Copy and work each problem.

a. $2\frac{8}{9}$
$4\frac{7}{9}$
$+5\frac{6}{9}$
____

b. $1\frac{5}{7}$
$3\frac{6}{7}$
$+4\frac{4}{7}$
____

c. $8\frac{2}{10}$
$5\frac{5}{10}$
$+1\frac{9}{10}$
____

Part 5 Some items tell about related units. Rewrite those items as a number and a different unit name.

a. $\frac{7}{3}$ yards

b. $\frac{7}{3}$ years

c. $\frac{7}{3}$ days

d. $\frac{4}{8}$ of a day

e. $\frac{4}{8}$ of a gallon

f. $\frac{4}{8}$ of a year

g. $\frac{4}{52}$ of a year

h. $\frac{4}{4}$ of a year

i. $\frac{4}{24}$ of a month

j. $\frac{4}{4}$ of a week

k. $\frac{4}{7}$ of a week

l. $\frac{15}{60}$ of an hour

Part 6 Copy and complete each table. Write answers as mixed numbers.

a.

	5	■
	3	■
total	8	9

b.

	1	■
	9	■
total	10	25

Lesson 16

Independent Work

Part 7 For each item, make a ratio equation and answer the question.

a. A mixture had 5 parts of alcohol for every 2 parts of sulphur. If there were 151 parts of sulphur in the mixture, how many parts of alcohol were in the mixture?

b. It takes a machine 13 seconds to grind off 7 ounces of material. How long does it take the machine to grind off 25 ounces of material?

c. A soup recipe calls for 2 quarts of water for every 3 onions. A cook uses 11 onions. How many quarts of water does the cook need?

Part 8 Write the fraction for each item.

a. The units are **minutes** and **hours**.
   1) What's the fraction for 16 minutes?
   2) What's the fraction for 1 hour?
   3) What's the fraction for 1 minute?

b. The units are **feet** and **yards**.
   1) What's the fraction for 1 foot?
   2) What's the fraction for 63 feet?
   3) What's the fraction for 1 yard?

Part 9 Write the number and unit name that completes each statement.

a. $\frac{1}{12}$ of a year is ▬▬▬.

b. $\frac{3}{4}$ of a year is ▬▬▬.

c. $\frac{2}{16}$ of a pound is ▬▬▬.

d. $\frac{1}{52}$ of a year is ▬▬▬.

e. $\frac{418}{365}$ years is ▬▬▬.

Part 10 Write each item as a column problem and work it.

a. .3 x 5.2

b. .003 x 100

c. 4.3 x .27

Part 11 Write each problem in columns and work it.

a. 4.03 – .27

b. 2 – 1.38

c. 206 – 152.8

Part 12 Find the area and perimeter of each triangle.

a.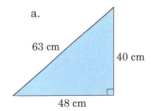
63 cm, 40 cm, 48 cm

b.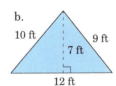
10 ft, 9 ft, 7 ft, 12 ft

Lesson 17

Part 1 For each item, write equations and answer the question.

a. The elevator started out with 9 people in it and the number increased by 15 at the second floor. At the third floor, the number of people on the elevator was divided by 4. At the fourth floor, all the remaining people got off and the elevator ended up empty. How many people got off at the fourth floor? ③

b. A dump truck started out with some dirt in it. The truck delivered 11 cubic feet of dirt. Then more dirt was added until the amount of dirt in the truck had been tripled. Later, another 21 cubic feet of dirt was added. Then the amount in the truck was divided by 2. The truck ended up with 36 cubic feet of dirt. How much dirt was in the truck to begin with? ④

c. There were 8 letters in a mailbox. 14 more letters were put in the box. Later, the number of letters in the box doubled. Then all the letters in the box were removed. The box was now empty. How many letters were removed from the box? ③

Part 2 Copy and complete each table.

a.
	2	■
	7	■
total	9	15

b.
	7	■
	4	■
total	11	8

Part 3 Copy and complete each equation. Cross out zeros in the numerator and denominator. Write the simplified fraction.

a. $\dfrac{210}{3800} =$ ■

b. $\dfrac{10500}{100} =$ ■

c. $\dfrac{280}{1000} =$ ■

d. $\dfrac{509000}{5000} =$ ■

Part 4

- Some **mixed numbers** have **fractions** that show related units.
- $2\frac{5}{12}$ **years** has a fraction that tells about the leftover months.
  - ✔ The denominator of the fraction is 12.
  - ✔ That's the number of months in one year.
  - ✔ So the numerator shows months.
- $2\frac{5}{12}$ **years** is **2** years and **5 months.**
- $4\frac{7}{12}$ **years** also tells about years and months.
- If the denominator of the fraction is not a number for related units, the numerator does not tell about units that have a name.
- $2\frac{5}{7}$ **years** is just **2** years and $\frac{5}{7}$ of the next year.

Part 5
Write the letter of each item that shows related units. Rewrite those items with two unit names.

a. $1\frac{3}{5}$ gallons   b. $3\frac{1}{4}$ gallons   c. $9\frac{2}{3}$ gallons

d. $4\frac{3}{8}$ gallons   e. $5\frac{6}{7}$ gallons   f. $2\frac{4}{16}$ gallons

Part 6
Write the letter of each item that shows related units. Rewrite those items with two unit names.

a. $2\frac{8}{12}$ years   b. $4\frac{2}{50}$ years   c. $2\frac{10}{24}$ years

d. $5\frac{3}{4}$ years   e. $2\frac{15}{365}$ years   f. $3\frac{5}{36}$ years

g. $6\frac{30}{52}$ years

68 Lesson 17

Part 7 Copy and work each problem.

a. $1\frac{8}{11}$
$\frac{10}{11}$
$+ 5\frac{9}{11}$
▬

b. $2\frac{4}{6}$
$1\frac{5}{6}$
$+ 7\frac{2}{6}$
▬

c. $4\frac{7}{9}$
$\frac{8}{9}$
$+ 3\frac{5}{9}$
▬

Independent Work

Part 8 Copy and complete the table.

	Fraction	Decimal	Mixed number
a.		6.08	
b.			$3\frac{2}{10}$
c.	$\frac{565}{10}$		
d.		2.94	

Part 9 Find the area and perimeter of each figure.

a.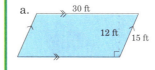

b.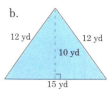

Part 10 Write a fraction for each item.

a. What fraction of a year is 11 months?
b. What fraction of a year is 33 days?
c. What fraction of a gallon is 3 quarts?
d. What fraction of a pound is 4 ounces?

Part 11 Write the number and unit name that completes each item.

a. $\frac{4}{12}$ of a year is ▬.
b. $\frac{3}{365}$ of a year is ▬.
c. $\frac{36}{24}$ days is ▬.
d. $\frac{8}{4}$ years is ▬.

Part 12 For each item, make a fraction number family and a ratio table. Answer the questions.

a. 80% of the children had flu shots. There were 25 children in all. How many had flu shots? How many did not have flu shots?

b. .4 of the tires were on sale. 66 tires were not on sale. How many were on sale? What was the total number of tires?

Part 13 Write the complete equation for each item. Show the proper mixed number for each mixed number shown.

a. $3\frac{7}{3}$ = ▬
b. $21\frac{11}{2}$ = ▬
c. $12\frac{20}{3}$ = ▬

Part J

a. $\frac{210}{380\cancel{0}} = \frac{21}{380}$ b. $\frac{10500}{100\cancel{0}} = \frac{105}{1}$ c. $\frac{280}{1000} = \frac{28}{100}$ d. $\frac{509600}{5000} = \frac{509}{5}$

Lesson 18

Part 1 Write an equation for each item.

> *Sample sentence 1*
> Some more material was added.   ■ + ■ = ■
>
> *Sample sentence 2*
> The amount was multiplied by a number.   ■ x ■ = ■

a. Then the amount was divided by a number.
b. Then some more fuel was added to the tank.
c. Then marbles were removed from the pile.
d. Then the size of the pile increased by a number of times.

Part 2 Copy and complete each item.

a. 19 x 2 = ■   ?
    ■ – ■ = ■
    ■ ÷ 5 = 7

b. 3 x 12 = ■   ?
    ■ – ■ = ■
    ■ + 15 = 19

c. 82 – 57 = ■   ?
    ■ x ■ = ■
    ■ – 100 = 0

Part 3 Write the letter of each item that tells about related units. Rewrite those items with two unit names.

a. $5\frac{3}{8}$ dollars
b. $2\frac{3}{4}$ years
c. $1\frac{3}{4}$ dollars
d. $1\frac{1}{52}$ years
e. $7\frac{5}{9}$ seconds
f. $1\frac{3}{8}$ gallons
g. $11\frac{3}{10}$ feet
h. $8\frac{2}{3}$ inches
i. $6\frac{2}{3}$ yards

Part 4

Copy and work each item. Cross out zeros if you can.

> **Rule** You can simplify values that are multiplied if you cross out the same value on top and in the denominator.

Sample $32\cancel{0} \times \dfrac{4\cancel{0}}{2\cancel{00}} = \dfrac{128}{2}$

a. $40 \times \dfrac{350}{200} = \boxed{}$

b. $50 \times \dfrac{13}{100} = \boxed{}$

c. $50 \times \dfrac{4}{100} = \boxed{}$

Part 5

Write each item as a column problem and work it.

a. .24 + 1.3 + .021
b. .06 x 3.1
c. 3.24 x .062
d. 17.8 − 2.36

Part 6

Make a fraction number family and ratio table. Answer the question.

.3 of the harvest was wheat. The rest was corn. The entire harvest weighed 600 tons. What was the weight of the wheat?

Independent Work

Part 7

Write a fraction for each item.

a. What fraction of a day is 3 hours?

b. What fraction of an hour is 7 minutes?

c. What fraction of a week is 5 days?

d. What fraction of a day is 19 hours?

Part 8

Write the number and unit name that completes each item.

a. $\dfrac{10}{36}$ of a yard is _____.

b. $\dfrac{2}{3}$ of a yard is _____.

c. $\dfrac{2}{12}$ of a foot is _____.

d. $\dfrac{2}{4}$ of a gallon is _____.

e. $\dfrac{29}{8}$ gallons is _____.

f. $\dfrac{4}{4}$ of a gallon is _____.

Lesson 18

Part 9 Copy and work each item. Show each answer as a proper mixed number.

a. $4\frac{5}{8}$
   $+ 3\frac{6}{8}$

b. $14\frac{1}{2}$
   $3\frac{1}{2}$
   $+ 5\frac{1}{2}$

c. 21
   $- 2\frac{1}{3}$

d. 5
   $- 4\frac{2}{7}$

Part 10 Work each item.

a. John had 100 stamps in his collection. On Monday, John sold 55 stamps. On Tuesday, his collection was divided by 3. On Friday, he bought some more stamps and ended up with 134 stamps. How many stamps did he buy?

b. A large elevator started out with a lot of people in it. The number was divided by 4 when the elevator stopped at the third floor. Then 11 people got on the elevator. The elevator ended up with 18 people in it. How many people were in the elevator to begin with?

Part 11 Copy and complete each table.

a.

	2	■
	■	■
total	13	55

b.

	4	3
	7	■
total	■	■

Part 12 Copy and complete the table.

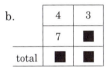

	Fraction	Decimal	Mixed number
a.			$2\frac{5}{100}$
b.		16.3	
c.		2.09	

Part J

a. .240
    1.300
    + .021
    [1.561]

b. .06
    × 3.1
    06
    +180
    [.186]

c. 3.24
    × .062
    648
    +19440
    [.20088]

d. 17.80
    − 2.36
    [15.44]

Lesson 19

Part 1 For each item that shows related units, rewrite the item with two unit names.

a. $10\frac{5}{12}$ hours d. $5\frac{7}{12}$ years f. $7\frac{3}{4}$ inches

b. $2\frac{3}{8}$ dollars e. $1\frac{9}{20}$ dollars g. $3\frac{29}{60}$ minutes

c. $2\frac{34}{36}$ yards

Part 2 Copy each problem and work it.

a. 11 x 3 = ■   ?
■ – ■ = ■
■ + 8 = 31

b. 100 – 90 = ■   ?
■ x ■ = ■
■ – 1 = 89

c. 12 – 7 = ■   ?
■ – ■ = ■
■ + 9 = 9

Part 3 For each item, make a fraction number family and a ratio table. Answer the questions.

a. 30% of the ribbon is blue. 7 yards of ribbon are not blue. How many yards of ribbon are there in all? How many yards are blue?

b. 80% of the corn was yellow. The rest was white. If there were 26 tons of corn in all, how many tons of white corn were there? How many tons of yellow corn were there?

Part 4
Write a mixed number for each item.

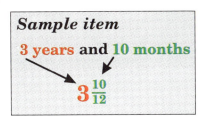

a. 3 quarts and 2 cups
b. 5 years and 2 seasons
c. 4 dollars and 3 nickels
d. 2 gallons and 3 quarts
e. 5 weeks and 6 days
f. 4 minutes and 33 seconds
g. 2 days and 7 hours

Independent Work

Part 5
Work each item.

a. If it takes 3 pints of paint to cover 61 square feet, how many pints of paint are needed to cover 20 square feet?
b. A recipe calls for 5 potatoes for every 2 pints of milk. A cook uses 6 potatoes. How many pints of milk are needed?
c. A car uses 3 gallons of gas for every 100 miles. How far can the car go on 7 gallons of gas?

Part 6
Copy and work each item. Cross out zeros if you can.

a. $3 \times \frac{50}{270} = $ ▉

b. $70 \times \frac{20}{100} = $ ▉

c. $200 \times \frac{2}{700} = $ ▉

Part 7
Work each item.

a. What fraction of a year is 99 months?
b. What is $\frac{3}{16}$ of a pound?
c. What is $\frac{12}{4}$ years?
d. What is $\frac{3}{7}$ of a week?
e. What fraction of a foot is 11 inches?
f. What fraction of a year is 9 days?
g. What fraction of a day is 18 hours?

Part 8
Write each item as a column problem and work it.

a. .2 x .5
b. .56 + 1.2 + .8
c. .03 x 25.6
d. 12 – 5.37
e. 5 x .007
f. 15.3 – 1.11

Part 9
Make a fraction number family and ratio table. Answer the questions.

30% of the mixture was water. If the water in the mixture weighed 11 pounds, how much did the entire mixture weigh? What was the weight of the part of the mixture that was not water?

Part 10
Copy and complete each equation.

a. ▉ x 7 = 6
b. 251 x ▉ = 17
c. ▉ x 7 = 23
d. 23 x ▉ = 7

Lesson 19

Lesson 20

Part 1 For each item that shows related units, rewrite the item with two unit names.

a. $9\frac{2}{3}$ years

b. $4\frac{1}{3}$ yards

c. $10\frac{5}{9}$ minutes

d. $5\frac{3}{12}$ yards

e. $8\frac{9}{100}$ dollars

f. $4\frac{3}{8}$ gallons

g. $11\frac{10}{52}$ years

Test 2

Part 1 Work each item.

a. What is $\frac{60}{24}$ days?

b. What is $\frac{3}{4}$ of a year?

c. What fraction of a pound is 15 ounces?

d. What fraction of a year is 200 days?

e. What fraction of a yard is 9 inches?

f. What fraction of a foot is 9 inches?

Part 2 Copy and complete each item.

a. 48 − 20 = ■ ?
■ + ■ = ■
■ × 3 = 87

b. 12 × 4 = ■ ?
■ − ■ = ■
■ + 9 = 9

Part 3　Work each item.

a. 4 identical tiles weigh 11 ounces. How much do 7 tiles weigh?

b. It takes a machine 16 seconds to make 3 holders. How long does it take the machine to make 15 holders?

Part 4　Work each item.

a. Ginger had $145. She spent $25. Then she bought something for $42. Then she received some money for her birthday. She ended up with $300. How much money did she receive for her birthday?

b. A tank of water was full. Then 45 gallons of water were removed from the tank. Then the amount of water remaining in the tank was doubled. There were 66 gallons in the tank. How much is in a full tank?

Part 5　Write each item in columns and work it.

a. 56 − 3.18

b. 20.5 + 2.05 + .205

c. .23 x .06

d. 50.35 x .2

Part 6　Copy and work each item. Cross out zeros if you can.

a. $2 \times \dfrac{280}{30} = $ ■

b. $100 \times \dfrac{50}{3000} = $ ■

c. $20 \times \dfrac{506}{100} = $ ■

Part 7 For each item, make a fraction number family and a ratio table. Answer the questions.

a. 26% of the crop was ripe. The entire crop weighed 160 tons. How much of the crop was ripe? How much of the crop was not ripe?

b. .7 of the soup was water. The soup contained 5 quarts of water. How much soup was there? How much of the soup was not water?

Part 8 Work each problem. Show the answer as a proper mixed number.

a. 56
   − 6 5/8
   ▪

b. 2
   12 9/10
   + 3 5/10
   ▪

c. 9
   − 7 3/20
   ▪

Lesson 21

Part 1 Work each item.

a. What is $\frac{7}{3}$ of 21?

b. What's 8% of 300?

c. What is 2% of 15?

d. What's $\frac{10}{9}$ of 8?

Part 2 For each item, write the mixed number.

a. 3 gallons and 6 pints

b. 5 years and 200 days

c. 1 dollar and 14 nickels

d. 3 dollars and 1 quarter

e. 4 yards and 11 inches

f. 2 feet and 3 inches

Part 3

- Some division problems that divide by a two-digit number have an answer with two digits.

- Here's a problem:

    $$21\overline{)869}$$

- The first digit of the answer goes above the last digit of 86.

    $$21\overline{)\underset{}{8\underline{6}9}}^{4}$$

- When you multiply 21 by 4, you get 84. You subtract 84 from 86.

    $$\begin{array}{r} 4 \\ 21\overline{)869} \\ -84 \\ \hline 2 \end{array}$$

- You bring down the ones digit of the number under the division sign.

- Now you have a division problem for the ones column: 29 ÷ 21.

    $$\begin{array}{r} 41 \\ 21\overline{)869} \\ -84\downarrow \\ \hline 29 \end{array}$$

- You multiply 21 by 1 and subtract from 29. The remainder is **8**.

- The remainder is also divided by 21, so you can show the remainder as $\frac{8}{21}$.

    $$\begin{array}{r} 41\frac{8}{21} \\ 21\overline{)869}\phantom{\frac{8}{21}} \\ -84\phantom{9\frac{8}{21}} \\ \hline 29\phantom{\frac{8}{21}} \\ -21\phantom{\frac{8}{21}} \\ \hline 8\phantom{\frac{8}{21}} \end{array}$$

- Remember these steps:
    - ✔ Work a problem for the underlined digits.
    - ✔ The answer goes in the tens column.
    - ✔ Multiply and write the number **below the underlined digits.**
    - ✔ Subtract.
    - ✔ Bring down the last digit.
    - ✔ Work another division problem.
    - ✔ The answer goes in the ones column.
    - ✔ Subtract and show the remainder as a fraction.

Lesson 21

Part 4 Copy and work each item.

Sample 52 | 4764

a. 49 | 1273

b. 19 | 506

Part 5 Make equations for each item. Answer the question.

Sample problem There were 15 letters in a mailbox. 10 letters were added. Then some letters were removed. Then 15 letters were added. The box ended up with 38 letters in it. How many letters were removed?

a. A garden had 42 plants in it. Then the number of plants was doubled. Then a storm destroyed some of the plants. 136 plants were planted and the garden ended up with 200 plants in it. How many plants were destroyed by the storm?

b. A chicken farm had 452 chickens on it. 210 chickens were sold. Then a lot of chickens hatched. Then the number of chickens on the farm was divided by 9. There were still 85 chickens on the farm. How many chickens hatched?

Independent Work

Part 6 Copy and complete the table.

	Fraction	Decimal	Mixed number
a.	$\frac{310}{100}$		
b.		13.5	
c.			$2\frac{7}{1000}$

Part 7 Work each item.

a. In a recipe, there are 7 eggs for every 5 cups of pecans. A cook uses 10 eggs. How many cups of pecans does he use?

b. The ratio of boards to nails is 2 to 11. If a builder uses 600 boards, how many nails does the builder use?

c. A machine produces 7 bottletops every 2 seconds. If the machine works for 86 seconds, how many bottletops does it make?

Part 8 Answer each question.

a. What fraction of a pound is 7 ounces?

b. What is $\frac{28}{24}$ days? (Use one unit name.)

c. What fraction of a year is 28 days?

d. What is $\frac{9}{4}$ gallons? (Use one unit name.)

e. What is $\frac{78}{100}$ dollars?

f. What fraction of a gallon is 3 pints?

Part 9 Find the area and perimeter of each figure.

a.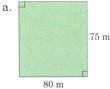
75 m, 80 m

b.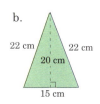
22 cm, 22 cm, 20 cm, 15 cm

Part 10 Work each item as a column problem.

a. 2.8 – 1.95

b. 2.8 x 3.05

c. 5.2 + .07 + 11

Lesson 21

Lesson 22

Part 1   The unit name is always the name of the larger unit.

2 years and 7 months is $2\frac{7}{12}$ **years.**

2 years and 44 weeks is $2\frac{44}{52}$ **years.**

3 dollars and 2 quarters is $3\frac{2}{4}$ ▓▓▓▓▓▓▓ .

Part 2   Write each item as a mixed number and **unit name.**

a. 4 feet and 11 inches

b. 5 years and 3 months

c. 8 gallons and 3 quarts

d. 2 years and 300 days

e. 7 days and 5 hours

f. 3 weeks and 1 day

Part 3

- Some ratio problems require a table. Those are problems that have **three names.** Problems that have only two names do not require a table.

- Here's a problem that requires a table:

  The ratio of <u>boys</u> to <u>children</u> is 2 to 5. If there are 70 children, how many <u>girls</u> are there?

  boys   ▪ ▪
  girls ▪ ▪
  children ▪ ▪

- The names are **boys, girls** and **children.** The problem requires a table because it has three names.

- Here's a problem that does not require a table:

  The ratio of <u>boys</u> to <u>children</u> is 2 to 5. If there are 30 boys, how many children are there?

  $\dfrac{\text{boys}}{\text{children}} \;\; \dfrac{\blacksquare}{\blacksquare}\left(\dfrac{\blacksquare}{\blacksquare}\right) = \dfrac{\blacksquare}{\blacksquare}$

- The names are **boys** and **children.** No table is needed.

Part 3 continued

- Remember, if there are **three names,** you need a table. If there are only two names, you don't need a table. Also remember that one of the names may be in the question.

Part 4 Read each problem. Figure out whether or not you need to make a table. Write table or no table.

a. 24% of the people were retired. 152 people were not retired. How many people were there in all?

b. At a swimming pool, there were 4 retired people for every 3 students. There were 81 students. How many retired people were there?

c. It takes 3 minutes for a machine to produce 5 yards of fabric. How many yards of fabric will the machine produce in 35 minutes?

Part 5 Figure out the mystery number for each item.

a. Start with 12 and multiply it by 3. Then divide by the mystery number. Then add 2. You'll end up with 8. What's the mystery number?

b. Start with 25 and subtract 7. Then multiply by a mystery number. Add 12 and you'll end up with 48. What's the mystery number?

c. Start with 10 and multiply by 8. Then multiply by a mystery number. Then subtract 15 and you'll end up with 65. What's the mystery number?

d. Start with 26 and divide by 2. Then add a mystery number. Then subtract 14. You'll end up with 10. What's the mystery number?

Part 6 Copy and work each item.

a. $23\overline{)979}$ b. $37\overline{)2031}$ c. $19\overline{)615}$

Lesson 22

Part 7 Work each item.

a. What's 175% of 8?

c. What's $\frac{3}{5}$ of 175?

c. What's 10% of 50?

d. What's 4% of 4?

Part 8 Make a fraction number family and ratio table for each item. Answer each question.

a. $\frac{3}{4}$ of the trees were conifers. The rest were not. There were 52 trees in all. How many were not conifers?

b. 40% of the sand was wet. There were 10 tons of sand. How many tons were wet? How many tons were not wet?

c. .7 of the pie had been eaten. The part that had not been eaten weighed 660 grams. What was the weight of the part that had been eaten? How much did the entire pie weigh to begin with?

Independent Work

Remember to complete the problems in part 4.

Part 9 Answer each question.

a. What fraction of a dollar is 99¢?

b. What fraction of a pound is 11 ounces?

c. What fraction of a year is 1 day?

d. What is $\frac{28}{8}$ gallons? (Use one unit name.)

e. What is $\frac{4}{52}$ of a year?

f. What is $\frac{3}{4}$ of a year?

Part 10 Write the missing value.

a. $5\left(\blacksquare\right) = 7$

b. $\frac{5}{8}\left(\frac{3}{3}\right) = \blacksquare$

c. $\frac{5}{3} = \frac{\blacksquare}{12}$

d. $\frac{2}{7} = \frac{14}{\blacksquare}$

e. $\blacksquare \times 9 = 3$

f. $9\left(\blacksquare\right) = 1$

Part 11 Write each item with two numbers and two unit names.

a. What's $3\frac{11}{356}$ years?

b. What's $2\frac{4}{16}$ pounds?

c. What's $4\frac{2}{3}$ yards?

d. What's $5\frac{2}{36}$ yards?

e. What's $7\frac{8}{24}$ days?

f. What's $2\frac{1}{4}$ dollars?

Part 12 For each improper mixed number, write an equation to show the proper mixed number it equals.

a. $1\frac{13}{4} =$ ▪

b. $2\frac{7}{8} =$ ▪

c. $2\frac{8}{7} =$ ▪

d. $5\frac{17}{18} =$ ▪

e. $3\frac{11}{2} =$ ▪

f. $9\frac{1}{12} =$ ▪

g. $4\frac{20}{17} =$ ▪

Part 13 Work each item.

a. An elevator started out with some people in it. At the second floor, 3 people got off and 11 people got on. The elevator now had 16 people in it. How many were in the elevator to begin with?

b. Tom had $52. On his birthday, the amount he had tripled. Then he spent $34 on skates. He made another purchase and ended up with $111. How much did he spend on his last purchase?

Part J

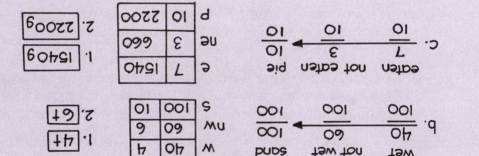

Lesson 23

Part 1 Copy and work each item.

  a. 48)733 b. 92)4759 c. 65)4207

Part 2 Rewrite each item as a mixed number and a unit name.

  a. 5 minutes and 3 seconds
  b. 7 gallons and 6 pints
  c. 8 dollars and 3 quarters
  d. 1 hour and 25 minutes
  e. 3 days and 17 hours

Part 3 Read each item. Figure out whether or not you need to make a table. Write **table** or **no table**.

  a. If there are 4 pounds of powder for every 11 pounds of sulphur, how many pounds of sulphur are needed for 6 pounds of powder?

  b. In a mixture of sand and water, there are 3 pounds of sand for every 5 pounds of water. If the entire mixture weighs 200 pounds, how many pounds of water are in the mixture?

  c. 8% of the workers ride bicycles to work. If 88 workers ride bicycles, how many workers do not ride bicycles?

Part 4

- You've learned that you can simplify some fractions by crossing out zeros.
- Remember the rules:
  - ✔ Cross out the same number in the numerator and the denominator.
  - ✔ The zeros must be at the end of each value.
- You can use the same rules to simplify long-division problems.

  - Here's a fraction: $\dfrac{2780}{30}$
- Here it is written as a long-division problem: $30\overline{)2780}$
  - You can cross out one zero in each value: $3\cancel{0}\overline{)278\cancel{0}}$
    - Now you can work a simpler problem: $3\overline{)278}$

Part 5
Simplify each problem and work it.

a. $100\overline{)240}$ b. $400\overline{)27000}$ c. $20\overline{)1860}$ d. $80\overline{)19050}$

Part 6
Work each item.

a. What's $\dfrac{7}{3}$ of $\dfrac{2}{3}$?   b. What's 15% of 90?

c. What's 120% of 5?   d. What's $\dfrac{5}{8}$ of 9?

Part 7 Make equations for each item and answer the question.

a. A train had 121 people in it. At the first stop, the number was reduced by 17. After the next stop, the number was divided by 2. At the third stop, a lot of people got off and the train ended up with 14 people in it. How many people got off at the last stop?

b. Start with 5 and triple it. Subtract a mystery number. Then add 18 and you'll end up with 20. What's the mystery number?

c. A nesting colony of penguins increased by 127 when new chicks hatched. Then 48 of the chicks died. Another 58 penguins joined the colony. There were then 238 penguins in the colony. How many penguins were there to start with?

d. A freight train had 111 cars on it. At the paper factory, the number of cars was doubled. A lot of cars were removed from the train at Hilltown. Another 75 cars were removed at Rivertown. The train still had 22 cars on it. How many cars were removed at Hilltown?

Independent Work

Remember to complete the items in part 3.

Part 8 Copy and work each item. Show each answer as a proper mixed number.

a. 14
   $- 3\frac{7}{8}$

b. $11\frac{1}{12}$
   $2\frac{9}{12}$
   $+ 1\frac{4}{12}$

c. $56\frac{7}{8}$
   $- 11$

Part 9 Simplify each problem that can be simplified. Write the answer as a whole number or mixed number.

a. $40 \times \frac{350}{200} = \blacksquare$

b. $\frac{4}{50} \times 325 = \blacksquare$

c. $20 \times \frac{30}{520} = \blacksquare$

Part 10 Answer each question.

a. What's $\frac{2}{3}$ of a yard?

b. What's $\frac{18}{10}$ dollars? (Use one unit name.)

c. What fraction of a pint is 1 cup?

d. What fraction of a year is 300 days?

e. What's $\frac{19}{12}$ feet? (Use one unit name.)

f. What fraction of a minute is 25 seconds?

Part 11 Find the perimeter and the area of each figure.

a.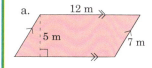

b.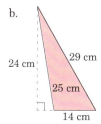

Lesson 23 91

Lesson 24

Part 1

- Here's a problem:

  Jane's age is 20% of her mother's age. Her mother is 30 years old. How old is Jane?

- You figure out 20% of her mother's age: $\dfrac{20}{100} \times m = \square$

- You work the problem: 20% of 30. $\dfrac{2\cancel{0}}{1\cancel{0}\cancel{0}} \times 3\cancel{0} = 6$

- Jane is $\boxed{6 \text{ years old}}$.

Part 2 Work each item.

a. A car had traveled $\frac{3}{5}$ of the total distance. The total distance was 200 miles. How far had the car traveled?

b. There were 150 people. 40% of them wore glasses. How many people wore glasses?

c. .3 of the days were sunny. There were 50 days. How many days were sunny?

Part 3 Copy and work each item.

a. $47\overline{)1767}$ b. $24\overline{)275}$ c. $71\overline{)506}$

Part 4 Here's how to round decimal numbers to the nearest hundredth:

- Look at the **third** digit after the decimal point.   7.38**5**1
- If that digit is 5 or more, you do not copy the hundredths digit. You replace it with the digit that is 1 more.   7.3**8**51
  7.3**9**
- If the third digit after the decimal point is less than 5, you just copy the hundredths digit.   7.38**4**1
  7.3**8**41
  7.3**8**
- Remember, if the digit after hundredths is 5 or more, change the hundredths digit. Otherwise, copy it.

Part 5 Round each decimal number to the nearest hundredth.

a. 8.6471
b. 12.05397
c. 10.273
d. .719
e. 5.0125
f. 5.0152

Lesson 24

Part 6

- When you work with related units, you can figure out the name for the numerator of a fraction if you know the name for the denominator.

- If the denominator shows **minutes in each hour,** the numerator of the fraction shows **minutes.**

$$\frac{\text{minutes}}{\text{minutes in each hour}}$$

- If the denominator of the fraction shows **hours in each day,** the numerator shows **hours.**

$$\frac{\text{hours}}{\text{hours in each day}}$$

- What does the numerator show?

$$\frac{\rule{2cm}{0.4pt}}{\text{pints in each gallon}}$$

- What does the numerator show?

$$\frac{\rule{2cm}{0.4pt}}{\text{feet in each mile}}$$

- When you write an equation, the unit for the whole number is the name for the **larger unit.**

$$\blacksquare = \frac{\blacksquare}{\blacksquare}$$

- Here's an equation that shows the relationship for years and months:

$$\text{years} = \frac{\text{months}}{\text{months in each year}}$$

Part 7 Write the complete equation for each item.

Sample equation $\quad 4 \;\rule{2cm}{0.4pt}\; = \dfrac{48\;\rule{2cm}{0.4pt}}{12 \text{ months in each year}}$

a. $2\;\rule{2cm}{0.4pt}\; = \dfrac{120\;\rule{2cm}{0.4pt}}{60 \text{ seconds in each minute}}$

b. $3\;\rule{2cm}{0.4pt}\; = \dfrac{72 \text{ hours}}{24\;\rule{2cm}{0.4pt}}$

c. $5\;\rule{2cm}{0.4pt}\; = \dfrac{180 \text{ inches}}{36\;\rule{2cm}{0.4pt}}$

d. $10\;\rule{2cm}{0.4pt}\; = \dfrac{40 \text{ quarts}}{4\;\rule{2cm}{0.4pt}}$

Lesson 24

Part 8

- You've found the distance around figures with straight sides. That distance is called the **perimeter**.

- A circle doesn't have any straight sides. So it doesn't have a perimeter. The distance around a circle is called the **circumference**.

- The first part of that name has the same letters as the word **circle: C-I-R-C**.

- One way to **measure** the circumference of a circle is to rotate the circle **one time** and see how long the path is.

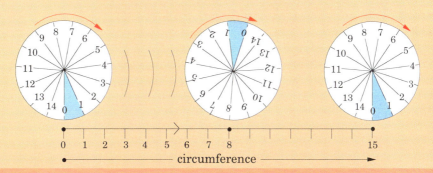

- The circumference of any circle is related to a line through the center of that circle. That line is called the **diameter**.

- The **circumference** of any circle is related to the **diameter** of the circle. The circumference is always 3.14 times the diameter.

- The number 3.14 has a special symbol: It's called **pi**. π

- Here's π with 5 decimal places: 3.14159
- We'll use π rounded to hundredths: 3.14
- Here's the equation you'll use: $\pi \times d = C$

Lesson 24   95

Part 9 Figure out the circumference for each circle. Use the equation: π x d = C.

a. 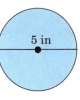 5 in

b. 3 m

c. 60 ft

d. 15 in

Part 10 Copy and work each item.

a. 30 ⟌ 4500

b. 600 ⟌ 40900

c. 880 ⟌ 4000

Independent Work

Part 11 For each item, write the mixed number and the unit name.

a. 4 years and 28 days
b. 4 years and 7 months
c. 4 years and 11 weeks
d. 3 hours and 8 minutes
e. 5 gallons and 2 quarts
f. 1 day and 9 hours

Part 12 Work each item.

a. A boat travels 13 miles every 20 minutes. If the boat travels 56 miles, how many minutes does the trip take?

b. 20% of the cars were blue. There were 56 cars that were not blue. How many cars were there in all? How many cars were blue?

c. .6 of the plants had blossoms. 48 plants had blossoms. How many plants did not have blossoms? How many plants were there?

d. Every 2 gallons of paint costs $22. A person spends $88. How many gallons of paint does the person buy?

e. The ratio of dogs to cats in a shelter is 5 to 4. There are 200 cats in the shelter. How many dogs are in the shelter?

Part 13 Copy and complete the table.

	Fraction	Decimal	Mixed number
a.			$2\frac{7}{100}$
b.		15.125	
c.	$\frac{37}{10}$		
d.		8.02	

Part 14 Find the mystery number for each item.

a. You start with a mystery number and multiply by 8. Then you subtract 200. Then you divide by 2. You end up with 12. What's the mystery number you started with?

b. You start with 10 and triple it. Then you add the mystery number. Then you subtract 9 and you end up with 200. What's the mystery number?

c. You start with a mystery number and subtract 20. Then you multiply by 350. Then you add 1. You end up with 1. What's the mystery number?

Part J

a. $37\frac{28}{47}$

$47\overline{)1767}$
$\underline{-141}$
357
$\underline{-329}$
28

b. $11\frac{11}{24}$

$24\overline{)275}$
$\underline{-24}$
35
$\underline{-24}$
11

c. $7\frac{9}{71}$

$71\overline{)506}$
$\underline{-497}$
9

She doesn't want to find the mystery number because it won't be a mystery anymore.

? □ × 3 = □   □ − 30 = 6

Lesson 25

Part 1 Copy and complete each equation.

> - The word **per** means **in each** or **in one**.
> - Another way of saying quarts **in each** gallon is quarts **per** gallon.
> - Another way of saying feet **in one** yard is feet **per** yard.

a. $4 \rule{1cm}{0.15cm} = \dfrac{12 \rule{1cm}{0.15cm}}{3 \text{ feet per yard}}$

b. $2 \rule{1cm}{0.15cm} = \dfrac{104 \text{ weeks}}{52 \rule{1cm}{0.15cm}}$

c. $7 \rule{1cm}{0.15cm} = \dfrac{168 \text{ hours}}{24 \rule{1cm}{0.15cm}}$

d. $1 \rule{1cm}{0.15cm} = \dfrac{100 \rule{1cm}{0.15cm}}{100 \text{ cents per dollar}}$

e. $9 \rule{1cm}{0.15cm} = \dfrac{72 \text{ pints}}{8 \rule{1cm}{0.15cm}}$

Part 2 Round each decimal number to the nearest hundredth.

a. 4.2765   b. 5.297   c. .1742   d. 10.495   e. 4.1405   f. 17.4928

Part 3 Work each item. Round answers to the nearest hundredth.

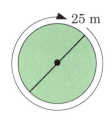
25 m

a. Figure out the diameter.

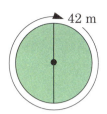
42 m

b. Figure out the diameter.

48 m

c. Figure out the circumference.

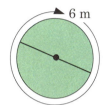
6 m

d. Figure out the diameter.

Part 4 Work each item.

a. $\frac{4}{5}$ of the mixture was carbon. The mixture weighed $\frac{2}{7}$ of a pound. What was the weight of the carbon?

b. The chimney's height was 180% of the school's height. The school was 60 feet tall. How tall was the chimney?

c. The water's weight is $\frac{7}{5}$ of the sugar's weight. The sugar weighs $\frac{3}{8}$ of a pound. What does the water weigh??

Part 5 Answer each question.

a. How many days are in 13 weeks and 1 day?
b. How many inches are in 5 feet and 9 inches?
c. How many ounces are in 2 pounds and 7 ounces?
d. How many hours are in 3 days and 6 hours?

Lesson 25

Part 6   Copy and work each item.

a. $74\overline{)183}$ b. $89\overline{)6715}$ c. $51\overline{)240}$

Independent Work

Part 7   Find the mystery number for each item.

a. You start with 111 and divide it by 3. Then you subtract 7. Then you divide by the mystery number and you end up with 10. What's the mystery number?

b. You start with a mystery number and double it. Then you subtract 50. Then you divide by 4 and you end up with 4. What's the mystery number?

c. You start with 5 and triple it. Then you add the mystery number. Then you divide by 3 and end up with 10. What's the mystery number?

Part 8   Copy and work each problem. Simplify the problem if you can.

a. $38\overline{)290}$ b. $50\overline{)290}$ c. $370\overline{)2080}$ d. $79\overline{)4360}$

Part 9   Work each item.

a. At a picnic, the ratio of egg-salad sandwiches to hot dogs was 5 to 4. There were 40 hot dogs. How many egg-salad sandwiches were there?

b. At the picnic, 30% of the children won prizes. If 35 children did not win prizes, how many children were at the picnic?

c. It took 5 minutes to prepare every 40 hot dogs. How long did it take to prepare 60 hot dogs?

d. $\frac{1}{4}$ of the people at the picnic came in cars. The rest came in buses. If 16 people came in cars, how many people did not come in cars?

Part 10   Write each item in a column and work it.

a. .3 x 20.8

b. 5.276 − 3.7

c. .57 + 3.008 + 1.5

Part 11   Rewrite each description as a mixed number and unit name.

a. 1 dollar and 4 dimes

b. 3 pounds and 3 ounces

c. 1 day and 20 hours

d. 1 hour and 42 minutes

e. 2 years and 1 season

Lesson 26

Part 1 Copy and complete each equation. Answer the questions.

Equations

a. $3 \_\_\_ = \dfrac{36 \text{ inches}}{12 \_\_\_}$

b. $5 \_\_\_ = \dfrac{300 \_\_\_}{60 \text{ minutes per hour}}$

c. $12 \_\_\_ = \dfrac{48 \_\_\_}{4 \text{ quarters per dollar}}$

d. $2 \_\_\_ = \dfrac{24 \text{ months}}{12 \_\_\_}$

Questions

a.
1) How many inches are in 3 feet?
2) How many feet are in 36 inches?
3) How many inches are in 1 foot?

b. How many hours are 300 minutes?

c. How many quarters are in $12?

d. How many years are 24 months?

Part 2 Work each item. Round answers to the nearest hundredth.

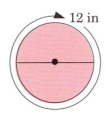

a. Figure out the diameter.

b. Figure out the circumference.

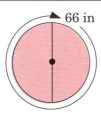

c. Figure out the diameter.

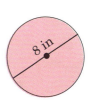

d. Figure out the circumference.

Part 3 Read each problem. Figure out whether or not you need to make a table. Write **table** or **no table**.

a. In a pond, there are 3 frogs for every 2 lily pads. There are 600 frogs in the pond. How many lily pads are there?

b. In another pond, the only fish are perch and bass. There are 4 perch for every 9 fish. If there are 45 bass, how many perch are there? How many fish are there?

c. In another pond, there are 7 water bugs for every 2 turtles. If there are 46 turtles, how many water bugs are there in the pond?

d. Near a river there are only two kinds of birds—herons and gulls. The ratio of herons to gulls is 3 to 16. There is a total of 228 birds near the river. How many herons are there?

Part 4 For each item, show the mixed number and the fraction it equals. Answer the question.

a. How many weeks are in 2 years and 3 weeks?

b. How many nickels are in 1 dollar and 5 nickels?

c. How many ounces are in 4 pounds and 7 ounces?

d. How many minutes are in 2 hours and 14 minutes?

Part 5

- You've worked problems that give a fraction of a value or a percent of a value. Some problems that work the same way use the word **as** instead of the word **of**. The problems tell about **as much as, as far as, as long as** or **as heavy as**.
- Here's part of a problem with the word **of**:

    Bill's weight is $\frac{7}{8}$ of his father's weight.

- Here's the same part with the word **as**:

    Bill's weight is $\frac{7}{8}$ as much as his father's weight.

- Here's an entire problem:

    The trip to Oregon takes $\frac{3}{5}$ as long as the trip to Texas. The trip to Texas takes 12 hours. How long does the trip to Oregon take?

- $\frac{3}{5}$ **as long as** the trip is $\frac{3}{5}$ **times** the trip.
    - You work the problem: $\frac{3}{5} \times 12 = \frac{36}{5}$ $\boxed{7\frac{1}{5} \text{ hr}}$
- The answer is $7\frac{1}{5}$ hours. That's how long it takes to get to Oregon.

Part 6 Work each item.

a. The car weighs 40% as much as the truck weighs. The truck weighs 6 tons. What does the car weigh?

b. The economy battery lasts .6 as long as the premium battery. The premium battery lasts 4.8 years. How long does the economy battery last?

c. 25% of the animals were on leashes. There were 20 animals. How many animals were on leashes?

d. There is $\frac{7}{10}$ as much chicken soup as vegetable soup. There are 9 gallons of vegetable soup. How much chicken soup is there?

Part 7

- You've worked with fractions that have denominators of 10, 100 or 1,000. $\frac{27}{10}$ $\frac{30}{100}$ $\frac{108}{1000}$

- You can show the decimal value the fraction equals.

  - Here's: $\frac{789}{100}$

- The digits in the numerator are 789. There are two decimal places. So it equals: **7.89**

- You do the same thing when the fraction is written as a division problem.

  - Here's: $100\overline{)789}$

- You're dividing by 100, so the answer has two decimal places:

  $100\overline{)789}^{\,7.89}$

- Notice where the answer is written. The whole-number part of the answer has one digit. So the whole number is over the last digit of 789.

- If you worked the problem the long way, you'd get the same answer with $\frac{89}{100}$ as the fraction:

  $$100\overline{)789}^{\,7\frac{89}{100}}$$
  $$\underline{-\,700}$$
  $$89$$

- Remember, division problems that divide by 10, 100 or 1,000 work just like fractions that have a denominator of 10, 100 or 1,000.

Part 8

Write each fraction as a division problem. Show the answer as a decimal value. Check the answer with your calculator.

a. $\frac{256}{100}$ b. $\frac{125}{10}$ c. $\frac{6204}{100}$ d. $\frac{1250}{1000}$

Independent Work

Remember to complete the problems in part 3.

Part 9
Copy and complete the table.

	Value	Decimal
Sample	$3\frac{2}{10}$	3.2
a.	$\frac{62}{100}$	
b.	$2\frac{2}{1000}$	
c.	$\frac{8}{10}$	
d.	$\frac{501}{100}$	
e.	$1\frac{12}{100}$	

Part 10
Write each item as a mixed number and a unit name.

a. 1 yard and 33 inches

b. 2 gallons and 1 quart

c. 2 years and 2 months

d. 1 year and 78 days

e. 4 weeks and 2 days

Part 11
Answer each question.

a. What's $\frac{2}{8}$ of 24?

b. What's $\frac{6}{5}$ of 10?

c. What's $\frac{1}{2}$ of $\frac{7}{8}$?

d. What's $\frac{5}{9}$ of 10?

Part 12
Round each number to the nearest hundredth.

a. 28.067

b. 3.0333

c. 17.297

Part 13
Work each item.

a. A truck starts out with some fuel in the tank and uses up 13 gallons. Then 42 gallons are added. Then the truck goes until the amount in the tank is divided by 2. The truck ends up with 24 gallons in the tank. How much did the truck start out with?

b. Start with a mystery number and triple it. Then subtract 25. Then multiply by 3. You end up with 105. What's the mystery number?

Part 14
Find the area and perimeter of each figure.

a. Rectangle: 15 ft by 10 ft

b.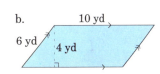

Lesson 27

Part 1 Copy and complete each equation.

a. ■ ■ = $\dfrac{240 \;\blacksquare}{\blacksquare \text{ minutes per hour}}$

b. ■ ■ = $\dfrac{72 \;\blacksquare}{\blacksquare \text{ inches per foot}}$

c. ■ ■ = $\dfrac{15 \text{ feet}}{3 \;\blacksquare}$

d. ■ ■ = $\dfrac{36 \text{ quarters}}{4 \;\blacksquare}$

e. ■ ■ = $\dfrac{80 \;\blacksquare}{\blacksquare \text{ nickels per dollar}}$

Part 2 Copy each problem and write the answer as a decimal value.

a. $100\overline{)62}$ b. $100\overline{)508}$ c. $10\overline{)5206}$ d. $1000\overline{)795}$

"I can't seem to multiply anything by pie."

Part 3

- The diameter goes through the center of a circle from one side to the other.

- Half the diameter is the **radius.** The radius goes from the edge to the center of the circle and then stops.

- Some circumference problems give information about the **radius** of the circle, not about the diameter.

- Here's a problem:

The radius is 4 feet. What's the circumference?

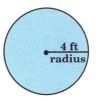 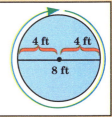

- If the radius is 4 feet, the diameter is twice that length–8 feet.

- So the circumference of the circle is π x 8.

π x d = C
3.14 x 8 = C
C = 25.12 ft

- If the problem gives the circumference and asks about the **radius,** you first figure out the **diameter.** Then you divide by 2 to find the radius.

- Here's a problem:

What is the radius?

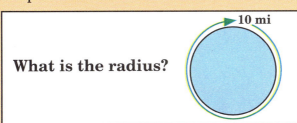

- The fraction you multiply by is $\frac{10}{3.14}$:

- The diameter is 3.18 miles.

- The radius is half that length: 3.18 ÷ 2.

π x d = C
3.14 ( ) = 10
3.14 ($\frac{10}{3.14}$) = 10

d = 3.18 mi

r = 1.59 mi

Part 4 Work each item. Round answers to the nearest hundredth.

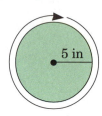

a. Figure out the circumference.

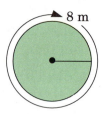

b. Figure out the radius.

c. Figure out the circumference.

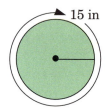

d. Figure out the radius.

Part 5 Work each item.

a. The cake's cost is 120% of the pie's cost. The pie costs $5. What does the cake cost?

b. The fence is .7 as long as the warehouse. The warehouse is 320 feet long. How long is the fence?

c. The bee egg weighs $\frac{3}{14}$ as much as the wasp egg. The wasp egg weighs $\frac{2}{3}$ of a gram. What does the bee egg weigh?

d. Team A ran $\frac{7}{5}$ as far as team B. Team B ran $\frac{8}{10}$ of a mile. How far did team A run?

Part 6 Show the mixed number and the fraction it equals. Answer the question.

a. How many feet are in 4 yards and 1 foot?

b. How many minutes are in 6 hours and 23 minutes?

c. How many centimeters are in 1 meter and 77 centimeters?

d. How many ounces are in 2 pounds and 11 ounces?

e. How many hours are in 3 days and 5 hours?

Part 7

- You've learned to work problems that multiply by a decimal value. You first do the multiplication. Then you count the decimal places in the problem and write the same number of decimal places in the answer.

    - Here's: $\begin{array}{r} 36 \\ \times\ .4 \\ \hline \end{array}$
    - The answer is: 14.4

- There's another way to work the same problem. You change each decimal value into a fraction and multiply.

    $36 \times \frac{4}{10} = \frac{144}{10} = 14.4$

- You end up with a fraction that equals the decimal answer, 14.4.

Part 8 Write each problem as a fraction-multiplication problem and work it.

a. $\begin{array}{r} 25 \\ \times\ .3 \\ \hline \end{array}$

b. $\begin{array}{r} 4 \\ \times\ .03 \\ \hline \end{array}$

c. $\begin{array}{r} .86 \\ \times\ .2 \\ \hline \end{array}$

d. $\begin{array}{r} 22 \\ \times\ .04 \\ \hline \end{array}$

Independent Work

Part 9 Write each item as a column problem and work it.

a. $14\frac{2}{3} + 9 + 11\frac{2}{3} = \blacksquare$
b. $14 - 9\frac{3}{8} = \blacksquare$
c. $17\frac{3}{100} + 2\frac{16}{100} = \blacksquare$

Part 10 Work each item.

a. 65% of the workers had dental problems. There were 105 workers who did not have dental problems. How many workers were there in all?

b. .3 of the documents had errors. There were 300 documents. How many did not have errors? How many did have errors?

c. A car used up 2 gallons of gas every 46 miles. The car went 90 miles. How many gallons of gas did it use?

Part 11 Copy and work each item.

a. $\blacksquare \times 7 = 5$
b. $2 \times \blacksquare = 1$
c. $80 \times \blacksquare = 3$
d. $8 \times \blacksquare = 7$

Part 12 Rewrite each item with two numbers and two unit names.

a. $3\frac{17}{60}$ hours
b. $1\frac{5}{12}$ feet
c. $2\frac{2}{4}$ gallons
d. $11\frac{3}{7}$ weeks
e. $20\frac{8}{10}$ dollars

Part 13 Copy and work each item.

a. $\frac{3}{4}\left(\frac{9}{9}\right) = \blacksquare$
b. $\frac{3}{4} = \frac{7}{\blacksquare}$
c. $\frac{12}{11} = \frac{7}{\blacksquare}$
d. $\frac{9}{5} = \frac{\blacksquare}{1}$
e. $\frac{2}{8}\left(\frac{7}{4}\right) = \blacksquare$

Part J

a. $\frac{120}{100} \times 5 = \frac{600}{100}$ $\boxed{\$6}$

b. $\frac{7}{10} \times 320 = 224$ $\boxed{224 \text{ ft}}$ or $\frac{320}{7} \times \frac{1}{} = \frac{2240}{7}$ $\boxed{224 \text{ ft}}$

c. $\frac{14}{3} \times \frac{2}{3} = \frac{42}{9}$ $\boxed{\frac{42}{9}}$

d. $\frac{7}{8} \times \frac{5}{10} = \frac{35}{50}$ $\boxed{\frac{9}{50} \text{ mi}}$

Lesson 28

Part 1

- You've worked problems that tell about a fraction of something. You've solved these problems by using multiplication.
- Here's part of a problem:

    Jane's age is $\frac{3}{4}$ of her mother's age.

- You can't work the problem as a multiplication problem unless you have a number for **her mother's age.**
- You can't work this problem as a multiplication problem:

    Jane is $\frac{3}{4}$ as old as her mother. Jane is 54 years old. How old is her mother?

- You'd write: $\frac{3}{4} \times m$
- The problem does not give a number for **m**. It gives a number for Jane. So you can't work the problem by multiplying.

Part 2

Figure out which items can be worked by multiplication, and work them.

a. Dan weighs $\frac{7}{5}$ as much as Mary. Dan weighs 80 pounds. How much does Mary weigh?

b. The train travels $\frac{3}{5}$ as far as the car. The car travels 60 miles. How far does the train travel?

c. The county is $\frac{1}{8}$ as large as the state. The county is 300 square miles. How large is the state?

d. The bug's weight is $\frac{8}{9}$ of the pebble's weight. The pebble weighs 20 grams. How much does the bug weigh?

e. The coast is $\frac{9}{5}$ as far away as the mountain. The mountain is 40 miles away. How far away is the coast?

Part 3 Read each problem. Figure out whether or not you need to make a table. Write **table** or **no table**.

a. At Jones Elementary School, there are 4 boys for every 5 girls. There are 225 children at Jones Elementary. How many boys attend the school?

b. The ratio of girls to boys on a bus was 6 to 5. There were 24 girls on the bus. How many children were on the bus?

c. The ratio of girls to boys on a playground was 3 to 4. There were 56 boys on the playground. How many girls were on the playground?

Part 4 Copy and complete each equation.

a. $\blacksquare \blacksquare = \dfrac{180 \text{ seconds}}{60 \ \blacksquare}$

b. $\blacksquare \blacksquare = \dfrac{32 \ \blacksquare}{\blacksquare \text{ quarts per gallon}}$

c. $\blacksquare \blacksquare = \dfrac{400 \ \blacksquare}{\blacksquare \text{ cents per dollar}}$

d. $\blacksquare \blacksquare = \dfrac{60 \text{ inches}}{12 \ \blacksquare}$

Part 5 Work each item.

a. Figure out the circumference.

b. Figure out the radius.

c. Figure out the circumference.

d. Figure out the radius.

Part 6 Write each decimal value as a fraction and multiply. Then write the answer as a decimal value.

a. 2.1
   x .02

b. .5
   x 1.8

c. 10
   x .42

d. 2.71
   x   .4

Part 7 Work each item. Use shortcuts.

a. 60 ⟌ 980

b. 100 ⟌ 24

c. 100 ⟌ 800

d. 640 ⟌ 880

e. 10 ⟌ 486

Independent Work

Remember to complete the problems in part 3.

Part 8 Work each item.

a. What's $\frac{2}{7}$ of 21?

b. Billy is $\frac{3}{5}$ as old as his horse. His horse is 27 years old. How old is Billy?

c. Mr. Johnson earns $\frac{7}{3}$ as much as his son. His son earns $1,000 a month. How much does Mr. Johnson earn in a month?

d. What's $\frac{3}{5}$ of 30?

e. What $\frac{7}{3}$ of 15?

Part 9 For each item, show the mixed number and the fraction it equals. Answer the question.

a. How many feet are in 5 yards and 1 foot?

b. How many inches are in 3 yards and 7 inches?

c. How many months are in 2 years and 6 months?

d. How many quarters are in 4 dollars and 3 quarters?

Part 10 For each item, make equations and answer the question.

a. Start with Jerry's age and divide it by 4. Then add 3. Then divide by 4. You end up with 2. How old is Jerry?

b. A train started out with 200 passengers. At the first stop, 33 people got off. Then some people got on the train. At the next stop, 24 people got off the train, and the train had 148 people on it. How many people got on at the first stop?

c. Start with the mystery number and subtract 50. Then divide the number by 3. Then subtract 8. Then multiply by 3. You end up with 24. What's the mystery number?

Lesson 29

Part 1

- You've learned to find the circumference of a circle. That's the distance around the circle.

- You can also find the area of a circle. That's the number of square units that fill the circle.

- Here's the equation for the area of a circle:

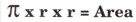

$\pi \times r \times r = \text{Area}$

- When you multiply the **radius** times the **radius,** you get a square that's as wide and as high as the radius.

- When you multiply **that square** times π, you end up with a little more than three of those squares.

- Parts of each square are outside the circle. When you move those parts around, the entire circle is filled and there are no leftover parts.

- Remember, the **radius** times the **radius** gives a **square.** When you multiply that square times π, you have the area of the circle.

  - Here's a circle:

- The diameter is 6. So the radius is 3.
- You multiply 3 x 3. And multiply that by 3.14. You get 28.26. That's the number of square units in the circle.

A = 28.26 square units

Part 2 Figure out the area of each circle.

$$\pi \times r \times r = A$$

a.  16 m

b. 9 in

c. 12 yd

d. 2 mi

Part 3 Copy each item and write the answer as a mixed number.

a. 100)156   b. 10)288   c. 100)2648   d. 10)892

Part 4

- You can write complete equations from questions like this:

  How many yards are in 27 feet?

- The units named in the question are **yards** and **feet**.

- The equation shows the larger unit on the left. So **yards** goes on the left and **feet** goes in the numerator of the fraction.

  ■ yards = $\dfrac{27 \text{ feet}}{}$

- The denominator of the fraction tells the number of feet in one yard. That's the number of feet per yard.

  ■ yards = $\dfrac{27 \text{ feet}}{■ \text{ feet per yard}}$

- The **name** for the denominator tells you the **number** for the denominator. It's 3.

  ■ yards = $\dfrac{27 \text{ feet}}{3 \text{ feet per yard}}$

- Now you can figure out the number of yards. It's 9.

  9 yards = $\dfrac{27 \text{ feet}}{3 \text{ feet per yard}}$

- Remember, put the name for the larger unit on the left and the name for the smaller unit as the numerator of the fraction. The denominator of the fraction shows how the two names are related.

Lesson 29 115

Part 5
Write an equation for each item.

a. How many years are in 360 months?
b. How many minutes are in 180 seconds?
c. How many gallons are in 12 quarts?
d. How many dollars are in 100 nickels?

Part 6
Figure out which items can be worked by multiplication. Then work those items.

a. The man spent $\frac{5}{4}$ the amount his son spent. The man spent $20. How much did his son spend?

b. The fence is $\frac{3}{5}$ as long as the sidewalk. The fence is 25 yards long. How long is the sidewalk?

c. The toy's weight is $\frac{9}{5}$ of the cat's weight. The cat weighs 20 pounds. What does the toy weigh?

d. The cost of the soil is $\frac{1}{8}$ the cost of the bulbs. The bulbs cost $24. What does the soil cost?

e. The fall crop was $\frac{7}{3}$ of the summer crop. The fall crop was 52 tons. What was the summer crop?

Part 7
For each item, work a fraction-multiplication problem. Then write the answer as a decimal value. Check each item by working the original problem.

a. .03   b. 1.5   c. 4.02   d. 5.2
    x 14   x .7   x .8   x 9

Independent Work

Part 8 Work each item. Round answers to the nearest hundredth.

a. Find the circumference.

b. Find the diameter.

Part 9 Work each item.

a. What's $\frac{3}{10}$ of 40?

b. What's $\frac{1}{2}$ of $\frac{5}{8}$?

c. $\frac{3}{5}$ of the apples were spoiled. There were 200 apples. How many were spoiled?

d. $\frac{2}{9}$ of the children were laughing. There were 162 children. How many were laughing?

Part 10 Find the perimeter and area of each figure.

a.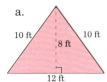

b.

Part 11 For each item, make a ratio table or write a ratio equation. Answer the question.

a. 30% of the telephones are cordless. There are 9 cordless phones. How many phones are there in all?

b. The ratio of red birds to yellow birds is 7 to 30. If there are 63 red birds, how many yellow birds are there?

c. A machine produces 11 bottle caps every 3 seconds. The machine works for 120 seconds. How many bottle caps does it produce?

Part 12 Write the mixed number and unit name for each item.

a. 4 pounds and 13 ounces

b. 2 years and 3 seasons

c. 7 dollars and 59 cents

d. 2 days and 3 hours

Lesson 30

Part 1 Figure out which items you can work by multiplication. Then work those items.

a. The woman earns $\frac{7}{5}$ the amount her husband earns. Her husband earns $3,000. What does the woman earn?

b. The road race is $\frac{1}{8}$ as far as the bicycle race. The road race is 6 kilometers. How far is the bike race?

c. The truck's weight is $\frac{8}{3}$ the elephant's weight. The elephant weighs 2 tons. What is the weight of the truck?

d. Dan has completed $\frac{4}{5}$ of the job. The entire job will take 25 hours. How many hours has Dan worked so far?

e. Bonnie is $\frac{2}{3}$ as old as her aunt. Bonnie is 20 years old. How old is her aunt?

Test 3

Part 1 For each item, show the mixed number and the fraction it equals. Answer the question.

a. How many inches are in $2\frac{3}{12}$ feet?

b. How many months are in 1 year and 11 months?

c. How many ounces are in 2 pounds and 3 ounces?

Part 2 Use shortcuts to work each problem.

a. $40\overline{)7080}$ b. $10\overline{)3789}$

c. $100\overline{)376}$ d. $600\overline{)4790}$

Part 3 Round each decimal to the nearest hundredth.

a. 2.397   b. 56.019

c. 3.074   d. 2.555

Part 4 Write each decimal value as a fraction and multiply. Then write the answer as a decimal value.

a. .04
   x .3

b. 1.05
   x 10

Part 5 Copy and work each each problem.

a. 16)356

b. 31)2037

Part 6 Work each item.

a. At a picnic, 3 out of every 4 children wore shorts. 20 children did not wear shorts. How many children were at the picnic?

b. 24% of the items were on sale. There were 300 items in all. How many items were not on sale?

c. 2 out of every 3 frogs had spots. There were 27 frogs. How many of them had spots?

Part 7 Copy and complete each equation.

a. ■ ■ = $\dfrac{36 \text{ months}}{12\ ■}$

b. 2 ■ = $\dfrac{■\ ■}{16 \text{ ounces per pound}}$

c. 5 hours = $\dfrac{■ \text{ minutes}}{■\ ■}$

Part 8 Figure the area of each figure.

a.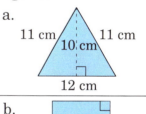

b.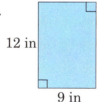

Part 9 Use your calculator to work each item.

a. Figure out the radius.

b. Figure out the circumference.

c. Figure out the diameter.

Lesson 31

Part 1

- Here's a statement:

    Pile A is $\frac{3}{4}$ the weight of pile B. $\frac{3}{4} \times B$

- You know that you can work a multiplication problem if you have a number for pile B.

- But even if you don't have numbers for pile A or pile B, you can show how large one of the piles is compared to the other pile. Here's why: One of the names in the problem already has a fraction. The other name is 1 whole.

- Pile A has the fraction $\frac{3}{4}$:

- Pile A is compared to pile B. So pile **B is 1 whole:**

- 1 whole is larger than $\frac{3}{4}$. The **larger value is the big number** in the number family.

- Here's another statement:

    The truck is $\frac{8}{3}$ the size of the car.

- One of the names has a fraction. That name is **truck**. The fraction is $\frac{8}{3}$. The other name in the sentence is **car**. It's 1 whole: $\frac{3}{3}$.

    - Here's the number family:

- The big number is $\frac{8}{3}$. That's the fraction for the truck. Remember, this fraction number family doesn't show the actual size of the car or the truck. It just shows how much larger the truck is than the car.

- Here are some picture pairs for the truck and the car. If the car is a certain size, the truck is so much bigger.

Part 2

- Here are the rules for making fraction number families from statements that compare:
  ✔ You find the name for the fraction.
  ✔ If the fraction is **more than 1,** the name is the **big number.**
  ✔ If the fraction is **less than 1,** the name is a **small number.**
- Here's a sentence:

    The pile's weight was $\frac{7}{3}$ the truck's weight.

- Here's another sentence:

    The dog's age is $\frac{7}{8}$ the cat's age.

- Remember, if the fraction is less than 1, the name for that fraction is not the big number.

Part 3 For each item, write a fraction number family with two names and two fractions.

> ***Sample sentence*** Bill is $\frac{7}{5}$ as old as his sister.

a. The sale price is $\frac{8}{10}$ of the regular price.

b. The distance to the coast is $\frac{11}{6}$ the distance to the river.

c. Lunch costs $\frac{5}{8}$ as much as dinner.

d. The man's age is $\frac{13}{12}$ his wife's age.

Part 4

- Some problems tell the value for each item and then tell how many items there are. You can work those problems by multiplying.

- Here's a problem:

    Each seed weighs 3 grams. There are 90 seeds. What is the weight of these seeds?

- You multiply 90 by 3.

    $$\begin{array}{r} 90 \\ \times\ 3 \\ \hline \end{array}$$

    The answer is 270 grams.   270 g

- Here's a problem that involves money:

    Each gram of medication costs 3¢. There are 56 grams of medication. What's the total cost?

- You multiply 56 by 3 cents. 3 cents is $\frac{3}{100}$ of a dollar. You can show that value as a decimal or as a fraction. The answer is $1.68.

    $$\begin{array}{r} 56 \\ \times\ .03 \\ \hline \$1.68 \end{array}$$

    $56 \times \frac{3}{100} = \frac{168}{100}$ $1.68

- Remember, if a problem gives a value for each item and asks about the value for a group of those items, you multiply. The value for each item x the number of items = the product. The product is the answer.

Part 5

Answer each question.

a. Each pint of paint costs $3.50. A painter buys 45 pints of paint. What's the cost of all the paint?

b. Stamps cost 7¢ each. How much do 80 stamps cost?

c. Each sheet of sandpaper costs 6¢. There are 50 sheets in a package. How much does the package cost?

d. Each donut weighs 4.5 ounces. What's the weight of 12 donuts?

Part 6 Make equivalent fractions for each problem and box the answer to each question.

a. How many months are in $\frac{5}{4}$ years?

b. How many months are in $\frac{2}{3}$ of a year?

c. How many quarts are in $\frac{9}{2}$ gallons?

d. How many seconds are in $\frac{7}{3}$ minutes?

e. How many pints are in $\frac{5}{2}$ gallons?

Part 7 Find the area of each circle.

a. 16 in

b. 9 yd

c. 15 m

d. 4 mi

Part 8 Write an equation for each item. Box the answer to the question.

a. How many years are in 72 months?

b. How many yards are in 63 feet?

c. How many dollars are in 100 quarters?

d. How many pounds are in 48 ounces?

Independent Work

Part 9 Work each item. Round answers to the nearest hundredths.

 54 in

 7 in

 345 mi

a. Figure out the circumference.

b. Figure out the diameter.

c. Figure out the radius.

Lesson 31 123

Part 10 Work each item.

a. $16\overline{)121}$ b. $43\overline{)146}$

c. $73\overline{)829}$

Part 11 Write each item in columns and work it.

a. 6.08 x 1.9 b. 1.63 + 2.304 c. 16.2 − .37

Part 12 For each item, make a ratio equation or a ratio table. Answer each question.

a. 2 of every 13 scissors needed repairs. 55 scissors did not need repairs. How many scissors needed repairs? How many scissors were there in all?

b. For every 7 workers, there are 4 workers in the union. 260 workers at a factory are in the union. How many workers are in the factory?

Part 13 Copy and complete each equation.

a. $\dfrac{8}{3} = \dfrac{32}{\blacksquare}$

b. $4(\blacksquare) = 37$

c. $\dfrac{2}{11} = \dfrac{\blacksquare}{4}$

d. $\dfrac{3}{4} = \dfrac{\blacksquare}{10}$

e. $\dfrac{\blacksquare}{2} = 4$

Part 14 Work each item.

a. Joe picked 174 more berries than he ate. Joe ate 196 berries. How many berries did he pick?

b. Jill picked blueberries and blackberries. Jill picked 196 berries in all. If she picked 174 blackberries, how many blueberries did Jill pick?

Part 15 Work each problem that can be worked by multiplying. Do not work the other problems.

a. The table costs $\dfrac{4}{5}$ as much as the couch. The table costs $250. How much does the couch cost?

b. The sofa costs $\dfrac{6}{4}$ as much as the chair. The chair costs $211. How much does the sofa cost?

c. Billy was $\dfrac{9}{7}$ the height of his brother. His brother was 49 inches tall. How tall was Billy?

d. The alligator was $\dfrac{3}{4}$ the length of the snake. The snake was 80 inches long. How long was the alligator?

e. The tank's weight is $\dfrac{5}{4}$ the weight of the barrel. The barrel weighs 457 pounds. What's the weight of the tank?

f. Bernie is $\dfrac{4}{7}$ as old as her aunt. Her aunt is 56 years old. How old is Bernie?

Lesson 32

Part 1 Make a complete equation for each item. Box the answer to the question.

a. How many pints are in 32 cups?
b. How many days are in 96 hours?
c. How many years are in 104 weeks?
d. How many dollars are in 80 dimes?
e. How many gallons are in 72 pints?

Part 2   Figure out the circumference and the area of each circle.

a. circle with radius 2.5 ft

b. circle with diameter 16 cm

Part 3   Answer each question.

a. How many inches are in $\frac{8}{3}$ feet?

b. How many minutes is $\frac{2}{5}$ of an hour?

c. How many hours are in $\frac{5}{4}$ days?

d. How many ounces are in $\frac{1}{2}$ pound?

Part 4   Answer each question. Remember the dollar signs.

a. Each hour that Dan worked, he earned $12.30. He worked for 4 and $\frac{2}{10}$ hours. How much did he earn?

b. Reggie earned $5.85 for each full hour he worked. He worked $\frac{5}{10}$ of an hour. How much did he earn?

c. Rita earned $14.80 for each full hour she worked. She worked $\frac{3}{10}$ of an hour. How much did she earn?

d. Donna earned $15.10 for each full hour she worked. How much did she earn if she worked $3\frac{2}{10}$ hours?

e. Sid worked $5\frac{5}{10}$ hours. If he earned $13.65 for each full hour he worked, how much did he earn altogether?

Part 5

- Sentences that compare tell about number families. Because these sentences compare, they always have a difference number. That's the first value shown in a complete family.

- Here's a sentence:

  Fran's height is $\frac{7}{5}$ of Ann's height.

- Fran has the fraction $\frac{7}{5}$. It's more than 1, so **Fran** is the big number.

- The sentence compares somebody to Ann. So **Ann** equals 1. She's a small number.

- The difference between Ann's height and Fran's height is shown with the fraction $\frac{2}{5}$.

- Below is a diagram of Ann's height, Fran's height and the difference.

- Remember, the difference does not mean that Ann is $\frac{2}{5}$ of an inch shorter than Fran. It means that if Ann is 5 units tall, Fran is 7 units tall. Fran is 2 units taller.

Lesson 32

Part 6
Make a complete fraction number family for each item.

a. Ann is $\frac{3}{8}$ as old as Fran.

b. Dan weighs $\frac{4}{3}$ the amount that Greg weighs.

c. The car travels at $\frac{11}{3}$ the speed of the bicycle.

d. The attendance at the football game was $\frac{9}{7}$ the attendance at the baseball game.

e. The new price is $\frac{4}{5}$ as much as the old price.

Independent Work

Part 7
Write each problem in columns and work it.

a. .064 + 8.14   b. 10.5 − 2.73   c. 3.06 − .257   d. 1.76 × 3

Part 8
Work each item.

a. One of the items costs $8.57 more than the backpack. Which item?

b. Jill bought the poster, the cap and the camera. How much did she spend?

Part 9
Work each problem that you can work as a multiplication problem.

a. The car went $\frac{7}{3}$ the speed of the bus. The bus went 30 miles per hour. How fast did the car go?

b. Ginger's dog is $\frac{5}{2}$ as old as her cat. Her dog is 11 years old. How old is the cat?

c. The bicycle costs $\frac{3}{8}$ as much as the TV. The TV costs $400. How much does the bicycle cost?

Part 10
Copy and work each problem. Figure out the missing number and write an equation to show what the letter equals.

a. 2314 − R = 169
R = ■

b. M + 82 = 356
M = ■

c. T = 643 + 12 + 34
T = ■

d. 8 + 174 + 301 = V
V = ■

e. 5 × R = 14
R = ■

f. 17 × 6 = M
M = ■

Part 11 For each problem, make a ratio equation or a ratio table. Answer each question.

a. $\frac{2}{3}$ of the days in September were sunny. There are 30 days in September. How many days were sunny? How many days were not sunny?

b. A truck travels at a steady rate of 12 miles every 17 minutes. If the truck travels for 51 minutes, how far does it travel?

c. Joe's car lot has 7 new cars for every 3 used cars. There are 56 new cars on the lot. How many cars are on the lot?

Part 12 Write the division problem for each fraction that is more than 1. Write the answer as a mixed number.

a. $\frac{3}{27}$ e. $\frac{27}{2}$ h. $\frac{15}{12}$

b. $\frac{17}{4}$ f. $\frac{4}{4}$ i. $\frac{100}{100}$

c. $\frac{4}{17}$ g. $\frac{39}{9}$ j. $\frac{38}{5}$

d. $\frac{17}{17}$

Lesson 33

Part 1 Make a complete equation for each item. Box the answer to the question.

a. How many months are in 4 years?

b. How many inches are in 14 feet?

c. How many nickels are in 15 dollars?

d. How many hours are in 3 days?

Part 2

- Here's a difficult problem:

  The sale price of a bed was $\frac{2}{5}$ the regular price. If the regular price of the bed was $550, how much was the sale price?

- The problem tells about fractions, so you can make a fraction number family.

- The problem indicates that the sale price is $\frac{2}{5}$. That's a small number.

- The regular price is the big number, $\frac{5}{5}$.

- The difference is $\frac{3}{5}$.

$$\xrightarrow{\frac{2}{5}}\text{sale price}$$

$$\underset{\frac{3}{5}}{\text{dif}} \underset{\frac{2}{5}}{\text{sale price}} \xrightarrow{} \underset{\frac{5}{5}}{\text{regular price}}$$

- You know that the numerators are ratio numbers. You can put them in a ratio table. Then you put in the **number** the problem gives. That's the regular price of the bed—$550.

dif	3	
sp	2	
rp	5	550

- Now you can figure out the sale price of the bed and how much you'd save if you bought the bed on sale. That's the difference number.

Part 3 Make a number family and a ratio table for each problem. Answer the questions.

a. The regular price of a chair is $\frac{5}{4}$ the sale price of the chair. If you bought the chair on sale, you'd save $12. What's the regular price of the chair? What's the sale price of the chair?

b. The elephant weighs $\frac{3}{8}$ as much as the rock. The elephant weighs 6,000 pounds. How much does the rock weigh? How much more does the rock weigh than the elephant weighs?

c. The cost of the sewing machine is $\frac{7}{5}$ the cost of the TV set. The TV set costs $280. How much does the sewing machine cost? What's the difference between the cost of the sewing machine and the cost of the TV set?

Part 4 Figure out the circumference and the area of each circle.

a.

b.

Part 5

- You've made fraction number families from statements that use a fraction to compare two things.

- The fraction number families don't tell the actual weight or height or age. They just give you a way of comparing the two values.

- Here's a sentence:

  The house was $\frac{1}{2}$ as tall as the pole.

- Here's the fraction number family:

  $$\xrightarrow{\text{dif} \quad \text{house} \quad \text{pole}} \quad \frac{1}{2} \quad \frac{2}{2}$$

- One of these diagrams shows what the statement says.

Part 6 For each item, make a fraction number family. Then write the number of the correct picture.

a. The pole is $\frac{10}{9}$ the height of the house.

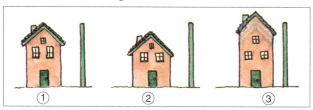

b. The dog is $\frac{1}{4}$ as tall as the pole.

c. The cat is $\frac{1}{8}$ the height of the pole.

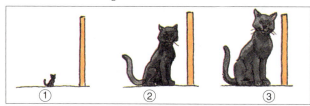

d. The pole is $\frac{9}{5}$ the height of the tree.

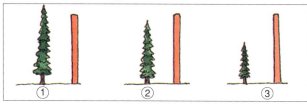

e. The tiger was $\frac{8}{5}$ the length of the alligator.

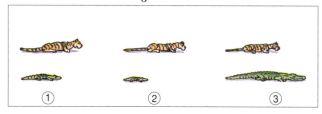

Part 7   Answer each question.

a. Mark earns $5.60 for each full hour he works. If he works $1\frac{8}{10}$ hours, how much does he earn?

b. Each full day that Martha works, she earns $38.75. If she works for $\frac{8}{10}$ of a day, how much does she earn?

c. Bill earns $3.50 an hour. How much would he earn for 15 hours' work?

Part 8   Answer each question.

a. How many hours are in $\frac{3}{8}$ of a day?

b. How many months are in $\frac{7}{3}$ years?

c. How many seconds are in $\frac{12}{10}$ minutes?

Independent Work

Part 9   Work each problem.

a. Start with Donna's age and add 20. Then divide by 3. Then subtract 25. You end up with 0. What's Donna's age?

b. Start with the mystery number. Subtract 100. Then divide by 3. You end up with 20. What's the mystery number?

c. Fred had $345 in the bank. Then Fred took out $120. Later, Fred put some money in the bank. He now has $490 in the bank. How much did he put in the bank?

Part 10   Work each item.

a. Find the circumference.

b. Find the radius.

Part 11   Answer each question.

a. There were 84 dirty cars in a lot. There was a total of 167 cars in the lot. How many of the cars were not dirty?

b. There were 83 fewer dirty cars than clean cars. There were 84 dirty cars. How many clean cars were there?

Part 12 For each item, make a ratio equation or a ratio table. Answer each question.

a. 35% of the cards were blue. There were 200 cards. How many were blue?

b. There are 2 cups of water in every 3 cups of soup. A chef makes 20 cups of soup. How many cups of water are needed?

c. The wheel turns 3 times every 8 seconds. If the wheel turns 26 times, how many seconds pass?

Part 13 Copy and complete the table.

	Fraction	Decimal	Mixed number
a.	$\frac{357}{10}$		
b.			$16\frac{2}{100}$
c.		8.067	
d.			$10\frac{76}{1000}$

Part 14 Copy each problem and write the answer.

a. $\frac{17}{4} - \frac{6}{4} =$

b. $\frac{3}{2} \times \frac{5}{4} \times \frac{1}{5} =$

c. $\frac{12}{5} + \frac{6}{5} =$

Part 15 Answer each question.

a. What fraction of a year is 7 months?

b. What fraction of a day is 5 hours?

c. What is $\frac{3}{4}$ of a gallon?

d. What is $\frac{17}{60}$ of a minute?

e. What fraction of a year is 6 days?

Part J

b. $38.75
  × 8
  $31.00̸0̸

c. $3.50
  × 15
  1750
  + 3500
  $52.50

Lesson 34

Part 1 Make a complete equation for each item. Box the answer to the question.

a. How many months are in 10 years?

b. How many minutes are in 4 hours?

c. How many days are in 72 hours?

d. How many hours are in 120 minutes?

e. How many hours are in 20 days?

Part 2

- You're going to make fraction number families and find the diagram that shows what your family shows.
- The fraction that is 1 whole gives you a clue for estimating which picture is correct.
- Here's a statement:

   The tiger is $\frac{7}{8}$ as long as the alligator.

- Here's the fraction number family: $\overset{\text{dif}}{\frac{1}{8}} \overset{\text{tiger}}{\frac{7}{8}} \longrightarrow \overset{\text{alligator}}{\frac{8}{8}}$

- The fraction for the alligator is $\frac{8}{8}$. So you think about dividing the alligator into 8 equal parts. The tiger would be the length of 7 parts.

- Remember, the fraction for 1 gives you information for estimating.

Part 3 For each item, make a fraction number family. Then write the number of the correct picture.

a. The alligator is $\frac{7}{5}$ the length of the tiger.

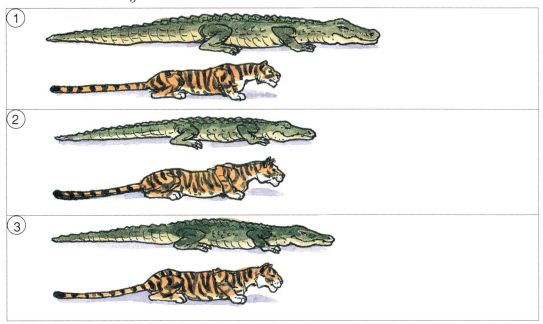

b. The tiger is $\frac{4}{10}$ as long as the alligator.

c. The alligator is $\frac{8}{4}$ the length of the tiger.

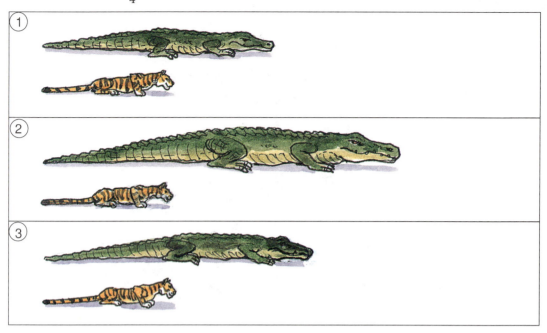

d. The tiger is $\frac{1}{3}$ as long as the alligator.

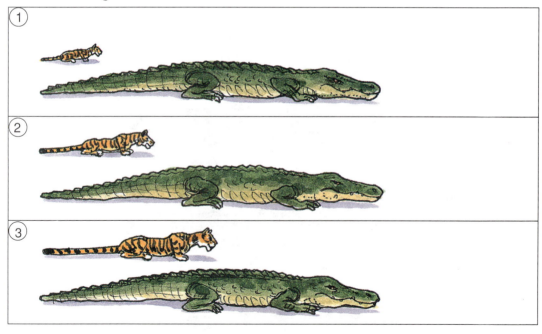

Part 4   **Answer each question.**

a. Each serving had 46 calories. How many calories are in $3\frac{5}{10}$ servings?

b. Each gallon of fuel costs $1.42. A tank of gas holds 20 gallons. How much does it cost to fill the tank?

c. Bo earns $7.25 per hour. She works $1\frac{5}{10}$ hours. How much does she earn?

Part 5   **Make a number family and a ratio table for each problem. Answer the questions.**

a. The area of the rug was $\frac{3}{2}$ the area of the living room. The installers had to cut 24 square meters from the rug before it would fit in the living room. What's the area of the living room? What was the area of the rug before the installers cut it?

b. The number of students on the field trip was $\frac{3}{5}$ the number of students attending the hockey practice. 35 students attended the hockey practice. How many students were on the field trip? How many fewer students were on the field trip than were at the hockey practice?

c. Lunch cost $\frac{4}{9}$ as much as dinner cost. Dinner cost $36. How much did lunch cost? How much more did dinner cost than lunch?

Part 6   **Complete each statement.**

> **Sample problem** $5\frac{2}{3}$ hours is ■ hours and ■ minutes.

a. $8\frac{3}{4}$ dollars is ■ dollars and ■ cents.

b. $4\frac{7}{8}$ days is ■ days and ■ hours.

c. $1\frac{5}{12}$ minutes is ■ minutes and ■ seconds.

d. $10\frac{4}{5}$ dollars is ■ dollars and ■ cents.

Independent Work

Part 7
Work each item.

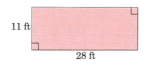
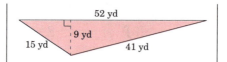

a. What's the perimeter? What's the area?

b. What's the perimeter? What's the area?

c. What's the circumference? What's the area?

Part 8
Work each item.

a. 94 ⟌ 7360

b. 12 ⟌ 485

c. 65 ⟌ 372

d. 37 ⟌ 78

Part 9
Work each item.

a. A water tank starts out with 400 gallons. Then 120 gallons are removed. Then the number of gallons in the tank is tripled. Then some water leaks from the tank. The tank ends up with 60 gallons in it. How much water leaked from the tank?

b. Start with the mystery number and double it. Then subtract 60. Then divide by 6. Then subtract 10. You end up with 0. What's the mystery number?

Part 10
For each item, make a ratio equation or a ratio table. Answer each question.

a. A factory produced 112 bottles every 4 minutes. The factory produced bottles for 36 minutes. How many bottles did the factory produce?

b. In the forest there are squirrels and rabbits. There are 7 squirrels for every 5 rabbits. There are 245 squirrels. How many rabbits are there?

c. 20% of the items in the store are on sale. 240 items are not on sale. How many items are in the store?

Part 11
Answer each question.

a. What is $\frac{2}{3}$ of a yard?

b. What is $\frac{8}{365}$ of a year?

c. How many months are in $\frac{5}{12}$ years?

d. What is $\frac{3}{16}$ of a pound?

Part J

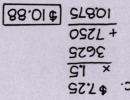
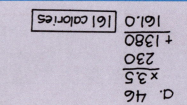

Lesson 35

Part 1 Work each item.

a. How many weeks are in 56 days?

b. How many days are in 28 weeks?

c. How many years are in 156 weeks?

d. How many weeks are in 12 years?

Part 2

- Some problems are made up of simpler problems. To work these problems, you solve the simpler problems and then use the answers to work the final problem.

- Here's an example:

    A rectangular field is 80 feet by 200 feet. A farmer fences the field. The fencing costs $1.30 per foot. How much does the fence cost?

    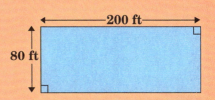

- Before we can figure out the cost of the fence, we have to figure out how much fence to use. So we figure out the perimeter of the field:

    ```
      80
      80
     200
    +200
    ```
    P = 560 ft

- We need fencing for each foot of the perimeter. So we multiply the cost of the fencing by the number of feet.

    ```
    $1.30
    x 560
    ```
    $728.00

- The total cost of fencing the field is $728.

- Remember, work the simpler problems. Then use the answers to work the final problem.

Part 3 Work each item.

a. A farmer plants a field with wheat. The field is 240 feet long and 360 feet wide. The cost of wheat is $.03 per square foot. How much does it cost to plant the entire field?

b. A farmer wants to fence a square field that is 90 feet on each side. The cost of fencing is $2.58 per foot. What's the cost of fencing for the field?

c. A farmer gets $.90 per gallon of milk and $.55 for each dozen eggs. In April, the farmer sold 1,235 gallons of milk and 165 dozen eggs. How much money did the farmer receive?

d. A farmer receives $2.10 for each bushel of corn and $.50 for each dozen eggs. During one month, the farmer sold 1,600 bushels of corn and 284 dozen eggs. How much did the farmer earn in all?

Part 4 Make a number family and a ratio table for each problem. Answer the questions.

a. The tank holds $\frac{7}{5}$ as much as the barrel. The barrel holds 65 gallons. How much does the tank hold? How much more does the tank hold than the barrel holds?

b. Michael earned $\frac{2}{3}$ the amount that Walter earned. Walter earned $145 more than Michael. How much did Walter earn? How much did Michael earn?

c. Sarah's weight is $\frac{12}{5}$ her dog's weight. Sarah weighs 96 pounds. How much does Sarah's dog weigh? How much more does Sarah weigh than her dog weighs?

Part 5

- You've worked division problems that have a mixed-number answer.

  - Here's 8 ÷ 5: $5\overline{)8} = 1\frac{3}{5}$

  - The answer's $1\frac{3}{5}$.

- You can work those same problems so they have a decimal answer. The decimal answer will show exactly the same value as the mixed-number answer.

- Here are the steps for working division problems so the answer shows hundredths.

- Write a decimal point and two zeros after the decimal point: $5\overline{)8.00}$

- Then write a decimal point in the answer directly above the other decimal point: $5\overline{)8.00}$ with $1.$ above

  - Then work the problem: $5\overline{)8.00} = 1.60$

- The answer is 1.60. That's the same value as $1\frac{3}{5}$.

- Remember the steps:
   ✔ Make a decimal point after the whole number.
   ✔ Make two zeros.
   ✔ Put the decimal point in the answer.
   ✔ Work the problem.

Part 6   Copy each division problem. Write the decimal point and two zeros. Then work the problem.

a. $4\overline{)13}$ b. $2\overline{)7}$ c. $8\overline{)12}$

Part 7 Complete each statement.

a. $1\frac{3}{4}$ yards is ■ yard and ■ inches.

b. $6\frac{2}{3}$ feet is ■ feet and ■ inches.

c. $3\frac{1}{2}$ years is ■ years and ■ weeks.

Independent Work

Part 8 Work each item.

a. Find the radius.

b. Find the circumference.

c. Find the area.

d. Find the diameter.

e. Find the circumference.

Part 9 Copy and complete each equation.

a. $\frac{■}{2} = 8$

b. $\frac{7}{4} = \frac{28}{■}$

c. $5(■) = 36$

d. $17(■) = 2$

e. $\frac{5}{35} = \frac{■}{7}$

f. $\frac{3}{8} + \frac{7}{8} = ■$

Part 10 Copy and complete the table.

	Fraction	Decimal	Mixed number
a.	$\frac{3074}{1000}$		
b.		10.60	
c.	$\frac{807}{10}$		
d.			$7\frac{5}{100}$

Part 11 Work each item.

a. 80% of the vacation days were sunny. 12 days were not sunny. How many vacation days were there?

b. $\frac{2}{9}$ of the people in the audience wear glasses. There are 243 people in the audience. How many people wear glasses? How many people do not wear glasses?

Part 12 For each statement, make the fraction number family. Write the number of the correct diagram.

a. The elephant was $\frac{3}{7}$ the height of the tree.

b. The apartment building is $\frac{5}{2}$ the height of the pole.

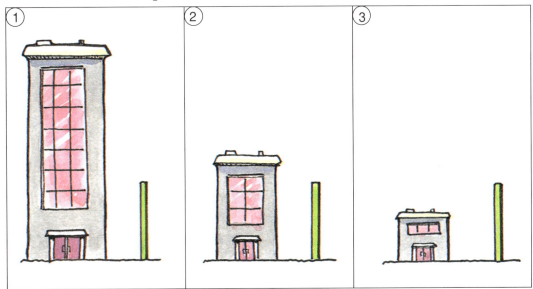

Part 13 Work the decimal-multiplication problem for each item.

a. Roger earns $12.50 per hour. He works for $\frac{3}{10}$ hour. How much does he earn?

b. Each foot of fencing costs $14.60. A garden has a perimeter of 46 feet. How much is the cost of fencing for the garden?

Lesson 36

Part 1

- Some money problems involve **tax**. The **tax** is a percent of the cost.
- Here's a problem:

    The cost of a cap is $3.50, and the tax is 5%. What's the total cost of the cap?

- To find the total, you figure out the amount of tax. You add that amount to the cost of the cap.
- Here's the problem for the tax:

    $3.50
    x   .05
    .1750

- The answer rounds to 18 cents. $.18

- You add 18¢ to $3.50. So the cap would cost the person $3.68.

    $3.50
    + .18
    $3.68

- Remember, figure out the tax. Then add the tax to the price of the item. That gives the total amount somebody pays.

Part 2   Work each item.

a. An item costs $36.15. The tax is 4%. How much would the person have to pay for the item?

b. An item costs $18.49. That tax is 5%. How much would a person pay for the item?

c. A radio costs $68.88. The tax is 6%. How much would a person pay for the radio?

d. Glasses cost $74.50. The tax is 8%. How much is the total purchase price of the glasses?

Part 3 Copy each division problem. Write the decimal point and two zeros. Then work the problem.

a. 5)56   b. 4)129   c. 2)17   d. 8)102

Part 4

- Some ratio-table problems that compare two things tell about **percents.** You make the number family with **fractions for the percents.** Then you use the numerators in a ratio table.

- Here's a problem:

    Ginger's height was 120% of Amy's height. Amy was 10 inches shorter than Ginger. How tall was Ginger? How tall was Amy?

- The first sentence tells how to make the number family:

    $$\frac{20}{100} \xrightarrow{} \frac{\text{Amy}}{\frac{100}{100}} \quad \frac{\text{Ginger}}{\frac{120}{100}}$$

- The numerators are ratio numbers for the table.

- The problem gives a difference number of 10 inches.

dif	20	10
A	100	
G	120	

- You figure out the missing numbers and answer the questions the problem asks.

Part 5 Make a fraction number family and a ratio table for each problem. Answer the question.

a. Fran's savings were 65% as much as Linda's savings. Fran's savings were $130. How much were Linda's savings? How much more were Linda's savings than Fran's savings?

b. The rainfall in July was 15% of the rainfall in April. The rainfall in July was 45 millimeters. What was the rainfall in April? How much less rain fell in July than in April?

c. The amount of fuel used by the car was 360% the amount used by the scooter. The scooter used 1,800 pints of fuel. How much more fuel did the car use than the scooter used? How much fuel did the car use?

Part 6

- You can figure out the area of some complicated figures shown on the coordinate system by figuring out the area of the parts that make up the whole figure.
- First, you find the area of **each part.**
- Then you **add the areas** to find the area of the whole figure.

- Here's a figure:
- It is made up of a triangle and a rectangle.

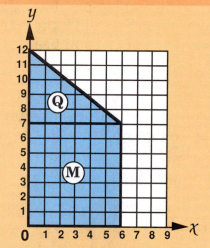

- To find the area of the entire figure, you find the area of the triangle and the rectangle.

triangle Q

$$\frac{b \times h}{2} = A$$

$$\frac{6 \times 5}{2} = \frac{30}{2}$$

15 sq units

rectangle M

$$b \times h = M$$

$$6 \times 7 = 42$$

42 sq units

entire figure

- Then you add those areas:

15
+ 42
Area = 57 sq units

Part 7 Find the area of each entire figure.

a.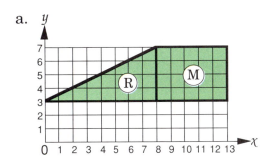

b.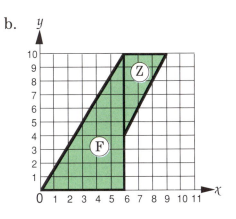

Part 8 Make an equation for each item. Box the answer to the question.

a. How many hours are in 120 minutes?

b. How many hours are in 12 days?

c. How many days are 96 hours?

d. How many minutes are in 5 hours?

Independent Work

Part 9 For each item, make a ratio equation or a ratio table. Answer each question.

a. There were 3 sparrows for every 2 robins. If there were 36 robins, how many sparrows were there?

b. 4 out of every 7 birds were robins. If there were 105 birds, how many were not robins?

c. 2 out of every 9 birds were sparrows. If there were 300 sparrows, how many birds were there?

d. $\frac{3}{5}$ of the birds were flying. 108 birds were not flying. How many birds were there in all?

Part 10 For each item, make a pair of equivalent fractions. Answer the question.

a. How many minutes are in $\frac{5}{6}$ of an hour?

b. How many ounces are in $\frac{9}{8}$ pounds?

c. How many months are in $\frac{2}{3}$ of a year?

d. How many hours are in $\frac{5}{4}$ days?

Part 11 For each circle, figure out the area and circumference.

 a.   b.

Part 12 Copy and complete each equation.

a. $3(\blacksquare) = 5$

b. $36(\blacksquare) = 1$

c. $\blacksquare(8) = 7$

d. $\blacksquare(2) = 11$

Part 13 Rewrite each problem in columns and work it.

a. 11.3 − 7.45

b. 17.6 + 4.08 + .759

c. 37 x .06

Lesson 37

Part 1 Work each problem two times. First show a mixed number answer. Then show a decimal answer.

a. $4\overline{)114}$ b. $8\overline{)26}$ c. $5\overline{)39}$ d. $4\overline{)53}$

Part 2 Make an equation for each item. Box the answer to the question.

a. How many days are in 79 hours?

b. How many dollars are in 33 nickels?

c. How many feet are in 66 inches?

d. How many weeks are in 75 days?

Part 3 Work each item.

a. A radio costs $28. That tax is 7%. How much would a person pay for the radio?

b. Socks cost $1.70. The tax is 5%. What is the total purchase price of the socks?

c. A TV costs $365. If the tax is 8%, how much would a person pay for the TV?

Part 4 Find the area of each complex figure.

a.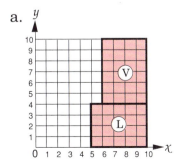

b.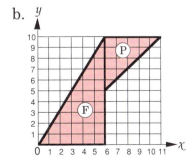

c.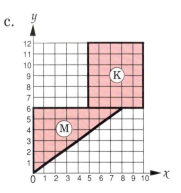

Part 5 For each item, write an equation with three names and one number.

> *Sample item*   There are 6 bottles per carton.

a. There are 13 dogs in each kennel.

b. The machine makes 25 buttons in each second.

c. There are 23 students in each class.

d. The trolley moves 4 miles per hour.

e. There are 8 slices in each pie.

Part 6 Make a fraction number family and a ratio table for each problem. Answer the questions.

a. The brick's weight is 25% of the dog's weight. The dog weighs 12 pounds. How much does the brick weigh? How much more does the dog weigh than the brick weighs?

b. The regular price is 120% of the sale price. The sale price is $20. What is the regular price? How much would you save if you bought the item on sale?

Independent Work

Part 7
Find the area and the perimeter of each figure.

a.

25 cm, 39 cm, 15 cm, 56 cm

b.

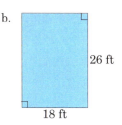
26 ft, 18 ft

Part 8
Answer the questions.

a. $\frac{3}{4}$ of the flowers were daisies. 27 flowers were not daisies. How many flowers were there?

b. $\frac{5}{17}$ of the lights were on. 65 lights were on. How many lights were not on?

Part 9
Answer each question.

1. 2 in

2. 48 mi

3. 2 yd

a. What is the circumference of circle 1?

b. What is the radius of circle 2?

c. What is the area of circle 1?

d. What is the area of circle 3?

Part 10
Rewrite each item with two numbers and two unit names.

a. $3\frac{2}{7}$ weeks

b. $1\frac{12}{60}$ hour

c. $7\frac{2}{3}$ yards

d. $4\frac{10}{36}$ yards

e. $3\frac{4}{24}$ days

Part 11
Show the multiplication for each item. Answer each question.

a. .58 of a building's wall surface has been painted. The total area is 280 square yards. How many square yards have been painted?

b. What is 75% of 12?

c. Jane petted $\frac{2}{5}$ of the rabbits. There were 200 rabbits. How many did Jane pet?

d. 14% of the products were damaged. There were 50 products. How many were damaged?

e. Tim earns $12.60 each hour. He works for 1.3 hours. How much does he earn?

Part 12 For each statement, make the fraction number family. Write the number of the correct diagram.

a. The horse is $\frac{7}{5}$ as tall as the boy.

b. Pile A is $\frac{5}{11}$ as tall as pile B.

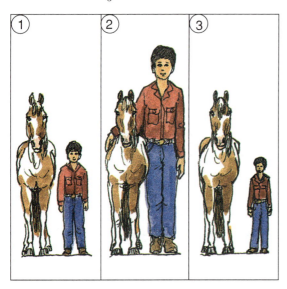

c. The snake was $\frac{10}{9}$ the length of the rope.

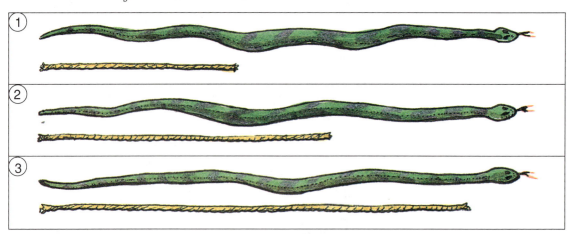
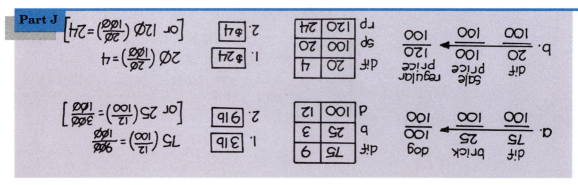

Lesson 38

Part 1   **Work each item.**

a. Fran purchases a radio for $44.60 and a pair of gloves for $9.80. The tax is 5%. What is the cost of both items? What is the tax? What is the total purchase price of the items including tax?

b. Dan bought a pair of shoes for $56.20. He bought some paper for $2.88. He bought sunglasses for $7.72. The sales tax is 6%. What's the cost of the items? What's the tax? What's the cost of the three items including tax?

c. Bonnie bought pencils for 60¢. She bought an eraser for 29¢ and she bought a notepad for 82¢. The sales tax is 8%. What's the cost of the items? What the tax? How much did Bonnie pay for all three items including tax?

Part 2   **Make an equation for each item. Box the answer to the question.**

a. There are 8 shoes in each bin. There are 13 bins. How many shoes are there in all?

b. There were 12 caps in each bin. There were 240 caps. How many bins were there?

c. There were 7 pieces in each pie. There were 11 pies. How many pieces were there?

d. There are 8 pieces in each pie. If there is a total of 128 pieces, how many pies are there?

Lesson 38   **155**

Part 3 Find the area of each complex figure.

a.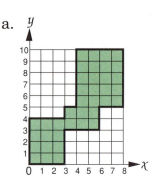

b.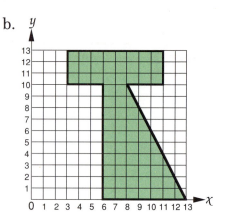

Part 4

- Some problems that tell about a fraction of something can be worked as multiplication problems. Others can't.

- Here's a problem that can be worked by multiplication:

    Sue is $\frac{3}{8}$ as old as her **mother**. Her **mother** is 40 years old. How old is Sue?

    $\frac{3}{8} \times m$

    $\frac{3}{8} \times 40 = \frac{120}{8}$ **15 years**

- Here's a problem that can't be worked by multiplication:

    Jane is $\frac{3}{8}$ as old as her mother. **Jane** is 24 years old. How old is her mother?

- You can work that problem by making a fraction number family and a ratio table.

    - Here's the family:

        dif J   m
        $\frac{5}{8}$ $\frac{3}{8}$ → $\frac{8}{8}$

- Here's the table with the number for Jane's age:

dif	5	
J	3	24
m	8	

- Now you can figure out her mother's age.

Lesson 38

Part 5 Solve each problem by using either fraction multiplication or a ratio table.

a. The dog's weight is $\frac{3}{5}$ of the boy's weight. The boy's weight is 70 pounds. What does the dog weigh?

b. The cat's weight is $\frac{10}{3}$ of the rabbit's weight. The rabbit's weight is 2 pounds. What does the cat weigh?

c. A man works $\frac{7}{3}$ as long as his neighbor works. The man works for 40 hours. How long does the neighbor work?

d. A man worked $\frac{3}{8}$ as long as his wife worked. His wife worked for 25 hours. How long did the man work?

e. The regular price is $\frac{7}{5}$ the sale price. The regular price is $56. What is the sale price?

Part 6 Figure out the answer to each question. Then write the answer with two unit names.

a. How many gallons are in 60 pints?

b. How many dollars are in 430 cents?

c. How many years are in 32 months?

Independent Work

Remember to work items c and e in part 5 as ratio-table problems.

Part 7 For each item, write the multiplication with a letter. Work the problems that can be worked by multiplication.

a. $\frac{6}{7}$ of the children were healthy. There were 84 children. How many were healthy?

b. There were 20% as many blue chairs as white chairs. There were 36 blue chairs. How many white chairs were there?

c. $\frac{3}{7}$ of the lawn was cut. 260 square feet were cut. How many square feet of lawn were there?

d. Ginger was 80% as old as Britanny. Britanny was 15 years old. How old was Ginger?

Lesson 38

Part 8 Work each item.

a. $3\frac{2}{7}$ weeks is ▇ ▇ and ▇ ▇.

b. How many pounds is 5 pounds and 7 ounces?

c. How many hours is 11 hours and 23 minutes?

d. $8\frac{11}{60}$ minutes is ▇ ▇ and ▇ ▇.

e. $1\frac{3}{4}$ years is ▇ ▇ and ▇ ▇.

Part 9 Copy and complete the table.

	Fraction	Decimal	Percent
a.			5%
b.	$\frac{7}{100}$		
c.	$\frac{203}{100}$		
d.			236%
e.		1.00	
f.		5.02	

Part 10 Use inverse operations to figure out each answer.

a. Start with the mystery number and add 11. Then triple the number. Then divide by 6. You end up with 6. What's the mystery number?

b. Dan starts out with some money. He buys a toaster for $17.12. He ends up with $3.80. How much did he start with?

c. A bus started out with 15 people in it. At the first stop, 12 more people got on the bus. At the second stop, the number of people in the bus was divided by 3. At the third stop, some people got off, then 4 people got on. There were now 5 people in the bus. How many people got off at the third stop?

d. A tank was full. 27 gallons were drained from the tank. Then the amount left in the tank was divided by 3. The tank ended up with 1 gallon in it. How many gallons does the tank hold?

e. A man had land. When he sold some of his land, he divided the amount he had by 4. He ended up with 12 acres. How many acres did he start out with?

Lesson 39

Part 1   Answer each question.

     a. How many gallons are in 42 cups?

     b. How many weeks are in 58 days?

     c. How many yards are in 211 inches?

     d. How many hours are in 211 minutes?

Part 2   Work each problem two times. First show a mixed number answer. Then show a decimal answer.

     a. $5\overline{)41}$ b. $10\overline{)52}$ c. $8\overline{)54}$ d. $4\overline{)283}$

Part 3   Find the area of each figure.

a.

b.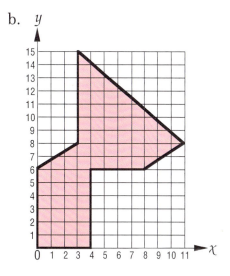

Part 4   Work each item.

a. A man goes into a store and buys a mug for $5, a shirt for $18 and a radio for $11.50. Sales tax is 7%. What is the cost of the items before tax? How much is the tax? How much does the man pay for his purchases?

b. Fencing costs $2.80 per foot. How much will fencing cost for a rectangular area 50 feet long and 27 feet wide?

c. A company wants to tile a section of roof that is 15 yards long and 12.5 yards wide. Roofing shingles cost $14 per square yard. How much will it cost to purchase enough shingles for the job?

d. Mary buys 5 boxes of greeting cards. Each box costs $8.25. Sales tax is 5%. What is the cost of the cards without tax? What is the tax on that amount? How much do the cards cost, including tax?

Part 5   For each item, make an equation. Answer the question.

a. There were 5 players on each basketball team. In Roper Park, there were 23 teams. How many players were there in Roper Park?

b. There were 24 stamps per sheet. Mary bought 360 stamps. How many sheets did she buy?

c. There were 36 stamps in each roll. Billy bought 4 rolls. How many stamps did Billy buy?

d. Each typewriter had 38 keys. The repair shop had 20 typewriters. How many typewriter keys were on those typewriters?

Part 6 Solve each problem by using either fraction multiplication or a ratio table.

a. The car's weight was 240% of the trailer's weight. The car weighed 3,600 pounds. How much did the trailer weigh?

b. Jan's age is 60% of her dad's age. Her dad is 45 years old. How old is Jane?

c. The rabbit's weight is $\frac{10}{9}$ the cat's weight. The cat weighs 14 pounds. What's the weight of the rabbit?

d. The distance to Funtown is $\frac{4}{9}$ the distance to Wonderworld. The distance to Funtown is 38 miles. What's the distance to Wonderworld?

Independent Work

Remember to work the problems in part 6.

Part 7 Figure out the answer to each question.

a. How much less does the frying pan cost than the electric can opener?

b. The toaster costs $4.16 less than one of the items costs. Which item?

c. Joan bought a crock pot, a frying pan and an electric can opener. How much did she spend?

Part 8 Figure out the answer to each question.

  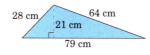 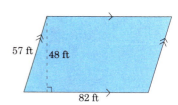

a. What is the perimeter of the triangle?

b. What is the area of the parallelogram?

c. What is the perimeter of the parallelogram?

d. What is the area of the triangle?

e. What is the radius of the circle?

Part 9 Make a fraction number family. Write the number of the correct picture.

a. The height of the pole is 125% the height of the tree.

b. The pole was $\frac{3}{8}$ the height of the tree.

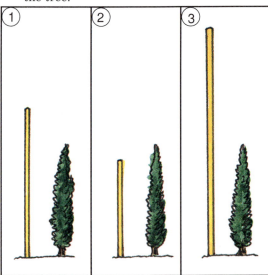
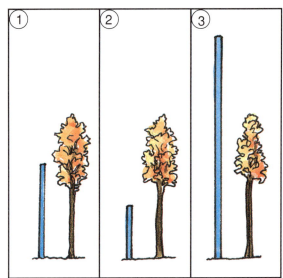

c. The length of the rope was .5 the length of the belt.

Part 10 Complete each equation.

a. $7 (\blacksquare) = 14$

b. $\frac{6}{5} = \frac{240}{\blacksquare}$

c. $2 \times \frac{1}{7} \times \frac{4}{3} = \blacksquare$

d. $\frac{3}{2} = \frac{\blacksquare}{1}$

e. $\frac{16}{5} - \frac{5}{5} = \blacksquare$

f. $\blacksquare \times 5 = 9$

g. $13 (\blacksquare) = 10$

h. $48 = \frac{\blacksquare}{3}$

Part J

Test 4

Part 1 Write the answer to each item. Show numbers and unit names.

  a. 6 dollars and 7 dimes is ■ dollars.
  b. $3\frac{5}{12}$ years is ■ ■ and ■ ■.
  c. $8\frac{6}{365}$ years is ■ ■ and ■ ■.
  d. 4 days and 1 hour is ■ days.

Part 2 Make a fraction number family for each item. Indicate the number of the correct picture.

a. The mug is $\frac{3}{2}$ the height of the glass.

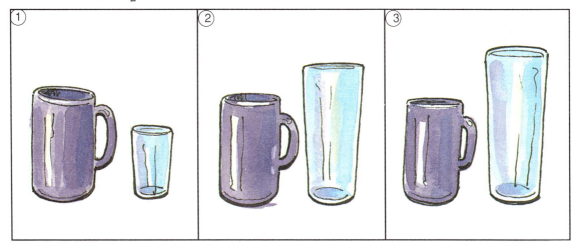

b. The snake was $\frac{2}{7}$ as long as the rope.

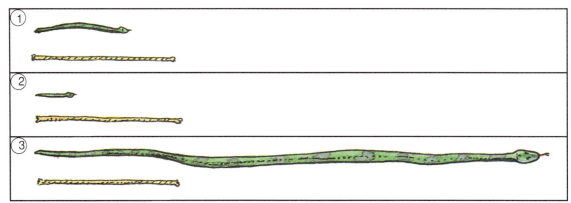

Part 3
Work each item as a multiplication problem if you can. Otherwise work it as a ratio-table problem.

a. The sale price of the bed is .65 of the regular price. The regular price of the bed is $260. What's the sale price?

b. The regular price of the table is 120% of the sale price. The regular price is $48. What's the sale price?

c. The number of eggs is $\frac{3}{5}$ the number of sweet rolls. There are 45 sweet rolls. How many eggs are there?

Part 4
Make an equation for each item. Box the answer to the question.

a. How many hours are in 2 days?

b. How many months are in 7 years?

c. How many hours are in 180 minutes?

Part 5
For each sentence, write the equation with three names and one number.

a. The machine makes 12 buttons per second.

b. There are 6 players on each team.

Part 6
Find the area of the green figure.

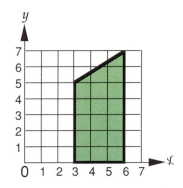

Part 7 Work each item. Show the cost of the items. Show the tax. Show the total.

a. Dan purchases the clock and the gloves. The tax is 6%. How much does Dan pay?

b. Ann purchases the hat, the glasses and the pen. The tax is 5%. How much does Ann pay?

Part 8 Work each division problem two times. Show the answer as a mixed number and as a hundredths decimal.

a. $8\overline{)46}$ b. $4\overline{)173}$

Part 9 Work each item.

1.   2. 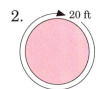 3.

a. Find the area of circle 1.
b. Find the radius of circle 2.
c. Find the circumference of circle 3.
d. Find the diameter of circle 2.

Test 4

Lesson 41

Part 1 — Facts about Percents

$\frac{1}{2}$ is 50%	is $\frac{1}{2}$ dollar.	 That's 50¢.
$\frac{1}{4}$ is 25%	is $\frac{1}{4}$ dollar.	 That's 25¢.
$\frac{1}{10}$ is 10%	is $\frac{1}{10}$ dollar.	That's 10¢.
$\frac{1}{20}$ is 5%	is $\frac{1}{20}$ dollar.	That's 20¢.

Part 2

- You've converted fractions into mixed numbers. You can do that by working the fraction as a division problem.
  - Here's $\frac{17}{4}$. That's: $4\overline{)17}$
- You can show the answer as a mixed number: $4\frac{1}{4}$, $4\overline{)17}$
- You can also show the answer as a decimal value: 4.25, $4\overline{)17.00}$
  - So: $4\frac{1}{4} = 4.25$

Part 3

Write each fraction as a division problem. Show the answer as a decimal.

a. $\frac{17}{5}$ b. $\frac{28}{8}$ c. $\frac{59}{4}$ d. $\frac{29}{5}$

Part 4 Make a fraction number family for each sentence.

a. The car's speed was 55% of the boat's speed.

b. 55% of the cars were wet.

c. 35% of the eggs were brown.

d. The cost of white eggs is 85% of the cost of brown eggs.

e. The book's weight was 78% of the bowl's weight.

f. 54% of the objects were books.

Part 5 Work each item.

a. For the parade, the Rex Company made a large circular disc. The disc was 11 feet in diameter. The Rex Company planned to paint it gold. The cost of painting each square foot was $1.20. How much was the cost of painting the entire disc?

b. Ms. Oozuloo and her son, Uk, have a large circular garden. The radius of the garden is 10 yards. They want to fence the garden. The type of fence they selected costs $5.17 per yard. How much will it cost to fence the garden?

c. Jamey and Hortence want to tile their kitchen floor. The room is 12 feet wide and 12 feet long. Tiling the room will cost $3.11 per square foot. How much will it cost to tile the entire room?

d. Sidney made purchases that cost $3.25, $2.70 and $11. The tax on these items was 8%. How much was the total price that Sidney paid?

Lesson 41

Part 6

- You've worked with problems that have related units. In the problems you've worked, you can easily identify the larger unit.

- If there are **5 bottles in each box,** **bottles** is the smaller unit and **box** is the larger unit. It contains the bottles.

  boxes = bottles / ▬▬▬

- If there are **7 slugs in each garden,** **garden** is the larger unit and **slugs** is the smaller unit.

  gardens = slugs / ▬▬▬

- **Each can contains 400 beans.**

  cans = beans / ▬▬▬

- For some problems, it is not as easy to identify the larger unit and the smaller unit.

- If a **car travels 45 miles per hour,** it's not easy to identify the larger unit.

- Here's how you do it.

- You write the name for the denominator of the fraction: = ▬▬▬ / **miles per hour**

- Then you write the numerator: = miles / **miles per hour**

- Then you write the larger unit: **hours** = miles / **miles per hour**

168   Lesson 41

Part 7

Copy each equation that is correct. Rewrite each equation that is incorrect.

Sample equation 1
$$\text{meters} = \frac{\text{seconds}}{\text{meters per second}}$$

Sample equation 2
$$\text{days} = \frac{\text{books}}{\text{books per day}}$$

Sample equation 3
$$\text{books} = \frac{\text{days}}{\text{days per book}}$$

a. $\text{cups} = \dfrac{\text{days}}{\text{cups per day}}$

b. $\text{miles} = \dfrac{\text{calories}}{\text{calories per mile}}$

c. $\text{mornings} = \dfrac{\text{trains}}{\text{trains per morning}}$

d. $\text{pages} = \dfrac{\text{dollars}}{\text{pages per dollar}}$

e. $\text{buildings} = \dfrac{\text{trees}}{\text{trees per building}}$

Independent Work

Part 8

For each item, make a complete equation with names and numbers. Box the answer to the question.

a. There were 6 cups in each box. There were 11 boxes. How many cups were there?

b. There were 6 cups in each box. There were 360 cups. How many boxes were there?

c. There were 9 players on each team. There were 810 players. How many teams were there?

d. There were 9 players on each team. There were 21 teams. How many players were there?

Part 9

For each problem, make a fraction number family and a ratio table. Answer the questions.

a. The regular price of a radio is $\frac{5}{4}$ as much as the sale price. The regular price is $65. How much is the sale price? How much would you save if you bought the radio on sale?

b. $\frac{9}{10}$ of the foxes live in the forest. 12 foxes do not live in the forest. How many foxes live in the forest? How many foxes are there in all?

Lesson 41

Part 10
Work each item.

a. What's $\frac{1}{4}$ of 52?
b. What's $\frac{7}{5}$ of 25?
c. What's $\frac{5}{4}$ of 100?

Part 11
Write the equation for the circumference of a circle.
Write the equation for the area of a circle.
Find the circumference and the area of each circle.

a.
b.

Part 12
Write each problem as a column problem, then work it.

a. 2.75 + 38.025 + .9
b. 118.7 − 99.97

Part 13
Work each item.

a. $1\frac{2}{4}$ years is ■ year and ■ months.
b. 3 weeks and 5 days is ■ weeks.
c. $5\frac{3}{8}$ pounds is ■ pounds and ■ ounces.
d. $10\frac{3}{20}$ dollars is ■ dollars and ■ cents.
e. 2 days and 5 hours is ■ days.

Part 14
Find the area of each colored figure.

a.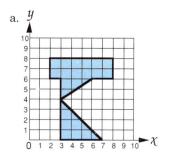
b.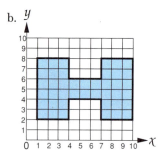

Part J

b. 8 ⟌ 28.00   [3.5]
c. 4 ⟌ 59.00   [14.75]
d. 5 ⟌ 29.00   [5.8]

Lesson 42

Part 1 Work each item.

a. A rectangular field is 40 yards wide and 28 yards long. The field will be turned into a parking lot. It will cost $13.80 per square yard. How much is the cost for preparing the entire lot?

b. A circular garden is 12 feet in diameter. It will be planted with 6 flowers per square foot. How many flowers will fit into the garden? (Round the area to the nearest whole number.)

c. Tina purchases the clock and the binoculars. The sales tax is 7%. How much does she have to pay in all?

Part 2 Write the correct equation for each item.

a. goats = $\dfrac{\text{shrubs}}{\text{shrubs per goat}}$

b. hours = $\dfrac{\text{dollars}}{\text{hours per dollar}}$

c. pens = $\dfrac{\text{dollars}}{\text{pens per dollar}}$

d. hours = $\dfrac{\text{dollars}}{\text{dollars per hour}}$

e. dollars = $\dfrac{\text{watches}}{\text{dollars per watch}}$

Part 3

- You can figure out simple fractions for these percents by using what you know.

75%   30%   20%

$25\% = \frac{1}{4}$

So 75% =

$30\% = \frac{30¢}{100¢}$

So $30\% = \frac{3}{10}$

$20\% = \frac{2¢}{100¢} = \frac{1}{5}$

So $20\% = \frac{1}{5}$

Part 4 Make a fraction number family for each sentence.

a. 18% of the days were rainy days.

b. 27% of all the rain fell in March.

c. The rainfall in February was 65% of the rainfall in March.

d. We traveled 56% of the distance by car and the rest of the distance by boat.

e. The cost of the hat was 45% of the cost of the scarf.

f. 85% of all the items were on sale.

Part 5 Write each fraction as a division problem. Show the answer as a decimal. Then write an equation.

Sample $\frac{3}{5}$

a. $\frac{3}{4}$ $4\overline{)3.00}$

$\frac{3}{4} = .\blacksquare$

b. $\frac{3}{12}$

c. $\frac{4}{8}$

d. $\frac{8}{25}$

Part 6 Make an equation for each item. Box the answer to the question.

a. How many years are in 40 months?

b. How many months are in 4 years?

c. How many days are in 24 weeks?

d. How many days are in 90 hours?

e. How many weeks are in 32 days?

Lesson 42

Independent Work

Part 7 Work each item as a fraction-multiplication problem or as a ratio-table problem.

a. The truck went $\frac{3}{4}$ as fast as the car. The truck went 40 miles per hour. How fast did the car go?

b. Jan was $\frac{6}{5}$ the height of her mom. Her mom was 60 inches tall. How tall was Jan?

c. The trip on the train lasted $\frac{8}{3}$ the length of time the rainstorm lasted. The rainstorm lasted 2 hours. How long did the trip last?

d. Frank made $\frac{3}{7}$ as many models as Rita made. Frank made 18 models. How many did Rita make?

Part 8 Write each problem in columns and work it.

a. 17 − 3.064
b. 2.073 × 12
c. 6.23 × .8
d. 14.38 + .068
e. 3.074 − .28

Part 9 For each sentence, write an equation with three names and one number.

a. There were 6 players on each team.
b. The train traveled 41 miles each hour.
c. They filled 89 bottles per hour.
d. The bees visited 4 flowers per minute.

Part 10 Work each item.

a. Start with the mystery number and subtract 20. Then multiply by 3. You end up with 60. What's the mystery number?

b. Start with the mystery number and divide by 4. Then subtract 15. Then divide by 5. You end up with 1. What's the mystery number?

Part 11 Copy and work each problem.

a. 18 + 74 + 707 = V
   V = ■

b. 6 × R = 14
   R = ■

c. 346 − T = 89
   T = ■

Part J

Lesson 43

Part 1 Answer each question.

a. The number of watches a dealer sells is 6 times the number of clocks. The dealer sells clocks for $23 each and watches for $11 each. During March, the dealer sold 56 clocks.
   1. How many watches did he sell?
   2. What was the amount he received for clocks?
   3. What was the amount for watches?
   4. What was the total amount the dealer earned?

Part 2 Make a number family for each sentence.

a. The sale price is 85% of the regular price.

b. The boy's height is 210% of the dog's height.

c. 46% of the trains were late.

d. The airplane is 20% the length of the train.

Part 3

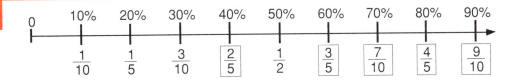

Part 4 Work each item. Write the complete equation. Box the answer to the question.

a. A ball was moving at the rate of 6 feet per second. The ball moved 366 feet. How many seconds did that take?

b. A machine makes 110 buttons per minute. How many buttons does it make in 5 minutes?

c. A man burns 150 calories each mile he walks. If he walks for 3 miles, how many calories does he burn?

d. A runner goes 25 feet per calorie. How many calories does he burn if he runs 100 feet?

Part 5

- You've divided to find the decimal number for fractions.

- Not all decimal numbers end after two digits. Some answers have three digits after the decimal point.

$$\frac{3}{4} \quad 4\overline{)3.0_20}^{.75}$$

$$\frac{3}{8} \quad 8\overline{)3.0_60_40}^{.375}$$

- Some answers go for as long as you want to figure the answer.

- Here's the division problem:

- The answer after two decimal places has a remainder of 1.

- So we can make more zeros under the division sign and figure the answer some more places.

- We keep getting the same remainder of 1. That would happen for as long as we made zeros.

$$\frac{1}{3} \quad 3\overline{)1.00}^{.}$$

$$3\overline{)1.0_10_1}^{.33}$$

$$3\overline{)1.0_10_10_10_10_10_1}^{.333333}$$

Part 6 Write each fraction as a division problem. Write the decimal point and three zeros. Then work the problem.

a. $\frac{5}{8}$ b. $\frac{1}{4}$ c. $\frac{1}{8}$ d. $\frac{7}{8}$ e. $\frac{3}{4}$

Part 7 Make a number family and ratio table for each item. Answer the questions.

a. 72% of the days were cloudy. The rest were sunny. There were 75 days. How many days were cloudy? How many days were sunny?

b. The new price is 150% of the old price. The new price is $27. What is the old price? What is the difference between the new price and the old price?

Independent Work

Part 8 Write the fraction for each item.

a. What's the simple fraction for 20%?
b. What's the simple fraction for 50%?
c. What's the simple fraction for 25%?
d. What's the simple fraction for 10%?

Part 9 Complete each statement.

a. $4\frac{1}{2}$ years is ■ years and ■ months.
b. $2\frac{1}{2}$ hours is ■ hours and ■ minutes.
c. 7 weeks and 1 day is ■ weeks.
d. 5 yards and 6 inches is ■ yards.
e. $7\frac{1}{2}$ gallons is ■ gallons and ■ pints.

Part 10 Find the area of each colored figure.

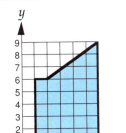
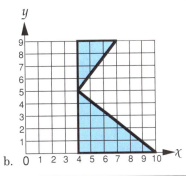

Part 11 Use inverse operations to find each missing value.

a. ■ ÷ 13 = 4
b. ■ x 7 = 9
c. ■ x 5 = 2
d. ■ + 52 = 81
e. ■ − 81 = 52
f. ■ x 3 = 81

Part 12 Work each item.

a. What's the radius of circle 1?
b. What's the area of circle 2?
c. What's the circumference of circle 2?
d. What's the diameter of circle 1?

Part 13 Make a ratio equation for each item. Answer the question.

a. The ratio of nuts to bolts was 4 to 3. There were 60 bolts. How many nuts were there?
b. There were 7 cats for every 3 bowls. There were 56 cats. How many bowls were there?
c. The mixture contained 3 pounds of sand for every 5 pounds of humus. There were 200 pounds of sand in the mixture. How many pounds of humus were in the mixture?
d. In a school, there were 17 books for every 3 students. There were 300 students in the school. How many books were in the school?

Part J

a. $\frac{\text{dif}}{15} \quad \frac{\text{sale price}}{85} \longrightarrow \frac{100}{100}$

b. $\frac{\text{sale price}}{100} \quad \frac{\text{regular}}{100} \longrightarrow \frac{100}{100}$

c. $\frac{\text{late}}{46} \quad \frac{\text{not late}}{54} \longrightarrow \frac{100}{100} \quad \text{trains}$

b. $\frac{\text{dif}}{110} \quad \frac{\text{dog}}{100} \longrightarrow \frac{100}{210} \quad \text{boy}$

d. $\frac{\text{dif}}{80} \quad \frac{\text{airplane}}{20} \longrightarrow \frac{100}{100} \quad \text{train}$

Lesson 43 177

Lesson 44

Part 1 Answer each question.

a. What percent is $\frac{1}{2}$?

b. What percent is $\frac{1}{10}$?

c. What percent is $\frac{1}{20}$?

d. What percent is $\frac{1}{4}$?

e. What percent is $\frac{3}{4}$?

f. What percent is $\frac{7}{10}$?

Part 2

- You can use your calculator to figure out answers to division problems that have remainders. The calculator shows the answer as a decimal value.

  $357 \div 5 = 71.4$

- Sometimes, the decimal answer shown will have many places.
  - Here's: $346 \div 7 = 49.428571$

- When you write the answer, you'll round it to hundredths.

- Look at the digit after hundredths. If that digit is 5 or more, you round the hundredths digit **up.** If the digit after hundredths is less than 5, you copy the hundredths digit.

  49.428571

  - Here's the rounded answer: 49.43

Part 3

Work each item as a division problem. Round the answer to hundredths if necessary.

a. $\dfrac{256}{237}$ b. $\dfrac{470}{25}$ c. $17\overline{)286}$ d. $\dfrac{139}{48}$ e. $4\overline{)718}$

Part 4

- Closed figures that have straight sides are called **polygons**.

- This is not a polygon because the figure is not closed:

- This is not a polygon because it doesn't have straight sides:

- These are polygons:

- Here are the names of some polygons:

- Polygons with **three sides** are called **triangles**.

- Polygons with **four sides** are called **quadilaterals**.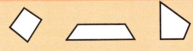

- Polygons with **five sides** are called **pentagons**.

- Polygons with **six sides** are called **hexagons**.

- Polygons with **eight sides** are called **octagons**.

Part 5

- You can write multiplication problems that show the number of equal fractions that are in 1 whole.

- Here's a problem:

    If a farm is divided into four equal parts, what's the simplest fraction for each part?

$\frac{1}{4} \times 4 = \frac{4}{4}$

- Here's another problem:

    If each part of a lot is $\frac{1}{7}$ of the total lot, how many parts are there?

- The answer is 7. The whole lot is $\frac{7}{7}$. Each part is $\frac{1}{7}$, and there are 7 parts.

- You can show the multiplication for the problem:

$\frac{1}{7} \times \boxed{7} = \frac{7}{7}$

- You multiply the **fraction for each part** by the **number of parts.** That's $\frac{1}{7}$ times 7 equals $\frac{7}{7}$.

Part 6

Write a complete equation for each item. Box the answer to the question.

a. Each part is $\frac{1}{5}$ of the total. How many parts are there?

b. Each piece of the pie is $\frac{1}{6}$ of the total pie. How many pieces are in the pie?

c. A deck of playing cards has 52 cards. What's the fraction for each card?

d. If there are 124 pages in a book, what's the fraction for each page?

e. A floor has an area of 34 square feet. What's the fraction of the floor in each square foot?

Part 7

For each item, write an equation with names and numbers. Box the answer to the question.

a. The team played 3 games per month. How many games did the team play in a 5-month period?

b. A truck traveled at the rate of 51 feet per second. The truck traveled for 300 seconds. How far did the truck travel during that time?

c. Each hat cost $8. Margie spent $240 on hats. How many hats did she buy?

d. The fencing weighed 13 pounds per yard. Dana had 24 yards of fencing. How much did it weigh?

Part 8

Answer each question.

a. Mr. James bought 8 times as many cans of oil as filters. He bought 64 cans of oil. Each can of oil cost $1.20. Each filter cost $2.30. The tax on all sales was 5%.

   1. What was the cost of the items before tax?
   2. What was the tax that Mr. James paid?
   3. What was the total amount that he paid?

Part 9

Make a number family and ratio table for each item. Answer the questions.

a. The sale price is 80% of the regular price. The regular price is $35. What is the sale price? How much would you save if you bought the item on sale?

b. The price of a radio this year is 138% of last year's price. This year's price is $19 more than last year's price. How much was last year's price? How much is this year's price?

c. There were 250 papers in all. They collected 82% of the papers. How many papers were not collected? How many papers were collected?

Lesson 44

Independent Work

Remember to complete the problems in part 9.

Part 10 For each sentence, write an equation with three names.

a. There were 13 acres in each plot.
b. The paint cost $14 per can.
c. The plane traveled 16 miles per minute.
d. There were 14 jars in each carton.

Part 11 Work each item.

 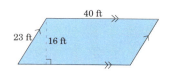

a. Find the area of the square.
b. Find the perimeter of the parallelogram.
c. Find the area of the triangle.
d. Find the perimeter of the triangle.

Part 12 Write a complete equation for each item. Box the answer to the question.

a. How many gallons are in 12 pints?
b. How many hours are in 3 days?
c. How many days are in 3 years?
d. How many seconds are in 2 minutes?
e. How many weeks are in 35 days?

Part 13 Make a number family for each sentence.

a. 58% of the workers are women.
b. There are 150% as many boys as girls.
c. 90% of the plates are cracked.
d. The regular price is 160% of the sale price.

Part 14 Work each item.

a. What's 20% of 300?
b. What's 70% of 90?
c. What's $\frac{3}{5}$ of 340?

Part 15 Work each item.

a. A farmer bought grass seed and tractor parts. Before tax, the seed cost $58 and the parts cost $112. The sales tax is 5%. How much did he pay in all?

b. Susie bought school supplies. Paper cost $20, books cost $85 and pens cost $7. There's a 6% sales tax. What's the amount Susie spent?

c. Jack bought a chair for $120, a desk for $85 and office equipment for $45. The sales tax was 4%. What was the total amount Jack paid?

Part J

b. 300 seconds = $\dfrac{\boxed{15{,}300 \text{ feet}}}{51 \text{ feet per second}}$

c. $\dfrac{240 \text{ dollars}}{8 \text{ dollars per hat}} = \boxed{30 \text{ hats}}$

d. 24 yards = $\dfrac{\boxed{312 \text{ pounds}}}{13 \text{ pounds per yard}}$

Lesson 45

Part 1 Answer each question.

a. A dinner makes 7 servings. What's the fraction for each serving?

b. Each page of a book is $\frac{1}{240}$ of the total book. How many pages are in the book?

c. If a farm is divided into 16 equal-sized lots, what is the fraction for each lot?

d. If each cup is $\frac{1}{9}$ of the set, how many cups are in the set?

e. If each part of the total is $\frac{1}{12}$ the total, how many parts are there?

Part 2 For each item, work a division problem. Round answers to two decimal places if necessary.

a. $\frac{171}{15}$ b. $93\overline{)478}$ c. $8\overline{)14}$ d. $\frac{1004}{997}$ e. $\frac{456}{189}$

Part 3 Answer each question.

a. A quadilateral has how many sides?

b. An octagon has how many sides?

c. A pentagon has how many sides?

d. A hexagon has how many sides?

Part 4 Figure out the missing value for each item.

Sample problem

$3 = \frac{270}{\blacksquare}$

a. $8 = \frac{56}{\blacksquare}$

b. $7 = \frac{91}{\blacksquare}$

c. $17 = \frac{34}{\blacksquare}$

d. $5 = \frac{2}{\blacksquare}$

Part 5 Rewrite and complete each equation.

a. $\dfrac{1}{6}(\blacksquare) = 1$

b. $\dfrac{1}{20}(\blacksquare) = 1$

c. $\dfrac{1}{9}(\blacksquare) = 1$

d. $\dfrac{1}{43}(\blacksquare) = 1$

Part 6 Answer each question.

a. During one day, a store sells 7 times as many jeans as shirts. The store sells shirts for $14 each and jeans for $23 each. The store sells 16 shirts. The store took in 5% tax on the sale of jeans and shirts.
   1. How many pairs of jeans did the store sell?
   2. What was the amount the store received for shirts and jeans before tax?
   3. What was the tax that the store took in?
   4. What was the total amount that the store took in?

b. A jeweler made a circular medallion. The medallion has a diameter of 16 millimeters. The edge of the medallion has etchings on it. To etch the edge cost $2 per millimeter. The medallion is made of gold. The gold cost $1 per square millimeter.
   1. How much did the etching cost?
   2. How much did the gold cost?
   3. What was the total cost of the medallion?

E   F   G   H

Part 7 Make a fraction number family and a ratio table. Answer the questions.

a. 92% of the bugs had spots. 2 bugs did not have spots. How many bugs had spots? How many bugs were there in all?

b. The temperature in the afternoon was 130% of the temperature in the morning. The temperature was 80° in the morning. What was the temperature in the afternoon? How many degrees did the temperature rise that day?

Independent Work

Part 8
Work each item. Show each problem you work on your calculator.

a. With his birthday money, Billy bought a calculator for $8, a watch for $10, a hat for $4 and a game for $11. Sales tax is 5%. How much did he spend in all?

b. Donna wants to frame a circular mirror. The frame costs 85¢ an inch. The mirror is 16 inches in diameter. How much is the cost of the frame?

c. A farmer planted a rectangular field that was 100 yards long and 60 yards wide. He planted 5 plants per square yard. Each plant cost 60¢. How many plants did he plant? How much was the total cost of planting the field?

d. The Wacko Paper Company bought chemicals for $200, machinery for $1,200, floor tiles for $650 and paint for $115. There is a 6% sales tax on all items. What was the total cost of all the items?

Part 9
Answer each question.

a. What's $\frac{3}{5}$ of 15?

b. What's 60% of 15?

c. What 80% of 25?

d. What's $\frac{7}{9}$ of 81?

Part 10
Copy and complete the table.

	Fraction	Decimal	Mixed number
a.			$3\frac{2}{100}$
b.			$1\frac{7}{10}$
c.		4.023	
d.	$\frac{468}{10}$		

Part 11
For each item, make a ratio equation. Answer the question.

a. There were 7 pounds of dog food for every 3 dogs. There were 154 pounds of dog food. How many dogs were there?

b. If it takes 6 minutes to travel 5 miles, how long will it take to travel 88 miles?

c. In a pond, the ratio of frogs to worms is 17 to 9. There are 306 worms in the pond. How many frogs are in the pond?

d. Every 6 bricks cost $4. How much do 900 bricks cost?

Part 12
Answer each question.

a. What's the percent for $\frac{3}{4}$?

b. What's the simple fraction for 50%?

c. What's the simple fraction for 20%?

d. What's the simple fraction for 60%?

e. What's the percent for $\frac{7}{10}$?

f. What's the percent for $\frac{1}{10}$?

Part 13
Work each division problem two times. Show the answer as a mixed number, and as a hundredths decimal.

a. $4\overline{)7}$ b. $8\overline{)26}$ c. $5\overline{)56}$

Lesson 46

Part 1 For each item, work a division problem.

a. $40\overline{)790}$ b. $\dfrac{575}{323}$ c. $\dfrac{258}{20}$ d. $99\overline{)652}$ e. $\dfrac{48}{13}$

Part 2

- The reciprocal of any value is the value turned "upside down."

Value	Reciprocal
$\dfrac{2}{5}$	$\dfrac{5}{2}$
$\dfrac{1}{9}$	$\dfrac{9}{1}$ or 9
$\dfrac{7}{3}$	$\dfrac{3}{7}$
12	$\dfrac{1}{12}$

- Remember, to find the reciprocal of a whole number, think of the number over 1, then turn the fraction upside down.

Part 3 Write the reciprocal for each item.

a. $\dfrac{9}{7}$ b. 2 c. $\dfrac{2}{5}$ d. 11 e. $\dfrac{1}{10}$ f. $\dfrac{17}{44}$

Part 4 Write the missing number for each item.

a. An octagon has ■ sides.

b. A hexagon has ■ sides.

c. A quadrilateral has ■ sides.

d. A pentagon has ■ sides.

Part 5 Write a complete equation for each item. Box the answer to the question.

> *Sample* It takes a jogger 3 hours to travel 16 miles. How many miles per hour does the jogger travel?

a. A machine produces 126 parts in 6 seconds. How many parts per second does the machine produce?

b. A cook uses 3 onions for every 4 quarts of soup. How many onions per quart does the cook use?

c. A train travels 122 miles in 5 hours. How many miles per hour does the train travel?

Part 6 For each item, make a fraction number family and a ratio table. Answer the questions.

a. 75% of the houses had storm windows. The rest didn't. There were 150 houses that didn't have storm windows. How many houses were there in all? How many houses had storm windows?

b. Tim ran 130% the distance that Jan ran. Tim ran 24 miles farther than Jan ran. How far did Jan run? How far did Tim run?

Part 7 Work the item.

A trucking company buys 3 times as many tires as mufflers. Last year, the company bought 120 mufflers. The company paid $40 for each tire and $90 for each muffler. The company paid 5% sales tax on all tires and mufflers. How much did the company spend in all for the tires and mufflers?

Independent Work

Part 8 Answer each question.

a. If a book has 136 pages, what fraction of the book is each page?

b. If a gas tank holds 22 gallons, what fraction of the full tank is each gallon?

c. If each part of the cake is $\frac{1}{8}$ of the cake, how many pieces are in the cake?

d. If an acre is $\frac{1}{40}$ of the field, how many acres are in the field?

e. If a recipe makes 5 servings, what fraction is each serving?

Part 9 Work each item. If an answer is 1 or more, write it as a whole number or a mixed number.

a. $4 = \dfrac{24}{\blacksquare}$

b. $\dfrac{\blacksquare}{} = \dfrac{15}{2}$

c. $20 = \dfrac{\blacksquare}{8}$

d. $2 = \dfrac{\blacksquare}{42}$

e. $\dfrac{1}{5} \times \dfrac{3}{8} = \blacksquare$

f. $\dfrac{12}{5} \times \dfrac{5}{12} = \blacksquare$

g. $4 \times \dfrac{9}{7} = \blacksquare$

Part 10 Find the area of the colored figure.

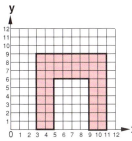

Part 11 Work each item.

a. It costs 20¢ to seed each square yard of a field. Find the area of the field and figure out the cost of seeding the entire field.

b. A team buys 7 bats and 20 baseballs. Each bat costs $18. Each baseball costs $3.50. The tax is 8%. Figure out the total cost of the purchase.

Part 12 For each item, write the complete equation with names. Box the answer to the question.

a. How many months are in 5 years?

b. How many years are in 27 months?

c. How many yards are in 12 feet?

d. How many minutes are in 3 hours?

e. How many hours are in 146 minutes?

Lesson 46   189

Lesson 47

Part 1 Work the item.

A farmer bought sacks of corn and sacks of grass seed. Each sack of grass seed cost 3 times as much as each sack of corn. The farmer paid $5 for each sack of corn. The farmer bought 11 sacks of corn and 10 sacks of grass seed. The sales tax was 8%. How much did the farmer pay for each sack of grass seed? How much did the farmer pay in all?

Part 2 Write the reciprocal for each item.

a. 100   b. 17   c. $\frac{3}{12}$ d. $\frac{18}{15}$ e. $\frac{1}{25}$

Part 3   Facts about Angles

- Degrees are units that tell about angles.
- Here is the symbol for degrees: °
- Here is how to write 50 degrees: **50°**

- A circle has 360°:

- Any triangle has 180°: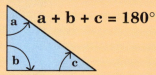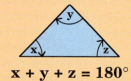

- Half a circle has 180°:

- A corner of a page has 90°:

Part 4 Make a complete equation for each item. Box the answer to the question.

a. An athlete runs 1,206 yards in 3 minutes. How many yards per minute does the athlete run?

b. A factory produces 17 cars per month. How many cars does the factory produce in 12 months?

c. An editor reads 7 books in 3 days. How many books per day does the editor read?

d. A machine makes 8 cartons per minute. How long does it take the machine to make 200 cartons?

Part 5

- If you multiply any value by its reciprocal, you'll end up with 1.
  - Here's: $\frac{3}{4}$
- If you start with $\frac{3}{4}$ and multiply by the reciprocal of $\frac{3}{4}$, you end up with 1.

  $$\frac{3}{4}\left(\frac{4}{3}\right) = \frac{12}{12} = 1$$

  - Here's: 33
- If you start with 33 and multiply by its reciprocal, you end up with 1.

  $$33\left(\frac{1}{33}\right) = \frac{33}{33} = 1$$

- Remember, if you multiply any value by its reciprocal, you end up with 1.

Part 6 Write the complete equation for each item. Show each value multiplied by its reciprocal.

a. $\frac{4}{7}$ b. 15   c. $\frac{20}{3}$ d. $\frac{1}{48}$

Lesson 47

Part 7 Work each item.

a. $\frac{2}{5}$ of the children had pet dogs. 30 children did not have pet dogs. How many children had pet dogs? How many children were there?

b. The crate weighed 20% as much as the books. The books weighed 240 pounds. How much more did the books weigh than the crate weighed? How much did the crate weigh?

Part 8 Write the name of each figure.

pentagon   octagon   hexagon   quadrilateral   triangle

a.   b.   c.   d.   e.

Independent Work

Part 9 Work each item.

a. In a pond, there are 4 frogs for every 3 logs. If the pond has 48 logs, how many frogs are there?

b. The building is $\frac{7}{3}$ the height of the tree. The difference in height is 36 feet. How tall is the tree? How tall is the building?

c. Every 5 ounces of touch-up paint costs $3. A painter spent $36 on touch-up paint. How much paint did the painter buy?

d. A machine grinds 3 tons of gravel every 7 seconds. How long does it take the machine to grind 200 tons of gravel?

e. The ratio of cats to dogs in a kennel is 7 to 3. If there are 42 cats, how many dogs are there?

f. A kennel has cats and dogs. The ratio of cats to dogs is 5 to 6. There are 253 pets in the kennel. How many are cats? How many are dogs?

Part 10 Show each value as a hundredths decimal. Round when necessary.

a. 14.028   b. 1.5   c. 3.096   d. 12.333

Part 11 Copy and complete each item. If an answer is 1 or more, show it as a whole number or a mixed number.

a. $3 = \frac{\blacksquare}{12}$ b. $10 = \frac{\blacksquare}{7}$ c. $\blacksquare = \frac{21}{6}$ d. $\blacksquare = \frac{45}{8}$

e. $10 = \frac{30}{\blacksquare}$ f. $\frac{1}{2} \times \frac{3}{8} = \blacksquare$ g. $15 \times \frac{2}{3} = \blacksquare$ h. $\frac{2}{8} \times \frac{8}{2} = \blacksquare$

Part 12 Make an equation. Answer each question.

a. How many hours are in $3\frac{1}{2}$ days?
b. How many hours are in 180 minutes?
c. How many minutes are in 2 hours?
d. How many ounces are in 3 pounds?
e. How many weeks are in 45 days?

Part 13 Find the area of the colored figure.

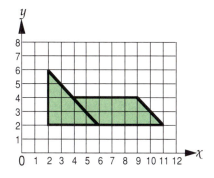

Lesson 48

Part 1

- Some sentences that compare two things give a number for **one of the things** that are compared.

- You've worked with sentences of that type:

    The book weighs 40% as much as the vase.

    dif   book   vase
    ────────────▶
          $\frac{40}{100}$

    The car traveled 120% as far as the truck traveled.

    dif   truck   car
    ────────────▶
                 $\frac{120}{100}$

- Some sentences that compare two things give the **difference** number.

- Here are sentences of that type:

    The book weighs 25% **less** than the phone.

    dif   book   phone
    $\frac{25}{100}$
    ────────────▶

    The car traveled 60% **farther** than the bus.

    dif   bus   car
    $\frac{60}{100}$
    ────────────▶

- Here's the rule:

    If the problem gives a number for the amount **more** or the amount **less**, it gives the difference number.

Part 2 Make a fraction number family for each item.

a. The hat costs 12% less than the gloves.

b. The cost of the hat is 120% the cost of the scarf.

c. The baby is 10% younger than the cat.

d. The phone weighs 82% more than the book.

e. Dan is 80% as old as his brother.

Part 3

- If you know how to multiply a fraction by a fraction, you can multiply mixed numbers. All you do is change each mixed number into a fraction. Then multiply.

- Here's a problem with mixed numbers: $\quad 2\frac{1}{3} \times 1\frac{4}{5} = \blacksquare$

- First, change the mixed numbers into fractions: $\quad \frac{7}{3} \times \frac{9}{5} = \blacksquare$

- The answer is $\frac{63}{15}$. That's $4\frac{3}{15}$. $\quad \frac{7}{3} \times \frac{9}{5} = \frac{63}{15} = \boxed{4\frac{3}{15}}$

- Remember, just change the mixed numbers into fractions. Then multiply.

Part 4
Change each mixed number into a fraction. Work each item.

a. $3\frac{1}{4} \times 3\frac{1}{2} = \blacksquare$

b. $2\frac{3}{5} \times 1\frac{1}{4} = \blacksquare$

c. $1\frac{2}{3} \times 6 = \blacksquare$

d. $\frac{7}{8} \times 2\frac{3}{4} = \blacksquare$

e. $4\frac{2}{7} \times 2\frac{1}{3} = \blacksquare$

Part 5
Write the complete equation for each item. Show each value multiplied by its reciprocal.

Sample
$\frac{2}{3}(\blacksquare) = 1$

a. $\frac{17}{2}$

b. 3

c. $\frac{2}{29}$

d. $\frac{1}{30}$

Lesson 48

Part 6

Find the area of each colored figure.

a.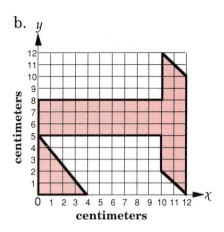

b.

Part 7

Write the answer to each question.

a. How many degrees are in this figure?

b. What's the name of this figure?

c. How many degrees in this figure?

d. How many degrees are in a whole circle?

e. How many degrees?

Part 8

Make a fraction number family for each item. Use simple fractions.

Sample The alligator is 20% as long as the pole.

a. The alligator is 50% as long as the pole.
b. The pole is 30% the length of the alligator.
c. The rope is 25% as long as the alligator.
d. The alligator is 60% as long as the broom.
e. The rope is 10% as long as the alligator.

Independent Work

Part 9 Work each item as a division problem. Show the answer as a hundredths decimal.

a. $\dfrac{27}{84}$ b. $17\overline{)324}$ c. $\dfrac{246}{38}$ d. $\dfrac{3}{8}$ e. $\dfrac{5}{9}$

Part 10 Answer each question.

a. If a pie has 5 equal pieces, what fraction of the pie is each piece?

b. If a cup holds 8 ounces, what fraction of a full cup is each ounce?

c. If each serving is $\dfrac{1}{8}$ of the total, how many servings are there?

d. If the troop of scouts contains 16 scouts, what fraction of the troop is each scout?

e. If each plot is $\dfrac{1}{12}$ of the garden, how many plots are there?

f. If each student is $\dfrac{1}{26}$ of the class, how many students are in the class?

Part 11 For each item, make an equation. Box the answer to the question.

a. How many days are 90 hours?

b. How many inches are $2\tfrac{1}{2}$ feet?

c. How many minutes are $1\tfrac{1}{2}$ hours?

d. How many feet are 48 inches?

Part 12 Find the area and perimeter of each figure.

a.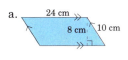

b.

c.

Part 13 Work each item.

a. Jane is $\dfrac{3}{5}$ the weight of her father. Her father weighs 210 pounds. How much does Jane weigh?

b. Jane is $\dfrac{2}{3}$ the age of an elm tree. Jane is 40 years old. What is the age of the elm tree?

c. The car traveled $\dfrac{1}{8}$ the distance the truck traveled. The truck traveled 20 miles. How far did the car travel?

d. The tractor used $\dfrac{8}{3}$ the amount of fuel the bus used. The tractor used 400 gallons of fuel. How much more fuel did the tractor used than the bus used?

Lesson 48

Lesson 49

Part 1 Work each item.

a. $4\frac{4}{5} \times 10 = \blacksquare$

b. $1\frac{2}{9} \times 2\frac{1}{3} = \blacksquare$

c. $\frac{3}{8} \times 2\frac{2}{3} = \blacksquare$

d. $2 \times 5\frac{4}{7} = \blacksquare$

e. $1\frac{1}{4} \times 3\frac{2}{5} = \blacksquare$

Part 2 Make a number family for each sentence. Show all fractions with a denominator of 100.

a. The boat weighs 130% more than the car.
b. The boat's weight is 130% of the car's weight.
c. The boat weighed 50% less than the trailer.
d. The weight of the boat was 12% of the truck's weight.
e. The truck's weight is 240% of the motorcycle's weight.

Part 3 Rewrite each item.

Sample item 1
6 pounds 20 ounces

Sample item 2
3 days 34 hours

a. 2 hours 72 minutes
b. 1 week 12 days
c. 5 dollars 35 nickels
d. 8 feet 20 inches

Part 4 Find the area of the colored figure.

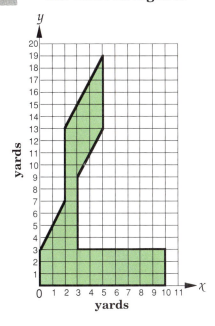

Part 5 Copy and complete each equation.

a. $\frac{11}{4}\left(\blacksquare\right) = \blacksquare = 1$

b. $\frac{1}{5}\left(\blacksquare\right) = \blacksquare = 1$

c. $\frac{3}{4}\left(\blacksquare\right) = \blacksquare = 1$

d. $27\left(\blacksquare\right) = \blacksquare = 1$

Part 6
Make a fraction number family for each item. Then write the number of the correct picture.

a. The tree is 75% the height of the building.

b. The boat is 90% as wide as the trailer.

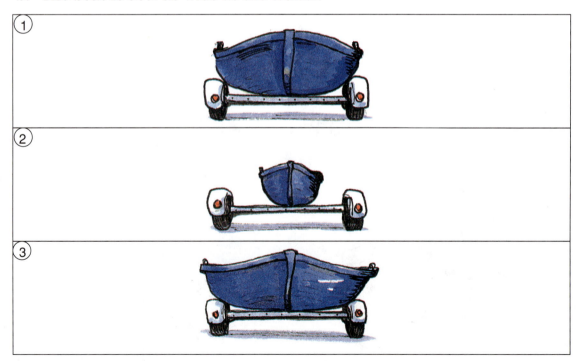

Part 6 continued

c. The snake is 20% the length of the rake.

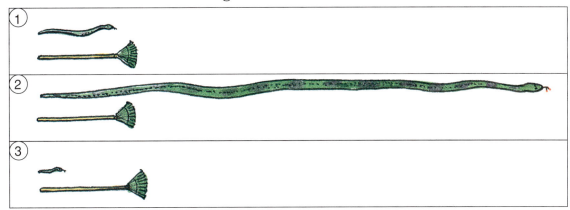

d. The snake is 40% the length of the alligator.

e. The pole is 50% the height of the tree.

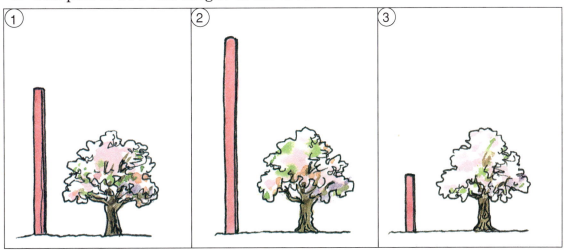

Independent Work

Part 7 **Work each item.**

a. .4 of the boats need repairs. There are 54 boats that do not need repairs. How many boats are there? How many boats do need repairs?

b. The new price of curtains is 120% of the old price. The old price was $80. How much more is the new price? What is the new price?

Part 8 **Take short cuts to work each division problem.**

a. $150\overline{)600}$

b. $100\overline{)268}$

c. $50\overline{)230}$

d. $10\overline{)88}$

e. $100\overline{)3}$

Part 9 **For each item, make an equation. Box the answer to the question.**

a. How many years are in 17 seasons?

b. How many months are in $4\frac{1}{2}$ years?

c. How many hours are in 80 minutes?

d. How many quarters are in 7 dollars?

e. How many yards are in 18 feet?

Part 10 **Work each item.**

a.
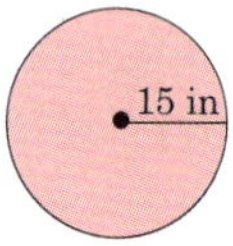

Find the area and circumference.

b.
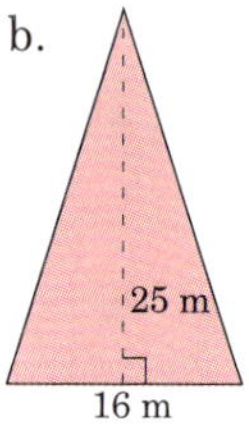

Find the area.

c.
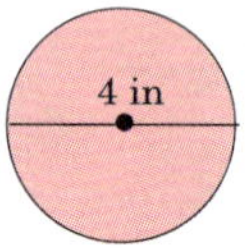

Find the area and circumference.

d.
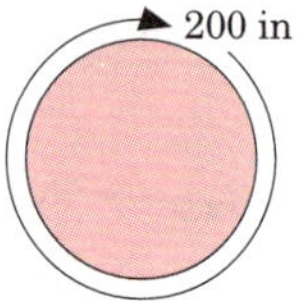

Find the diameter.

Part 11 **Work each item.**

a. A train starts out with some passengers. After the first stop, the number of passengers is tripled. After the next stop, the number in the train is 29 less than it was. The train now has 100 people in it. How many people did the train start out with?

b. Start with the mystery number and add 150. Then divide by 5. Then subtract 20. You end up with 10. What's the mystery number?

Part 12 **Rewrite each percent as fifths.**

a. 80%

b. 20%

c. 60%

d. 40%

Part J

b. dif $\frac{30}{100}$ car $\frac{100}{100}$ → boat $\frac{130}{100}$

c. dif $\frac{50}{100}$ boat $\frac{50}{100}$ → trailer $\frac{100}{100}$

d. dif $\frac{88}{100}$ boat $\frac{12}{100}$ → truck $\frac{100}{100}$

e. dif $\frac{140}{100}$ motorcycle $\frac{100}{100}$ → truck $\frac{240}{100}$

Test 5

Part 1   Answer each question.

  a. What's the reciprocal of $\frac{1}{7}$?

  b. What's the reciprocal of 15?

  c. What's the reciprocal of $\frac{12}{9}$?

Part 2   Answer each question.

  a. If a pie is divided into 9 equal pieces, what's the fraction for each piece?

  b. If a student is $\frac{1}{32}$ of the class, how many students are in the class?

  c. There are 220 students in a school. What's the fraction for each student?

Part 3   Work each item.

  a. $2\frac{1}{3} \times 7\frac{1}{2} = $ ▇   b. $3\frac{2}{5} \times 8 = $ ▇   c. $\frac{1}{2} \times 7 = $ ▇

Part 4   Write the simple fraction for each percent.

  a. 20%   b. 50%   c. 75%   d. 25%   e. 60%   f. 90%

Part 5   Write the name for each figure.

a.   b.   c.   d.   e.

Part 6 Answer each question.

a. How many degrees are in a triangle?
b. How many degrees are in the corner of a page?
c. How many degrees are in half a circle?
d. How many degrees are in a whole circle?

Part 7 For each item, make the complete equation with names. Box the answer to the question.

a. There are 56 bottles in 14 cartons. How many bottles per carton are there?
b. The train travels 50 feet per second. How many feet does the train travel in 20 seconds?
c. A car travels 55 miles. The car travels at the rate of 24 miles per hour. How long does the trip take?
d. A machine makes 60 nails in 4 seconds. How many nails per second does the machine make?

Part 8 Copy and complete each equation.

a. $\frac{7}{3}(\blacksquare) = \blacksquare = 1$

b. $\frac{32}{10}(\blacksquare) = \blacksquare = 1$

Part 9 Work each item.

a. 30% of the students walk to school. There are 260 students. How many students walk to school? How many don't walk to school?

b. The whale was 160% the length of the boat. The whale was 40 feet longer than the boat. How long was the whale? How long was the boat?

Part 10 Find the area of the colored figure.

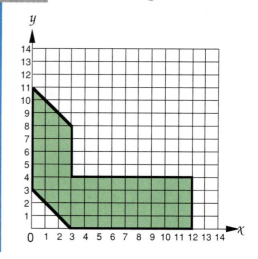

Part 11 Work each item.

a. The jeweler buys 3 times as many clocks as rings. He buys 50 rings. Each ring costs $45. Each clock costs $60. How many clocks are there? How much did the jeweler spend in all?

b. Fran purchases 3 caps and 12 baseballs. Tax is 6%. How much do the items cost before tax? What's the tax? How much does Fran pay in all?

c. A farmer fences the field and plants it. Planting it costs $2 for each square yard. Fencing it costs $6 per yard. What's the cost of planting? What's the cost of fencing? What's the total cost?

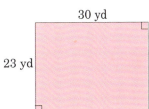

Part 12 Work each item as a division problem. Show the answer as a hundredths decimal.

a. $\dfrac{23}{4}$ b. $12\overline{)341}$ c. $\dfrac{3}{7}$

Lesson 51

Part 1 Make a number family for each sentence.

  a. The elm is 30% shorter than the maple.
  b. The sand weighed 25% more than the gravel weighed.
  c. The tank's volume is 138% of the box's volume.
  d. The waiter's wages are 80% as much as the cook's wages.
  e. The dinner was 45% more expensive than the breakfast.

Part 2

- Some figures have a hole. The simplest way to find the area of these figures is to compute the area of the **total figure,** compute the area of **the hole,** then subtract the area of the hole from the area of the total figure.
- Here's a figure:

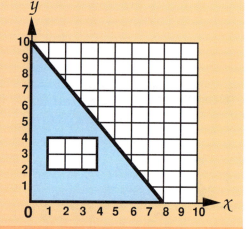

- First you find the area of the entire **triangle:**

  (triangle) $\dfrac{b \times h}{2} = A$

  $\dfrac{8 \times 10}{2} = \dfrac{80}{2} = A$

  40 sq units

- The hole is a **rectangle.** You find its area:

  (hole) $b \times h = A$

  $3 \times 2 = A$

  6 sq units

- Now you subtract the area of the hole from the area of the entire triangle:

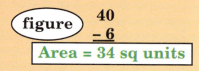

Part 3   Find the area of each colored figure.

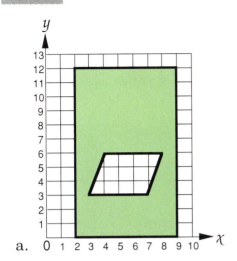
a.

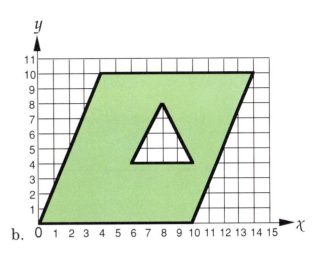
b.

Part 4   Work each item.

a. It takes $4\frac{3}{4}$ minutes to change 1 tire. How long does it take to change 8 tires?

b. Each carton weighs $5\frac{7}{8}$ ounces. How much do 9 cartons weigh?

c. Each load of sand weighs $3\frac{1}{5}$ tons. The workers used $7\frac{1}{2}$ loads. What was the weight of the sand they used?

d. The mower runs for $2\frac{5}{6}$ hours on a tank of gas. On Wednesday, the mower used $2\frac{4}{10}$ tanks of gas. How long did the mower run?

Part 5   Rewrite each item with a proper number for each unit name.

a. 4 wk   13 d
b. 2 ft   20 in
c. $8   140¢
d. 7 lb   28 oz
e. 3 hr   82 min

Part 6 Rewrite each percent as a simple fraction. Complete each equation.

a. $50\% \left(\ \right) = \blacksquare = 1$

b. $75\% \left(\ \right) = \blacksquare = 1$

c. $10\% \left(\ \right) = \blacksquare = 1$

d. $25\% \left(\ \right) = \blacksquare = 1$

e. $5\% \left(\ \right) = \blacksquare = 1$

Part 7 Copy and work each problem.

Sample $\frac{3}{8} \times 264 = \blacksquare$ Enter: $3 \div 8 \times 264 =$

a. $\frac{5}{4} \times 180 = \blacksquare$

b. $\frac{5}{6} \times 84 = \blacksquare$

c. $\frac{7}{8} \times 44 = \blacksquare$

d. $\frac{8}{5} \times 106 = \blacksquare$

Independent Work

Part 8
Work the item.

A person buys a dog house and a bird cage. The cost of the dog house is 9 times the cost of the bird cage. The bird cage costs $38.50. The tax is 8%. What is the total amount of this purchase?

Part 9
Copy and complete each equation. If the missing value is more than 1, write it as a whole number or a mixed number.

a. $5 = \dfrac{9}{\blacksquare}$ b. $12 = \dfrac{\blacksquare}{9}$ c. $28 = \dfrac{3}{\blacksquare}$ d. $\blacksquare = \dfrac{58}{5}$ e. $3.5 = \dfrac{\blacksquare}{20}$

Part 10
For each item, make a complete equation. Box the answer to the question.

a. A train moves at the steady rate of 45 miles per hour. How many hours does it take for the train to go 200 miles?

b. Another train travels 65 miles in 3 hours. How many miles per hour does that train travel?

c. A third train travels at the rate of 52 miles per hour. How many miles does the train travel in 12 hours?

Part 11
Work each item.

a. $15 - 3\dfrac{1}{7} = \blacksquare$

b. $2\dfrac{1}{2} \times \dfrac{1}{3} = \blacksquare$

c. $5\dfrac{3}{12} + 1\dfrac{10}{12} = \blacksquare$

d. $5\dfrac{25}{60} + 8\dfrac{38}{60} = \blacksquare$

e. $3 - 2\dfrac{12}{60} = \blacksquare$

f. $4\dfrac{1}{2} \times 3 = \blacksquare$

g. $10 - 5\dfrac{3}{10} = \blacksquare$

Part 12
Work each item.

a. At Muddy Lake, there are 2 perch for every 8 bass. There are 240 perch in the lake. How many bass are in the lake?

b. The number of fish in Loon Lake is $\dfrac{5}{4}$ the number of fish in Arrow Lake. There are 68 more fish in Loon Lake than in Arrow Lake. How many fish are in Arrow Lake?

c. At Loon Lake, there are 3 herons for every 7 loons. If there are 84 loons, how many herons are there?

d. Two kinds of fish live in Blue Lake—perch and bass. There are 5 perch for every 2 bass. There is a total of 700 fish in the lake. How many bass are in Blue Lake? How many perch are in Blue Lake?

Lesson 51

Lesson 52

Part 1 Work each item.

a. A machine produces $2\frac{1}{5}$ pounds of sawdust each minute. How much sawdust does the machine produce in $3\frac{1}{2}$ minutes?

b. The diameter of a tree trunk increases by $1\frac{3}{4}$ inches each year. How much wider does the tree get in $8\frac{1}{2}$ years?

c. Each bag holds $4\frac{3}{8}$ pounds of salt. How much salt do 8 bags hold?

d. A tractor moves 18 yards per minute. How far does the tractor move in $2\frac{1}{3}$ minutes?

Part 2 For each item, write a statement for Y and a statement for the difference.

Sample:
$$\text{dif} \quad \frac{Z}{100} \xrightarrow{} \frac{Y}{130}$$
$$\frac{}{100} \quad \frac{}{100}$$

Y is ■% of Z.
Y is ■% ■ than Z.

a. dif $\frac{Y}{80} \xrightarrow{} \frac{Z}{100}$
   $\frac{}{100} \quad \frac{}{100}$

b. dif $\frac{Z}{100} \xrightarrow{} \frac{Y}{105}$
   $\frac{}{100} \quad \frac{}{100}$

c. dif $\frac{Y}{45} \xrightarrow{} \frac{Z}{100}$
   $\frac{}{100} \quad \frac{}{100}$

d. dif $\frac{Y}{60} \xrightarrow{} \frac{Z}{100}$
   $\frac{}{100} \quad \frac{}{100}$

Part 3 Work each item.

Sample
```
  3 lb   5 oz
+ 1 lb  12 oz
  4 lb  17 oz
  5 lb   1 oz
```

a. 3 lb 12 oz
  + 9 lb 7 oz

b. 2 yr 11 wk
  + 5 yr 50 wk

c. 3 d 15 hr
  + 4 d 19 hr

d. 1 yd 25 in
  + 8 yd 30 in

e. 10 hr 45 min
  + 6 hr 15 min

Part 4 Find the area of each blue figure.

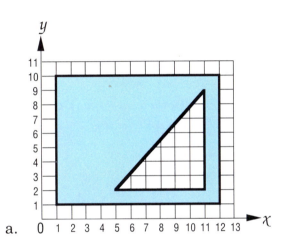
a.

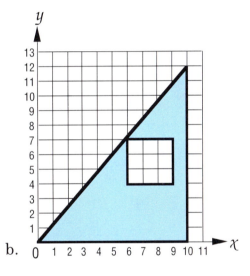
b.

Part 5

For each item, make a complete equation. Answer the question.

> **Sample** Each part of the pie is 20% of the pie. How many parts are there?

a. Each piece of the pie is 25% of the pie. How many pieces are in the pie?

b. Each section of the farm is 50% of the total. How many sections are there?

c. Each stamp is 10% of the entire collection. How many stamps are in the collection?

d. Each part of the rectangle is 5% of the rectangle. How many parts are in the rectangle?

Part 6

Write each item as a multiplication problem and work it.

a. $\frac{3}{5}$ of 21 = ■

b. $\frac{9}{8}$ of 50.57 = ■

c. $\frac{5}{4}$ of 96.5 = ■

d. $\frac{1}{2}$ of 125 = ■

e. $\frac{2}{9}$ of 11.8 = ■

Independent Work

Part 7

Answer each question.

The area of Mr. Green's farm is 3 times the area of Mr. Brown's farm. Mr. Brown's farm has 120 acres. It takes a crew .7 of an hour to plant each acre. A crew plants both farms.

a. How many hours does it take to plant Mr. Green's farm?

b. How long does it take to plant Mr. Brown's farm?

c. How long does it take to plant both the farms?

Part 8

Figure out the area of the colored figure.

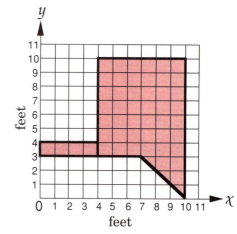

Part 9 Write a complete equation for each item. Box the answer to the question.

a. How many days are in 17 weeks?
b. How many weeks are in 40 days?
c. How many hours are in 500 minutes?
d. How many minutes are in 100 seconds?
e. How many hours are in 7 days?

Part 10 Work each item. If the missing value is more than 1, show the answer as a whole number or a mixed number.

a. ■ × 7 = 3
b. $\frac{2}{3}$ × 12 = ■
c. 14(■) = 6
d. 7 × ■ = 6
e. ■ × 15 = 32
f. 8 × $1\frac{3}{5}$ = ■

Part 11 Work each item.

a. The distance to the lodge is $\frac{3}{5}$ the distance to the lake. The distance to the lake is 25 miles. How far is it to the lodge?

b. The car costs $\frac{3}{8}$ as much as the truck. The truck costs $12,000. How much does the car cost?

c. The cost of the china is $\frac{8}{5}$ the cost of the table. The china costs $900. What's the cost of the table?

Lesson 52

Lesson 53

Part 1 Work each item.

a. Each slice of the pie is $\frac{1}{6}$ of the pie. Each slice costs 95¢. How much does the whole pie cost?

b. Each pile is $\frac{1}{5}$ of the total weight. Each pile weighs 13 pounds. What is the total weight?

c. Each serving is $\frac{1}{8}$ of the recipe. Each serving weighs 13 ounces. What does the entire amount weigh?

d. Each parcel of land is $\frac{1}{12}$ of the total. Each parcel costs $24,000. What's the total cost of the land?

Part 2 Work each problem.

a. $2\overline{)15.52}$ b. $8\overline{)7.848}$ c. $7\overline{)130.9}$

d. $9\overline{)1.08}$ e. $4\overline{)6.292}$

Part 3 For each item, write a statement for H and a statement for the difference.

a. $\underline{\text{dif}} \quad \dfrac{K}{100} \rightarrow \dfrac{H}{210}$
$\phantom{\text{dif}\ \ } \dfrac{}{100} \quad \dfrac{}{100}$

b. $\underline{\text{dif}} \quad \dfrac{H}{92} \rightarrow \dfrac{K}{100}$
$\phantom{\text{dif}\ \ } \dfrac{}{100} \quad \dfrac{}{100}$

c. $\underline{\text{dif}} \quad \dfrac{H}{45} \rightarrow \dfrac{K}{100}$
$\phantom{\text{dif}\ \ } \dfrac{}{100} \quad \dfrac{}{100}$

d. $\underline{\text{dif}} \quad \dfrac{K}{100} \rightarrow \dfrac{H}{125}$
$\phantom{\text{dif}\ \ } \dfrac{}{100} \quad \dfrac{}{100}$

e. $\underline{\text{dif}} \quad \dfrac{K}{100} \rightarrow \dfrac{H}{200}$
$\phantom{\text{dif}\ \ } \dfrac{}{100} \quad \dfrac{}{100}$

Part 4 Work each addition problem. Rewrite the answer if you need to.

a. 2 hr 25 min
  + 6 hr 55 min

b. 4 ft 5 in
  + 8 ft 6 in

c. 3 lb 15 oz
  + 4 lb 12 oz

d. 5 yr 8 mo
  + 2 yr 9 mo

e. 3 hr 15 min
  + 2 hr 28 min

Part 5 Work each item.

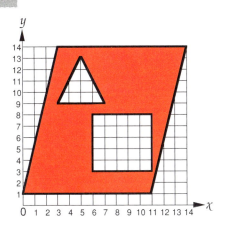

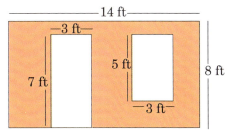

A builder wants to figure out the cost of siding for this wall. The wall will have a hole for the door and a hole for the window. The rest of the wall will be covered with siding.

a. Find the area of the red figure.

b. Find the area of the wall that needs siding.

Independent Work

Part 6 Answer each question.

a. Jill buys 2 frying pans and a clock. The tax is 5%. How much does she pay?

b. Alex buys 1 clock, 1 jacket and 2 pairs of shoes. How much does he pay? (Don't forget the tax.)

Part 7 Copy and complete each equation. If the missing value is more than 1, write it as a whole number or a mixed number.

a. $24 = \dfrac{\blacksquare}{9}$

b. $16 = \dfrac{50}{\blacksquare}$

c. $\blacksquare = \dfrac{86}{3}$

d. $\blacksquare \times 16 = 5$

e. $5 = \dfrac{85}{\blacksquare}$

Lesson 53   215

Part 8 Show the complete equation. Box the answer.

a. How many days are in $5\frac{3}{7}$ weeks?
b. How many weeks are 88 days?
c. How many hours are in $3\frac{1}{4}$ days?
d. How many feet are 99 inches?
e. How many inches are in $35\frac{1}{3}$ feet?

Part 9 Work each item.

a. $5\frac{2}{7} \times 2\frac{1}{2} = \blacksquare$

b. $\frac{3}{13} \times 1\frac{1}{3} = \blacksquare$

c. $12 - 2\frac{30}{60} = \blacksquare$

d. $5\frac{1}{8} + 7\frac{7}{8} = \blacksquare$

e. $10 - 2\frac{4}{13} = \blacksquare$

Part 10 Work each item.

a. At Camp Arnold, the ratio of boys to girls is 3 to 5. If there are 30 girls, how many boys are there?

b. At Camp Boontown, the ratio of boys to all children is 3 to 7. There are 40 girls at the camp. How many children are at Camp Boontown?

c. At Camp Carlos, the ratio of girls to all children is 5 to 9. There are 60 girls at this camp. How many boys are at Camp Carlos? How many children are there in all?

Part 11 Work each item.

a. 28 ft, 11 ft — Find the area and perimeter.

b. 14 cm — Find the area and circumference.

Part J

c. 7)130.9 [18.7]
d. 9)1.08 [.12]
e. 4)6.292 [1.573]

Lesson 54

Part 1 Copy and work each item. Rewrite the answer if you need to.

a. 1 hr   35 min
  + 3 hr   20 min

b. 5 ft   11 in
  + 2 ft   9 in

c. 6 gal   2 qt
  + 4 gal   1 qt

d. 6 gal   1 qt
  + 1 gal   6 qt

e. 2 yr   10 mo
  + 3 yr   5 mo

Part 2 Work each item.

a. Each part of the circle is $\frac{1}{4}$ the area of the circle. If each part is 46 square inches, what is the area of the entire circle?

b. Each serving is $\frac{1}{6}$ of the total meal. Each serving has 780 calories. How many calories are in the total meal?

c. Each delivery was $\frac{1}{9}$ of the total shipment. Each delivery cost $12.30. What was the cost of the total shipment?

d. The area of the triangle was $\frac{1}{5}$ the area of the entire figure. The area of the triangle was 12 square yards. What was the area of the entire figure?

Part 3 For each item, write two statements. First tell about one of the values that is shown. Then tell about the difference.

a. dif   R   M
         $\frac{100}{100}$ → $\frac{115}{100}$

b. dif   P   Q
         $\frac{90}{100}$ → $\frac{100}{100}$

c. dif   J   K
         $\frac{75}{100}$ → $\frac{100}{100}$

d. dif   N   R
         $\frac{100}{100}$ → $\frac{135}{100}$

Part 4

Copy each item. Rewrite the numbers for each unit.

Sample

2 11
3̸ wk 4̸ d

a. 5 wk   2 d
b. 4 lb   1 oz
c. 8 yd   2 ft
d. 6 min 17 sec
e. 5 d   11 hr

Part 5

Work the item.

This diagram shows a wall with holes for 2 windows. Find the area of the wall that will have siding.

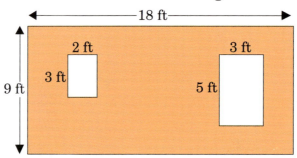

Part 6

Work each problem.

a. $8\overline{).456}$

b. $9\overline{)63.45}$

c. $4\overline{)48.8}$

d. $5\overline{)2.655}$

e. $7\overline{)148.4}$

Part 7

Work each item.

a. The area of a circle is 34.67 square feet. What is $\frac{1}{4}$ of the area?

b. The perimeter of a rectangle is 34.59 inches. What is $\frac{4}{5}$ of the perimeter?

c. The area of a circle is 20.81 square inches. What is $\frac{3}{5}$ of the area?

d. The circumference of a circle is 11.6 feet. What is $\frac{3}{2}$ of the circumference?

e. The area of a triangle is 52.54 square centimeters. What is $\frac{2}{7}$ of the area?

Independent Work

Part 8   Work the item.

This diagram shows a field. The cost of mowing is $.03 per square meter. How many square meters are mowed? What is the cost of mowing the entire field?

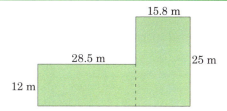

Part 9   Make a complete equation for each item. Box the answer to the question.

a. A car travels for 8 hours. The car goes 320 miles. How many miles per hour does the car go?

b. A farmer collects eggs at the rate of 16 dozen per day. The farmer collected 90 dozen eggs. How many days did that take?

c. A machine makes 15 cards per minute. How many minutes does it take for the machine to make 600 cards?

d. Another machine makes 45 cards. That takes 6 minutes. How many cards per minute does the machine make?

e. Another machine makes 11 cards per minute. The machine works for 33 minutes. How many cards does the machine make?

Part 10   Find the area of the figure.

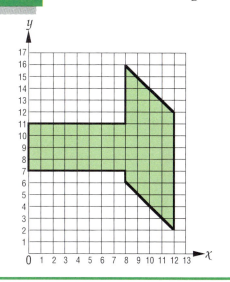

Part 11   Work each item.

a. A train started out with 152 people in it. At the first stop, some people got off. 28 people got in the train. There were now 118 people in the train. How many people got off at the stop?

b. Divide my age by 3. Then add 50. Then multiply by 2. You end up with 124. How old am I?

c. A mail truck starts out with some packages in it. It drops off 11 packages at the first stop. At the next stop, it doubles the number of packages it has. At the next stop, it drops off 400 packages. It ends up with 2 packages. How many did it start out with?

Lesson 54

Lesson 55

Part 1 Find the area of the figure.

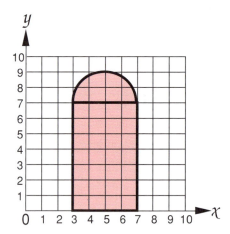

Part 2

- For some related-unit problems, you have to borrow.

- Here's a problem:

     5 wk 3 d
  − 1 wk 4 d

- You can't subtract 4 days from 3 days. So you borrow 1 week from the 5 weeks.

     4   10
     5̷ wk 3̷ d
  − 1 wk 4 d

- Now you can subtract. You end up with:

     3 wk 6 d

Part 3 Copy and work each item.

a.   7 gal 1 qt
  − 2 gal 3 qt

b.   5 d 3 hr
  − 4 d 20 hr

c.   5 ft 7 in
  − 3 ft 9 in

d.   10 lb 0 oz
  − 5 lb 11 oz

Part 4

For each item, write two statements. First tell about one of the values that is shown. Then tell about the difference.

a. $\dfrac{\text{dif}}{\frac{100}{100}} \;\; \dfrac{N}{\frac{88}{100}} \longrightarrow \dfrac{T}{\frac{100}{100}}$

b. $\dfrac{\text{dif}}{\frac{100}{100}} \;\; \dfrac{V}{\frac{20}{100}} \longrightarrow \dfrac{D}{\frac{100}{100}}$

c. $\dfrac{\text{dif}}{\frac{100}{100}} \;\; \dfrac{Q}{\frac{100}{100}} \longrightarrow \dfrac{F}{\frac{152}{100}}$

d. $\dfrac{\text{dif}}{\frac{100}{100}} \;\; \dfrac{M}{\frac{100}{100}} \longrightarrow \dfrac{R}{\frac{240}{100}}$

e. $\dfrac{\text{dif}}{\frac{100}{100}} \;\; \dfrac{H}{\frac{8}{100}} \longrightarrow \dfrac{C}{\frac{100}{100}}$

Part 5

Work each item.

a. The field was divided into 9 parcels of equal size. The entire field was 720 acres. How many acres were in each parcel?

b. Each pile of gold dust weighs $\frac{1}{5}$ of the total. The entire amount of gold dust weighs 260 ounces. How much does each pile weigh?

c. Each piece of pizza is $\frac{1}{10}$ of the total. The total pizza has 6,000 calories. How many calories are in each piece of pizza?

d. The circle's circumference was divided into 3 equal lengths. The circumference was 360 centimeters. What was the length of each part?

Lesson 55

Part 6 Work the item.

This diagram shows a wall with holes for two windows and a door. Siding costs $2.80 per square foot. Figure out the **cost** of siding for the part of the wall that does not have holes.

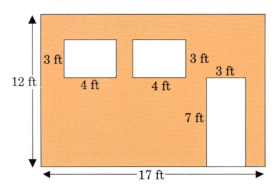

Part 7 For each item, work the fraction as a division problem.

a. $\dfrac{.3}{5}$ b. $\dfrac{15}{4}$ c. $\dfrac{.324}{6}$ d. $\dfrac{1.35}{5}$ e. $\dfrac{2}{8}$ f. $\dfrac{.20}{10}$

Independent Work

Part 8   Work each item.

a. Jan starts out with some money. On Tuesday, she spends $340. On Wednesday, she divides the amount she has left by 4. On Thursday, she receives $600. She ends up with $800. How much did she start out with?

b. Start out with 52 and divide by 4. Add the mystery number. Divide by 7. You end up with 3. What's the mystery number?

c. Start out with the mystery number and subtract 20. Then divide by 5. Then multiply by 3. You end up with 3. What's the mystery number?

Part 9   Work each item.

a. The sale price of the bed is .7 the regular price of the bed. The regular price is $450. How much would a person save by buying the bed on sale?

b. A painter paints house A and house B. Painting house A takes 125% the amount of time it takes to paint house B. It takes 12 hours longer to paint house A than house B. How long does it take to paint house A? How long does it take to paint house B?

c. John earns $50 for every 3 hours he works. If he works 21 hours, how much does he earn?

Part 10   Work each item.

A painter will paint the rectangle blue and the circle gold. Gold paint is 5 times as expensive as blue paint. It costs $.35 to paint each square meter blue.

a. What's the area of the rectangle?
b. What's the area of the circle?
c. How much will it cost to paint the rectangle?
d. How much will it cost to paint the circle?
e. How much will it cost to paint both areas?

Part 11   Write the complete equation. Box the answer.

a. How many weeks are in 44 days?
b. How many inches are in 34 feet?
c. How many inches are $3\frac{7}{12}$ feet?
d. How many quarts are in $6\frac{1}{4}$ gallons?
e. How many hours are $5\frac{1}{5}$ days?

Part 12   Answer each question.

a. How many degrees are in $\frac{1}{2}$ a circle?
b. How many degrees are in the corner of a page?
c. What's the name of this figure?
d. What's the simple fraction for 75%?
e. How many degrees are in a triangle?

Lesson 56

Part 1 Write each fraction as a division problem and work it.

a. $\dfrac{4.65}{5}$ b. $\dfrac{.324}{4}$ c. $\dfrac{6}{8}$ d. $\dfrac{11}{5}$ e. $\dfrac{8.16}{3}$

Part 2 Copy and work each item.

a. 8 gal 6 pt
   − 1 gal 7 pt

b. 6 ft 9 in
   − 2 ft 8 in

c. 7 yd 2 in
   −   30 in

d. 9 lb 4 oz
   − 4 lb 12 oz

e. 6 d 11 hr
   − 2 d   8 hr

Part 3

- If a problem tells about the whole and asks about **one of the equal parts,** you can work the problem by multiplying **or** by dividing.

- Here's a problem:
  The area of the whole rectangle is 400 square units.

$\dfrac{1}{4} \times 400 = \dfrac{400}{4}$ ⟶ 100 sq units

or

          100 sq units
     4 ⟌ 400

Part 4 Find the area of each colored part. Work each problem as a multiplication problem and as a division problem.

a. The area of the square is 160 square centimeters.

b. The area of the circle is 220 square inches.

c. The area of the rectangle is 189 square feet.

Part 5 Work the item.

This is a diagram of a roof. A builder is going to put roofing on the parts of the roof that are not red. The red parts are for the chimney and for a skylight. The cost of roofing is $3 per square foot. Find the area that will have roofing. Then find the cost of roofing that area.

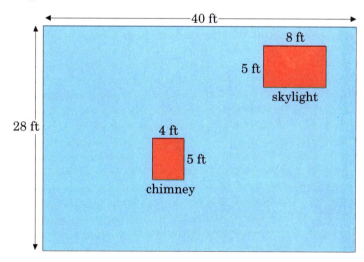

Lesson 56 **225**

Part 6 Work each item.

a. Each part of the quadrilateral is $\frac{1}{3}$ the total area. The entire quadrilateral has an area of 240 square centimeters. What is the area of each part?

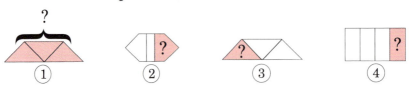

b. Each part of the rectangle is $\frac{1}{8}$ the total area. Each part has an area of 45 square feet. What is the area of the entire rectangle?

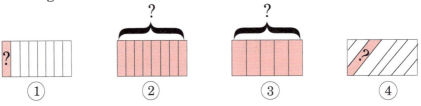

c. Each piece of the pie is $\frac{1}{6}$ of the total. Each piece costs 65¢. What is the cost of the entire pie?

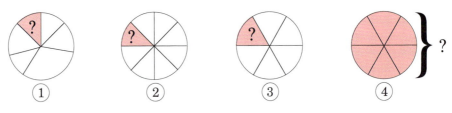

d. A rectangle is divided into 4 equal parts. The area of the rectangle is 160 square inches. What is the area of each part?

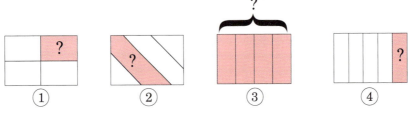

Part 6 continued

e. Each slice is $\frac{1}{7}$ the area of the total circle. The area of the circle is 700 square inches. What's the area of each slice?

 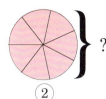 } ?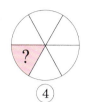

① ② ③ ④

Part 7 Write two statements for each item.

a. $\xrightarrow{\text{dif}\quad\dfrac{R}{\dfrac{72}{100}}\quad\dfrac{P}{\dfrac{100}{100}}}$

b. $\xrightarrow{\text{dif}\quad\dfrac{V}{\dfrac{100}{100}}\quad\dfrac{Q}{\dfrac{180}{100}}}$

c. $\xrightarrow{\text{dif}\quad\dfrac{N}{\dfrac{41}{100}}\quad\dfrac{F}{\dfrac{100}{100}}}$

d. $\xrightarrow{\text{dif}\quad\dfrac{H}{\dfrac{54}{100}}\quad\dfrac{W}{\dfrac{100}{100}}}$

e. $\xrightarrow{\text{dif}\quad\dfrac{X}{\dfrac{100}{100}}\quad\dfrac{Y}{\dfrac{117}{100}}}$

Part 8 Make a number family and ratio table for each problem. Answer the questions the problem asks.

a. The crane was 40% lighter than the tractor. The crane weighed 24 tons. How much did the tractor weigh? How much more did the tractor weigh than the crane weighed?

b. The crane held 36% of the amount the truck held. The truck held 1,500 pounds. How much did the crane hold? How much less did the crane hold than the truck?

c. The goose weighed 60% more than the hawk. The goose weighed 6 pounds more than the hawk. How much did the hawk weigh? How much did the goose weigh?

Lesson 56

Independent Work

Remember to finish the problems in part 8.

Part 9 Work each item.

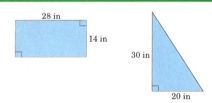

a. What's the area of the rectangle?
b. What's the area of the triangle?
c. What's the difference in the area of the two figures?

Part 10 Copy each mixed number. Write the fraction it equals.

a. $4\frac{7}{8}$ b. $7\frac{1}{2}$ c. $2\frac{8}{9}$

d. $11\frac{3}{8}$ e. $3\frac{2}{10}$

Part 11 Rewrite each item with two unit names.

a. $3\frac{6}{8}$ gallons   d. $8\frac{56}{60}$ hours

b. $5\frac{7}{365}$ years   e. $3\frac{8}{24}$ days

c. $1\frac{5}{20}$ dollars

Part 12 Write the multiplication problem and the answer for each problem.

a. Each bag weighs $7\frac{3}{4}$ ounces. What do 4 bags weigh? What does $\frac{1}{2}$ a bag weigh?

b. A machine produces 120 bottle tops each minute. How many bottle tops does the machine produce in $1\frac{3}{4}$ minutes? How many bottle tops does the machine produce in 3 minutes?

c. Each can of paint weighs $4\frac{3}{7}$ pounds. How much do $3\frac{1}{2}$ cans of paint weigh?

Part 13 Work each item. Round each answer to hundredths.

a. What's $\frac{2}{3}$ of 150.75?   b. What's $\frac{7}{5}$ of 208.3?

c. What's $\frac{5}{8}$ of 52.2?   d. What's $\frac{3}{7}$ of 100?

Part J

a. $5\overline{)4.65}$ .93
b. $4\overline{)3.24}$ .081
c. $8\overline{)6.00}$ .75
d. $5\overline{)11.0}$ 2.2
e. $3\overline{)8.16}$ 2.72

Lesson 57

Part 1 Find each colored area.

a. The area of the circle is 100 square inches.

b. The area of the circle is 52 square miles.

c. The area of the rectangle is 60 square feet.

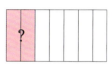

d. The area of the rectangle is 150 square meters.

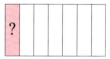

Part 2 Work each item.

a. Each barrel holds $3\frac{1}{4}$ cubic feet of oil. Each jug holds $\frac{1}{4}$ cubic foot of oil. Somebody buys a barrel of oil and a jug of oil. How much oil does the person buy?

b. The container had 12 pounds of flour. The cook used $5\frac{3}{8}$ pounds. How much flour was left in the container?

c. Each barrel holds $3\frac{1}{4}$ cubic feet of oil. How much oil do $1\frac{2}{5}$ barrels hold?

d. Each block of wood weighs $5\frac{2}{7}$ pounds. Each bag of wood chips weighs $1\frac{6}{7}$ pounds. What is the weight of one block and one bag?

Part 3

Copy and work each problem. Rewrite the answer if you need to.

a. 4 lb   7 oz
  + 6 lb 12 oz
  ───────────

b. 9 d 20 hr
  − 2 d 11 hr
  ───────────

c. 3 ft   6 in
  −   10 in
  ───────────

d.   3 min 27 sec
  + 18 min 32 sec
  ─────────────────

e. 8 gal 3 qt
  +   2 qt
  ───────────

f. 7 yr   8 mo
  − 1 yr 11 mo
  ───────────

Part 4

Work each item.

a. The carpenter earned 110% more than the mason. The mason earned $88 less than the carpenter. How much did the carpenter earn? How much did the mason earn?

b. The time that John worked was 110% the time that Fred worked. John worked 44 hours. How long did Fred work? What was the difference in the amount of time the two men worked?

Part 5

Work each item.

a. A box was divided into compartments. Each compartment held $\frac{1}{5}$ the amount the entire box held. If the entire box held 75 cups, how much did each compartment hold?

b. A board was cut into equal-sized pieces. Each piece was 60 square inches. Each piece was $\frac{1}{12}$ of the total area. What was the total area of the board before it was cut?

c. Each piece of a pizza was $\frac{1}{9}$ of the total. Each piece cost $1.20. What was the cost of the entire pizza?

d. Each piece of pizza was $\frac{1}{7}$ of the total. The entire pizza weighed 38 ounces. What was the weight of each piece?

Part 6   Work the item.

Mr. Dennis wants to plant grass in the land area that is green. The cost of planting grass is 6¢ per square yard. Find the area that will be planted. Then find the cost of planting that area.

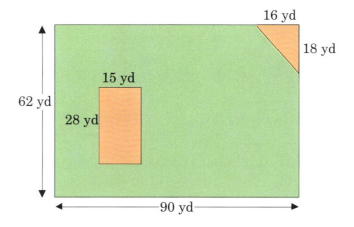

Independent Work

Part 7   Write each problem as a division problem and work it.

a. $\dfrac{3.45}{5}$ b. $\dfrac{52}{8}$

c. $\dfrac{60.24}{4}$ d. $\dfrac{58.4}{8}$

Part 8   Copy and work each item.

a. 2 d   9 hr
  + 1 d 16 hr

b.   1 gal 3 qt
  + 10 gal 3 qt

c. 1 yr   90 d
  + 1 yr 300 d

d. 16 min 50 sec
  + 3 min 18 sec

Part 9   Write each problem in columns and work it.

a. 1.06 − .824

b. 62.1 + .70

c. 4.2 + .652

Part 10   Use estimation to work each problem.

a. 94 ⟌ 750

b. 26 ⟌ 243

Lesson 57

Part 11
Work each item.

a. What's the area of Mr. Tom's field?

b. What's the area of Ms. Green's field?

c. How much larger is Ms. Green's field than Mr. Tom's field?

Ms. Green's field

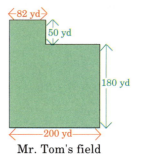
Mr. Tom's field

Part 12
Write the simple fraction for each percent.

a. 75%   b. 30%   c. 50%   d. 20%   e. 25%

Part 13
Answer each question.

a. How many degrees are in a triangle?

b. How many degrees are in a half circle?

c. How many degrees are in a corner?

d. How many sides does a quadrilateral have?

e. How many sides does an octagon have?

f. How many sides does a pentagon have?

g. Each page of a newspaper is $\frac{1}{32}$ of the newspaper. How many pages are in the newspaper?

h. There are 28 equal-sized compartments. What's the fraction for each compartment?

Part 14
Copy and complete each item.

a. $\frac{2}{3}(\blacksquare) = \blacksquare = 1$ b. $\frac{7}{5}(\blacksquare) = \blacksquare = 1$ c. $27(\blacksquare) = \blacksquare = 1$

Part J

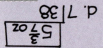

b. 60 × 12 720 sq. in

c. $120 × 9 $10.80

Lesson 58

Part 1 Find the area of the red part of the figure.

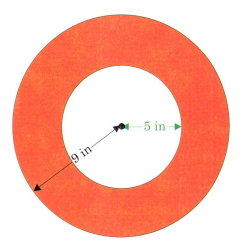

Part 2 Work each item.

a. A car moves $11\frac{1}{2}$ feet. A truck moves 8 feet. How much farther does the car move than the truck?

b. A car travels 12 feet per second. How far does the car travel in $6\frac{3}{4}$ seconds?

c. A small truck pulls $2\frac{1}{2}$ tons. A larger truck pulls $7\frac{1}{2}$ tons. How much would the two trucks pull together?

d. A tractor pulls 16 tons. A medium-sized truck pulls $9\frac{3}{8}$ tons. How much more does the tractor pull than the truck pulls?

Part 3

- You can work problems that involve either addition or subtraction **and** multiplication.

- Here's a problem:
- Here's the same problem with 11 written as 4 + 6 + 1:

$$\begin{array}{r} 11 \\ \times\ 2 \\ \hline \boxed{22} \end{array}$$

$$\begin{array}{r} 4 + 6 + 1 \\ \times\ 2 \\ \hline \end{array} = \boxed{}$$

- Here's how to work the problem:
  - ✔ Copy the plus signs in the answer.
  - ✔ Then do the multiplication for each part.

- The problem has two plus signs. So you write two plus signs in the answer.

$$\begin{array}{r} 4 + 6 + 1 \\ \times\ 2 \\ \hline +\quad + \end{array}$$

- Then you do the multiplication for each part.

$$\begin{array}{r} 4 + 6 + 1 \\ \times\ 2 \\ \hline 8 + 12 + 2 \end{array} = \boxed{}$$

- Now you add the parts: 8 + 12 + 2.
- That's 22. And that's the same answer you get when you multiply 11 x 2.

$$\begin{array}{r} 11 \\ \times\ 2 \\ \hline \boxed{22} \end{array}$$

$$\begin{array}{r} 4 + 6 + 1 \\ \times\ 2 \\ \hline 8 + 12 + 2 \end{array} = \boxed{22}$$

Part 4   Copy and complete each problem that is not boxed.

a.
$$\begin{array}{r} 5 \\ \times\ 4 \\ \hline \boxed{20} \end{array}$$
$$\begin{array}{r} 10 - 8 + 3 \\ \times\ 4 \\ \hline \end{array} = \boxed{}$$

b.
$$\begin{array}{r} 3 \\ \times\ 6 \\ \hline \boxed{} \end{array}$$
$$\begin{array}{r} 9 - 4 - 2 \\ \times\ 6 \\ \hline \end{array} = \boxed{}$$

c.
$$\begin{array}{r} 2 \\ \times\ 5 \\ \hline \boxed{} \end{array}$$
$$\begin{array}{r} 6 + 3 - 7 \\ \times\ 5 \\ \hline \end{array} = \boxed{}$$

Part 5 Copy and work each item.

a. 4 hr 10 min
   − 1 hr 25 min

b. 8 lb 7 oz
   − 2 lb 11 oz

c. 11 hr 15 min
   + 10 hr 50 min

d. 2 yr 7 mo
   + 8 yr 4 mo

e. 3 d 2 hr
   − 1 d 5 hr

Part 6 Find the area of the green part of each figure.

a.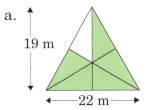
19 m, 22 m

b.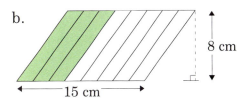
8 cm, 15 cm

Lesson 58 235

Part 7 For each item, make a number family.

a. A father is 160% the height of his son. The son is 50 inches tall. How tall is his father? How much taller is the father than the son?

b. Jane's mom is 140% taller than Jane. Jane is 42 inches shorter than her mom. How tall is Jane? How tall is Jane's mom?

Part 8 Write the number of the correct picture for the items in part 7.

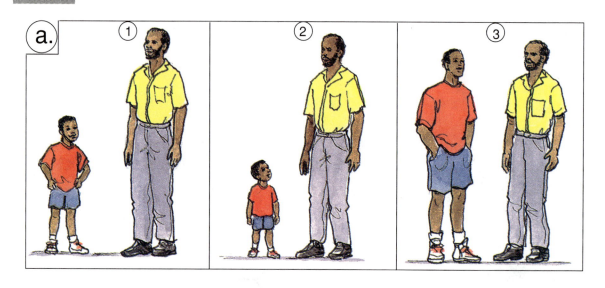

Independent Work

Remember to complete the problems in part 7.

Part 9 Work each item.

a. How many hours is $2\frac{1}{2}$ days?

b. Write 4 hours 26 minutes as a mixed number and unit name.

c. Write 10 years and 17 weeks as a mixed number and unit name.

d. How many days is 36 hours?

e. How many hours is 90 minutes?

f. How many quarts are in $3\frac{1}{2}$ gallons?

g. Write 8 weeks and 5 days as a mixed number and unit name.

Part 10 Work the item.

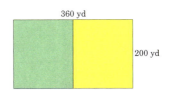

Farmer Davis divides his field in half and plants one half in grass and one half in corn. Planting a square yard of corn costs 9¢. Planting a square yard of grass costs 2¢.

a. What is the cost of planting the grass?

b. What is the cost of planting the corn?

c. What is the total cost?

Part 11 For each family, make two statements that use **both** letters shown in the family.

a.
```
      dif    R      P
            20 →  100
           ---    ---
           100    100
```

b.
```
      dif    V      T
           100 →  259
           ---    ---
           100    100
```

Part 12 Find the area of the figure.

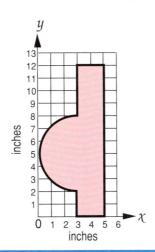

Part 13 Use inverse operations to work each item.

a. Jan had some stamps in her collection. After she sold some stamps, her collection had been divided in half. Then she sold 12 more stamps. Then she bought some stamps and tripled her collection. She now had 90 stamps. How many did she start out with?

b. Peter had $103 in his savings account. He received some money for his birthday, which he put into his account. He took out $23 for tennis shoes. Then he took out another $55 for buying presents. He had $68 left in his account. How much money did Peter receive for his birthday?

Part J

a.
```
   3
   70
  4 hr  45 min
 -1 hr  10 min
  2 hr  25 min
```

b.
```
   7
   23
   5 lb  12 oz
  -2 lb  11 oz
       
```

c.
```
  22 hr   5 min
  21 hr  65 min
 +10 hr  50 min
  11 hr  15 min
```

d.
```
    2
    26
    10 yr 11 mo
   + 8 yr  4 mo
     2 yr  7 mo
```

e.
```
     2
    3 d
   -1 d  
    5 hr
   2 hr
   14 hr  21 hr
```

Lesson 59

Part 1 For each item, write an addition or subtraction problem with unit names. Answer the question.

a. The brick weighed 3 pounds, 15 ounces. The board weighed 8 pounds, 12 ounces. How much heavier was the board than the brick?

b. What's the total weight of the board and the brick in item a?

c. It takes 2 hours and 45 minutes to paint the shed. It takes 5 hours and 20 minutes to paint the garage. What's the total time for both jobs?

d. How much longer does it take to paint the garage than the shed in item c?

e. A sack had 4 pounds, 3 ounces of flour in it. 1 pound, 11 ounces of flour were removed. How much flour was left in the sack?

Part 2 Find the yellow area in each figure.

a.
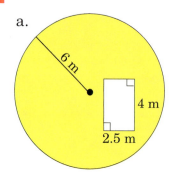

b.
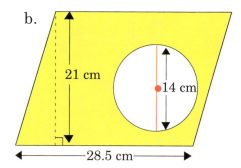

Part 3

- Some problems subtract more than one value. There are two ways to work these problems.
- You can start at the beginning and work the problem a step at a time. Or, you can figure out the total you subtract and then subtract that number.

- Here's:
$$\begin{array}{r} 14 \\ -4 \\ -2 \\ \underline{-6} \end{array}$$

- Here's how to work it a step at a time: $14 - 4 = 10$
  $10 - 2 = 8$
  $8 - 6 = 2$

- Here's how to work the problem by first figuring out the **total you subtract**.
- You subtract: 4 and 2 and 6. That's 12.
- So 14 minus 12 is 2.

$$\begin{array}{r} 14 \\ -4 \\ -2 \\ \underline{-6} \\ 2 \end{array} \Big\} -12$$

- You get the same answer either way.

Part 4   Work each item. First, figure out the total you subtract.

a. $88 - 15 - 13 - 19 = \blacksquare$

b. $\begin{array}{r} 62 \\ -48 \\ \underline{-14} \\ \blacksquare \end{array}$

Lesson 59

Part 5 Copy and complete each problem that is not boxed.

a.
```
   1          3 + 2 − 4
  x 7             x 7
  ▆▆        ▆▆▆▆▆▆▆▆ = ▆
```

b.
```
   2          8 − 5 − 1
  x 4             x 4
  ▆▆        ▆▆▆▆▆▆▆▆ = ▆
```

c.
```
   0          9 − 7 − 2
  x 6             x 6
  ▆▆        ▆▆▆▆▆▆▆▆ = ▆
```

Part 6 Work each item. Round your answers to hundredths.

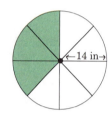

a. Find the area of the green part.

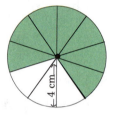

b. Find the area of the green part.

c. Find the green section of the circumference.

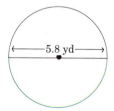

d. Find the green section of the circumference.

Part 7
Make a number family and ratio table for each item. Answer the questions.

a. 36% of the days were wet. The rest were dry. There were 150 days. How many wet days were there? How many dry days were there?

b. The new price is 120% of the old price. The new price is $30. What is the old price? What is the difference between the new price and the old price?

c. The time spent working is 25% more than the time spent sleeping. 8 hours are spent sleeping. How much time is spent working? How much less time is spent sleeping than working?

Independent Work

Remember to finish problems b and c in part 7.

Part 8
Copy and complete each equation.

a. 3 days = ■■ / ■ hours per day

b. ■ gallons = 7 quarts / ■■

c. ■ minutes = 70 seconds / ■■

d. 7 years = ■■ / ■ months per year

e. 7 years = ■■ / ■ weeks per year

Part 9
Work each item.

a. Milly had 128 buttons in her collection. She gave 39 buttons to her sister to start her own collection. Milly found 27 buttons in her mother's dresser and bought 25 buttons at the store. She gave 14 of those buttons to her sister. How many buttons does Milly have left in her collection?

b. There were 27 people in the bus when it started. At the first stop, 14 people got off the bus, and 31 people got in. At the second stop, 15 people got in the bus, and some more people got off. There were 41 people left in the bus. How many people got off the bus at the second stop?

Part 10
Work each item. Round each answer to hundredths.

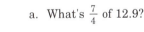

a. What's $\frac{7}{4}$ of 12.9?

b. What's $\frac{2}{10}$ of 1.64?

c. What's $\frac{3}{8}$ of 55.5?

d. What's $\frac{2}{7}$ of 30?

e. What's $\frac{56}{60}$ of 12?

Part 11 Answer each question.

Each pair of gloves costs $4.50. A hat costs 3 times as much as one pair of gloves. Tim buys 3 pairs of gloves and 1 hat. The tax on his purchase is 8 percent.
   a. What's the cost of all the items before tax?
   b. What's the total purchase price with tax?

Part 12 Copy and work each item.

   a. 14 lb   3 oz
      + 2 lb 15 oz

   b. 8 gal 2 pt
      − 3 gal 5 pt

   c. 3 hr 20 min
      + 1 hr 52 min

Part 13 Work each mixed-number problem.

   a. The broom is $1\frac{3}{8}$ feet tall. The pole is $3\frac{5}{8}$ feet tall. How much taller is the pole than the broom?

   b. Dan completes $3\frac{1}{3}$ cabinets each week. He works $2\frac{5}{7}$ weeks. How many cabinets does he complete?

   c. The chair weighs $45\frac{1}{5}$ pounds. The table weighs $36\frac{4}{5}$ pounds. What's the total weight of the two pieces of furniture?

   d. A machine uses $4\frac{6}{10}$ liters of fuel each hour. How much fuel does the machine use in $4\frac{3}{5}$ hours?

Lesson 60

Part 1 Work each item.

a. Erin was 5 feet, 3 inches tall. Her brother was 7 inches shorter than Erin. How tall was her brother?

b. The blue tub weighed 23 pounds, 8 ounces. The red tub weighed 14 ounces more than the blue tub. How much did the red tub weigh?

c. It takes 2 minutes, 15 seconds to sprint to the gate. It takes 45 seconds longer to sprint to the lake. How long does it take to sprint to the lake?

d. The original board was 3 feet, 9 inches long. After 1 foot, 11 inches was cut from the board. How much of the board remained?

e. Brenda worked a math problem for 2 minutes, 20 seconds. Later, she worked for another 4 minutes, 35 seconds. What was the total amount of time she worked?

Part 2 For each item, figure out the missing part of the top value. Then copy and complete the problem.

a.
$\begin{array}{r} 3 \\ \times\ 4 \\ \hline \blacksquare \end{array}$ $\begin{array}{r} 1+4\ \blacksquare \\ \times\ 4 \\ \hline \blacksquare \end{array} = \blacksquare$

b.
$\begin{array}{r} 2 \\ \times\ 5 \\ \hline \blacksquare \end{array}$ $\begin{array}{r} 7-6\ \blacksquare \\ \times\ 5 \\ \hline \blacksquare \end{array} = \blacksquare$

c.
$\begin{array}{r} 0 \\ \times\ 8 \\ \hline \blacksquare \end{array}$ $\begin{array}{r} 3+4\ \blacksquare \\ \times\ 8 \\ \hline \blacksquare \end{array} = \blacksquare$

Test 6

Part 1
Write each item as a division problem and work it.

a. $\dfrac{7.8}{4}$ b. $\dfrac{3.64}{7}$ c. $\dfrac{.285}{3}$

Part 2
Find the area of the yellow part.

a. The area of the entire circle is 50 square feet.

b. The area of the rectangle is 75 square inches.

Part 3
For each number family, make two statements that use both letters.

a. $\xrightarrow[\ \ \ \dfrac{100}{100}\ \ \ ]{\text{dif}} \begin{array}{c} J \\ \dfrac{100}{100} \end{array} \begin{array}{c} R \\ \dfrac{120}{100} \end{array}$

b. $\xrightarrow[\ \ \ \ \ \ \ \ \ \ ]{\text{dif}} \begin{array}{c} Q \\ \dfrac{55}{100} \end{array} \begin{array}{c} D \\ \dfrac{100}{100} \end{array}$

c. $\xrightarrow[\ \ \ \ \ \ \ \ \ \ ]{\text{dif}} \begin{array}{c} V \\ \dfrac{100}{100} \end{array} \begin{array}{c} X \\ \dfrac{250}{100} \end{array}$

Part 4
Work each item. Answer each question.

a. Each can holds $6\tfrac{5}{8}$ pounds of flour. How much flour do $3\tfrac{1}{2}$ containers hold?

b. Each can of flour weighs $6\tfrac{5}{8}$ pounds. Each bag of flour weighs $2\tfrac{3}{8}$ pounds. What's the total weight of a bag and a can of flour? How much more does the can weigh than the bag weighs?

Part 5 Work the item.

This diagram shows a wall with holes for a door and a window. Figure out the area of the wall that will have siding.

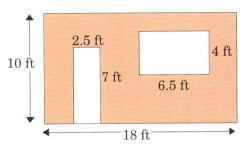

Part 6 Copy and work each item.

a.   7 lb 14 oz
   − 2 lb 15 oz

b.   8 hr 25 min
   + 3 hr 35 min

c. 12 gal 3 qt
   − 3 gal 1 qt

Part 7 Work each item.

a. A board is cut into 5 equal-sized pieces. The area of the whole board is 260 square inches. What's the area of each part?

b. $\frac{1}{5}$ of a window pane is 36 square inches. What's the area of the entire window pane?

Part 8 For each item, make a fraction number family and ratio table. Answer the questions.

a. The adults ate 40% more than the children ate. The children ate 40 pounds of food. How much less food did the children eat then the adults ate? How much food did the adults eat?

b. 5% of the students in a school won a prize. 18 students won a prize. How many students did not win a prize? How many students attended the school?

c. The low temperature was 25% of the high temperature. The high temperature was 24°. What was the low temperature? What was the difference between the high temperature and the low temperature?

Part 9 For each item, write the problem you'll work. Round the answer to two decimal places.

a. What's $\frac{2}{3}$ of 50?

b. What's $\frac{8}{5}$ of 20.6?

c. What's $\frac{12}{17}$ of 3?

Lesson 61

Part 1

- You're going to work common denominator problems. Remember, you can't add or subtract fractions the way they are written if they do not have the same denominator. You can multiply them, but you can't add or subtract.

- To work addition or subtraction problems that don't have the same denominator, you find the **lowest common denominator.** There are different ways to do that.

$$\frac{1}{4} + \frac{5}{6} = \blacksquare$$

- Here's the way we'll use: You'll write the numbers for counting by each denominator shown.

$$\frac{1}{4} \quad 4 \quad 8 \quad \boxed{12} \quad 16 \quad 20$$
$$+\frac{5}{6} \quad 6 \quad \boxed{12} \quad 18 \quad 24$$

- The first common number you write is the **lowest common denominator.**

$$\frac{7}{8} \quad 8 \quad 16 \quad 24 \quad 32 \quad \boxed{40} \quad 48$$
$$-\frac{3}{10} \quad 10 \quad 20 \quad 30 \quad \boxed{40} \quad 50$$

- After you find the common denominator, you write equivalent-fraction problems.

$$\frac{7}{8}\left(\frac{\ }{\ }\right) = \frac{\ }{40}$$
$$-\frac{3}{10}\left(\frac{\ }{\ }\right) = -\frac{\ }{40}$$

- When you complete the equivalent fractions, you get the new problem: $\frac{35}{40} - \frac{12}{40}$

$$\frac{7}{8}\left(\frac{5}{5}\right) = \frac{35}{40}$$
$$-\frac{3}{10}\left(\frac{4}{4}\right) = -\frac{12}{40}$$
$$\boxed{\frac{23}{40}}$$

- The answer is: $\frac{23}{40}$

Part 2 Copy and work each item.

a. $\dfrac{1}{6} + \dfrac{5}{8}$

b. $\dfrac{5}{3} - \dfrac{2}{5}$

c. $\dfrac{3}{4} + \dfrac{1}{12}$

Part 3

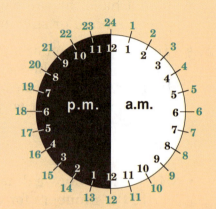

- The simplest way to work some time problems is to use the 24-hour clock. For that clock, the morning hours are the same as they are for the regular clock. The difference comes after 12. The number that follows 12 is not 1. It's 13. So the afternoon hours start with 13 and go all the way to 24. That's midnight.

- Here's how to convert p.m. hours into hours for the 24-hour clock:

    You add 12 to the p.m. hours.

- If the p.m. hour is 4 p.m., you add 12 to 4. The answer is 16.

    4:00 p.m.
    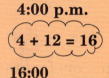
    16:00

- That's the hour for the 24-hour clock.

- Remember, for p.m. hours, add 12.

Part 4 Write the 24-hour time for each item.

a. 2:15 p.m.
b. 8:20 a.m.
c. 1:45 p.m.
d. 11:50 p.m.
e. 12:00 noon
f. 1:05 a.m.

Part 5

For each item, combine the values added. Combine the values subtracted. Work a new problem.

a. 0 + 26 − 15 + 104 − 2 − 8 = ■

b. 0 − 13 + 28 + 120 + 89 − 99 − 43 = ■

c. 0 + 51 − 141 − 68 + 312 = ■

Part 6

- When you multiply decimal values by 10, 100 or 1,000, you can show the answer by just moving the decimal point to the right.

- The rules are:

    ✔ **If you multiply by 10, the decimal point moves 1 place.**

    ✔ **If you multiply by 100, the decimal point moves 2 places.**

    ✔ **If you multiply by 1,000, the decimal point moves 3 places.**

- In this problem, the decimal point moves 1 place:

    ```
      .375
    x  10
     3.75
    ```

- In this problem, the decimal point moves 2 places:

    ```
      .375
    x 100
     37.5
    ```

- In this problem, the decimal point moves 3 places:

    ```
      .375
    x1000
      375
    ```

Lesson 61

Part 7 Write the answer to each problem.

a. .75
   × 100

b. 13.06
   ×   10

c. .135
   × 1000

d. .379
   × 100

e. .8
   × 10

f. 1.238
   ×   10

Part 8

- Some problems refer to clock time. You can work those problems by showing the hours and minutes separated by a colon.

- Here's a problem:

    Jim worked from 7:30 a.m. until 11:10 a.m. How long did he work?

    ```
      10 70
      11:10
    −  7:30
       3:40
    ```

    - Jim worked for: | 3 hr 40 min |

- Here's a different type of problem:

    Donna started work at 8:15 a.m. She worked for 2 hours and 45 minutes. When did she stop working?

- For this problem, you can show 2 hours and 45 minutes as 2:45.

    ```
       8:15
    + 2:45
      10:60
    ```

    - Donna stopped working at: | 11:00 a.m. |

Part 9 Work each item. Answer the question the problem asks.

a. Hilda left home at 7:40 a.m. She returned home at 10:15 a.m. How long was she away from home?

b. Fred worked for 5 hours, 50 minutes. If he started work at 2:15 p.m., at what time did he finish work?

c. Andrew started work at 7:30 a.m. Sally started work 3 hours and 20 minutes later. At what time did Sally start work?

Independent Work

Part 10 Copy and complete each problem that is not boxed.

a. | 5 | 7 − 6
    | ×3 | ×3
            ───── =

b. | 2 | 1 + 7
    | ×8 | ×8
            ───── =

c. | 4 | 20 − 5
    | ×3 | ×3
            ───── =

Part 11 Work each item.

a. Rita bought a pair of socks for $2.45 and a book for $7.80. The tax was 5%. How much did she pay in all?

b. Harry bought 2 cups. The cups were $3.90 each. The sales tax was 5%. How much did he pay in all?

Part 12 Make two statements for each number family. Tell the percent for one of the letters. Then tell about the difference.

a. dif   J   R
          100 →   120
          ───   ───
          100   100

b. dif   T   M
           48 →   100
          ───   ───
          100   100

c. dif   V   N
          100 →   240
          ───   ───
          100   100

Part 13 Work each item.

a. A board is 4 feet, 3 inches long. We cut off a piece that is 2 feet, 7 inches long. How long is the remaining part of the board?

b. Pile A weighs 5 pounds, 4 ounces. Pile B weighs 2 pounds, 10 ounces. How much heavier is pile A than pile B?

c. Roger went on a trip that lasted 4 weeks, 5 days. Then he went on another trip that lasted 2 weeks, 4 days. How many weeks and days was he gone on trips?

d. A tank has 3 quarts of fuel. We add 5 gallons, 1 quart. How much fuel is in the tank now?

Part 14 Find each green area.

a.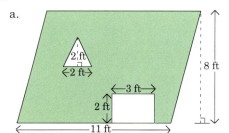

b.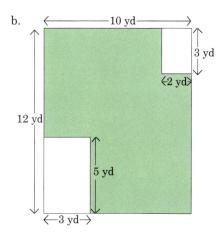

Part 15 Work each item.

a. Write $5\frac{1}{2}$ feet as feet and inches.

b. Write $2\frac{3}{4}$ gallons as gallons and pints.

c. Write $2\frac{3}{4}$ years as years and months.

d. Write $1\frac{2}{3}$ days as days and hours.

Lesson 62

Part 1 Copy and work each item.

a. $\dfrac{5}{6} - \dfrac{3}{4}$

b. $\dfrac{7}{20} - \dfrac{1}{5}$

c. $\dfrac{5}{7} + \dfrac{1}{3}$

Part 2 Work each item and write the answer to the question.

a. The store closed at 2:45 p.m. It reopened at 5:15 p.m. For how long was the store closed?

b. Bonnie arrived at work at 10:20 a.m. Sandra arrived 2 hours and 20 minutes earlier. At what time did Sandra arrive?

c. A train started out at 10:25 p.m. It arrived at its destination 50 minutes later. At what time did it arrive?

Part 3 For each item, figure out the total added and the total subtracted. Then work the simple problem.

a. 0 − 33 + 86 − 17 + 42 + 110 − 85 = ■
b. 0 + 128 − 16 − 120 + 95 = ■
c. 0 − 152 − 289 − 61 + 342 + 160 = ■

Part 4 Write the answer to each problem.

a. 5.235
   x 100

b. .621
   x 1000

c. 3.596
   x   10

d. 11.72
   x 100

e. .65
   x 10

Part 5 Copy and complete each item.

Sample 1
.27 (■) = 2.7

Sample 2
.35 (■) = 35

a. .4 (■) = 4
b. .3589 (■) = 358.9
c. .62 (■) = 62
d. .1102 (■) = 11.02

Folks, if you sit near the front of the train, you'll have a long walk when we reach our destination 50 minutes from now.

Lesson 62

Part 6 Write the 24-hour time for each item.

a. 6:25 p.m.   b. 12:00 midnight   c. 7:59 a.m.
d. 4:40 p.m.   e. 2:00 a.m.   f. 10:48 p.m.

Part 7 Write the 12-hour time for each item.

a. 20:08   b. 7:15   c. 23:40   d. 1:10   e. 15:30   f. 22:01

Part 8

- You've worked problems that add or subtract related units. You can also multiply related units.
- You work the problem by multiplying for the minutes and multiplying for the hours. You end up with 10 hours and 100 minutes.

- Here's:
$$\begin{array}{r} 2\text{ hr }20\text{ min} \\ \times 5 \\ \hline 10\text{ hr }100\text{ min} \end{array}$$

- That's: $\boxed{11\text{ hr }40\text{ min}}$

Part 9 Copy and work each item.

a. 7 wk 2 d
   x   4

b. 5 yd 7 in
   x   6

c. 7 lb 6 oz
   x   5

d. 2 min 15 sec
   x   4

Independent Work

Part 10 Work each item.

a. Start with the mystery number and triple it. Then subtract 55. Then divide by 4. You end up with 2. What's the mystery number?

b. To find Jan's age, you start with 60 and subtract her age. Then you divide by 4. You end up with 12. What's her age?

Part 11 Rewrite each fraction as a division problem and work it.

a. $\dfrac{.36}{9}$ b. $\dfrac{38.8}{4}$ c. $\dfrac{7.92}{2}$

Part 12 Copy and work each problem. Show the answer as a decimal value.

a. $4\overline{)15}$

b. $5\overline{)276}$

Part 13 Work each item.

Jan's age: 9 years   200 days
Tim's age: 10 years 10 days

a. How much older is Tim than Jan?

b. Together, how many years have Jan and Tim lived?

c. Andy is 1 year, 50 days younger than Jan. How old is Andy?

d. How much older is Tim than Andy?

Part 14 Work each item.

a. A farmer wants to plant the field and fence it. Fencing the field costs $8 per yard. Planting the field costs $2.30 per square yard. What's the cost of planting the field? What's the cost of fencing the field? What's the total cost?

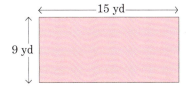

b. Roofing costs $2.15 per square foot. What is the area that will have roofing? What is the cost of roofing that area?

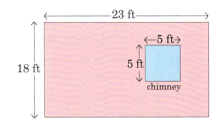

Part 15 For each problem, write the complete equation with names and numbers. Box the answer to the questions.

a. The machine produced 13 buttons per minute. How many buttons would the machine produce in 7 minutes? How long would it take the machine to produce 182 buttons?

b. A person walks at the rate of 180 feet per minute. How far will the person walk in one hour? How many minutes will it take for the person to walk 2,400 feet?

c. A train travels 140 miles in 4 hours. How many miles per hour does the train travel?

Lesson 62

Lesson 63

Part 1

- You've worked problems that have more than one value added and subtracted. You worked those problems by totaling all the values added, then totaling all the values subtracted.

    $52 - 12 - 3 + 8 = \blacksquare$

    $60 - 15 = \boxed{45}$

- There's another way to work these problems on your calculator. You just start with the first value and do the operation for each number that is shown.

- For the problem: $\qquad 15 - 3 - 5 = \blacksquare$

- You would enter: $\boxed{1}\boxed{5}\boxed{-}\boxed{3}\boxed{-}\boxed{5}\boxed{=}$

    - The answer is: $\boxed{7}$

- You'll end up with 7 if the values are in any order, but you must make sure that each value has a sign.

- 15 does not have a sign in the original problem: $\qquad 15 - 3 - 5 = \blacksquare$

- If it is not the first value, it must have a sign in front of it.

- Here's the rule:

Numbers without signs are + numbers.

- Here's the problem rewritten with 15 as the second value: $\qquad -3 + 15 - 5 = \blacksquare$

- It's + 15. $\qquad \boxed{-}\boxed{3}\boxed{+}\boxed{1}\boxed{5}\boxed{-}\boxed{5}\boxed{=}$

Part 2
Rewrite each problem in the new order and work it.

a. $10 - 2 - 3 = $ ■

new order: 2   3   10

b. $18 - 12 - 4 = $ ■

new order: 4   12   18

c. $4 - 2 + 5 = $ ■

new order: 5   4   2

d. $56 - 20 - 35 = $ ■

new order: 35   56   20

Part 3
Write the 24-hour time for each item.

a. 8:16 p.m.
b. 4:00 a.m.
c. 3:25 p.m.
d. 6:30 p.m.
e. 11:48 a.m.
f. 12:45 p.m.

Part 4
Write the a.m. or p.m. time for each item.

a. 17:35   b. 13:12   c. 7:09   d. 3:11   e. 19:19

Part 5
Work each problem.

a. It takes 2 weeks and 4 days to build each house. How long does it take to build 3 houses?

b. Each box weighs 2 pounds and 3 ounces. How much do 8 boxes weigh?

c. It takes 4 minutes and 18 seconds to assemble each toy. How long does it take to assemble 5 toys?

d. Each section is 5 feet, 7 inches long. How long are 3 sections?

Lesson 63

Part 6

Write the missing value for each item.

a. .006 (1000) = ■
b. .035 (100) = ■
c. .008 (■) = 8
d. .004 (■) = .4
e. .05 (100) = ■
f. .007 (■) = .07
g. .056 (■) = 56

Part 7

Work each problem.

a. The bus journey took 3 hours and 17 minutes. If the bus arrived at its destination at 6:10 p.m., what time did the bus start out?

b. The race began at 7:25 a.m. The winner crossed the line at 9:05 a.m. How long did the winner run?

c. Linda started work at 8:15 a.m. She worked for 2 hours and 50 minutes. When did Linda finish work?

Independent Work

Part 8

Write the complete equation with names and numbers. Box the answer to the question.

a. How many yards are in 27 feet?
b. How many feet are in 27 yards?
c. How many inches are in 5 feet?
d. How many days are in 3 years?
e. How many years are in 480 days?

Part 9

Make two statements for each number family. Tell the percent for one of the letters. Then tell about the difference.

a. $\xrightarrow{\text{dif}\quad Z \quad\quad X}$ $\dfrac{100}{100}\quad \dfrac{105}{100}$

b. $\xrightarrow{\text{dif}\quad V \quad\quad Q}$ $\dfrac{100}{100}\quad \dfrac{215}{100}$

c. $\xrightarrow{\text{dif}\quad F \quad\quad T}$ $\dfrac{23}{100}\quad \dfrac{100}{100}$

Part 10

Copy and work each item.

a. 8 − 2 − 3
    _____
       × 4

b. 10 + 2 − 7
    _____
        × 6

c. 9 − 1 + 2
    _____
       × 7

Part 11 Work each item.

Jug M

Jug R

Jug Q

a. How much more fluid is in Jug Q than Jug R?
b. What is the total amount of fluid in all three jugs?
c. How much less fluid is in Jug R than Jug M?
d. What is the total amount of fluid in Jugs M and Q?

Part 12 Work the division problem for each item.

a. $\dfrac{3.84}{4}$

b. $2\overline{).038}$

c. $\dfrac{96.96}{12}$

d. $3\overline{).261}$

Part 13 Work each item.

a. It takes a machine 8 seconds to produce 9 yards of string. How much string will the machine produce in 27 seconds?

b. The ratio of bulls to cows is 2 to 7. There are 56 bulls. How many cows are there?

c. A machine makes bottle tops at the rate of 3 bottle tops every 2 seconds. How long does it take the machine to make 50 bottle tops?

Lesson 63 **259**

Lesson 64

Part 1 Write the new problem for each item and work it. Remember to write a sign for each value.

a. $32 - 10 = \blacksquare$

new order: 10   32

b. $46 - 22 - 23 = \blacksquare$

new order: 23   22   46

c. $56 - 12 + 4 = \blacksquare$

new order: 4   56   12

d. $52 - 45 = \blacksquare$

new order: 45   52

Part 2 Work each item.

a. A train leaves Danville at 10:35 a.m. and arrives at Mudville at 4:50 p.m. How long did the trip take?

b. Millie leaves home at 7:10 a.m. She arrives at her aunt's house at 6:50 p.m. How long did the trip take?

c. Bill left Bradford at 11:20 a.m. His trip to Fairfax took 5 hours and 30 minutes. When did he arrive at Fairfax?

Part 3 Write the missing value for each item.

a. $3.42 \,(\blacksquare) = 342$

b. $.083 \,(100) = \blacksquare$

c. $5.1 \,(\blacksquare) = 51$

d. $.035 \,(\blacksquare) = 3.5$

e. $.08 \,(\blacksquare) = 8$

f. $.009 \,(1000) = \blacksquare$

Part 4 Copy and work each item.

a. $\dfrac{8}{9} - \dfrac{5}{6}$

b. $\dfrac{1}{3} + \dfrac{2}{5}$

c. $\dfrac{12}{10} - \dfrac{15}{20}$

Part 5

- Here's a simple number line:

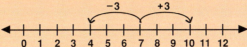

- You know that you add by going to the right. You subtract by going to the left.

- You can do the same thing when the numbers on the number line have signs.

- Here's a number line that shows signed numbers:

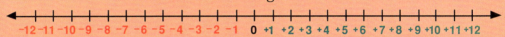

Numbers with a – sign are negative numbers. They are less than zero.

Numbers with a + sign are positive numbers. They are more than zero.

- You can start at any point on the number line and add or subtract.

- When you add, you go to the right: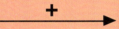

- When you subtract, you go to the left:

- Here's:

- That means, start at any place on the number line and go 3 places in the direction of the smaller numbers.

- When you start at +5, you end up at +2:

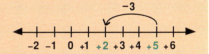

- When you start at +3, you end up at 0:

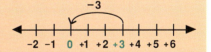

- When you start at +1, you end up at –2:

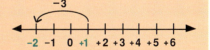

- When you start at –4, you end up at –7:

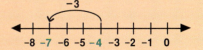

Lesson 64

Part 5 continued

- Here's: **+4**

- That means, start at any place on the number line and go 4 places in the direction of the larger numbers.

- If you start at +1, you end up at +5:
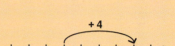

- If you start at −1, you end up at +3:
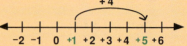

- If you start at −9, you end up at −5:
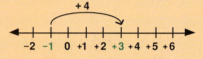

- Remember, the sign tells **the direction** you'll go. The number tells **how many places** you'll go.

Part 6 For each item, draw an arrow to show the direction you'd go to work the problem. Then write how many places you would go.

a. ■ − 3 = ■

Which direction?
How many places?

b. ■ − 11 = ■

Which direction?
How many places?

c. ■ + 6 = ■

Which direction?
How many places?

Part 7 Work both problems for each item. Show each direction with an arrow.

a. ■ + 5 = ■

■ − 5 = ■

b. ■ + 5 = ■

■ − 5 = ■

c. ■ + 5 = ■

■ − 5 = ■

Independent Work

Part 8
Write each value as a mixed number with a unit name.

a. 28 months b. 100 weeks c. 35 pints d. 12 days e. 15 inches f. 88 minutes

Part 9
Figure out each red area.

a.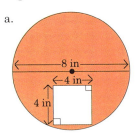

b.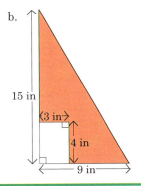

Part 10
Work each item.

Board F — 8 ft 8 in
Board G — 6 ft 2 in

a. How much longer is board F than board G?
b. What is the total length of boards F and G?
c. Board H is 3 feet, 8 inches longer than board F. What's the length of board H?

Part 11
Work each item.

a. There are 120 calories per serving of broccoli. How many servings have 1,000 calories?

b. A worker sews 8 shirts every 2 minutes. How many shirts per minute does the worker sew?

c. A snail moves at the rate of $7\frac{1}{2}$ inches per minute. How many inches does the snail move in 5 minutes?

d. A car gets 22 miles per gallon of gas. The car goes 400 miles. How many gallons of gas does the car use?

Lesson 65

Part 1 Write the new problem for each item and work it. Remember to write a sign for each value.

a. 3 + 15 − 7 = ■
    new order: 15 7 3

b. 26 − 1 − 22 = ■
    new order: 22 26 1

c. 32 + 17 − 18 = ■
    new order: 17 18 32

d. 32 − 28 = ■
    new order: 28 32

e. 56 − 12 − 20 = ■
    new order: 20 12 56

Part 2 Work each item.

a. William arrived in Durham at 4:50 p.m. He had been driving for 6 hours and 25 minutes. At what time had William started?

b. Fred worked for 6 hours and 20 minutes. He started work at 10:35 a.m. When did he finish?

c. Barbara finished work at 3:15 p.m. She had been working for 4 hours and 5 minutes. When had she started work?

d. Miriam started exercising at 6:45 a.m. She stopped exercising at 8:20 a.m. How long did she work out?

e. Sam worked on his motorcycle from 10:45 a.m. until 1:15 p.m. How long did he work?

Part 3

- For some **equivalent-fraction** problems, you multiply by: $\frac{10}{10}$, $\frac{100}{100}$ or $\frac{1000}{1000}$
- You can figure out the number you multiply by if you compare the starting value and the ending value.
- Here's a problem: $\frac{6.547}{.21} = \frac{\blacksquare}{21}$
- You know that you multiply by 10, 100 or 1,000 because the starting value and the ending value have the same digits.
- You can figure out the missing number by seeing how many places the decimal point moved.

$$\frac{6.547}{.21} \left(\frac{100}{100}\right) = \frac{\blacksquare}{21}$$

- Here's another problem: $\frac{11.6}{.5} = \frac{\blacksquare}{5}$
- The decimal point moved one place. The fraction that equals 1 is $\frac{10}{10}$.

$$\frac{11.6}{.5} \left(\frac{10}{10}\right) = \frac{\blacksquare}{5}$$

- Remember, see how many places the decimal point moved. That tells whether the missing fraction is $\frac{10}{10}$, $\frac{100}{100}$ or $\frac{1000}{1000}$.

Part 4

For each item, work the equivalent-fraction problem to figure out the missing value.

a. $\frac{5.81}{.07} = \frac{\blacksquare}{7}$

b. $\frac{.68}{.4} = \frac{\blacksquare}{4}$

c. $\frac{1.05}{.15} = \frac{\blacksquare}{15}$

d. $\frac{.0156}{.028} = \frac{\blacksquare}{28}$

Part 5

- You've worked with a number line that has negative numbers. That number line works just like a thermometer.

- The number line has numbers that are less than zero:

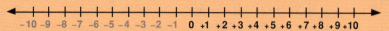

- The thermometer has numbers that are less than zero:

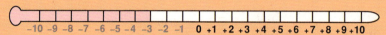

- On the vertical number line, the values are greater when you go up:

- You can go in that direction from any starting point on the number line or on the thermometer:

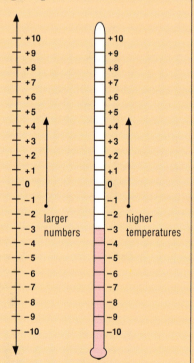

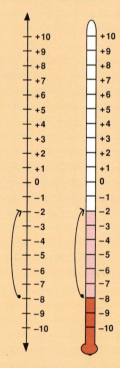

- On the thermometer, the temperatures are higher when you go up.

- You can end up with a number that is less than zero on either the number line or a thermometer.

- Remember, a day can start out with a temperature that is below zero. The temperature can increase, but it may stay below zero.

Part 5 continued

- You can think of the vertical number line as a water level. Numbers can be below the water or above it.
- If they are below, they are negative numbers. If they are above, they are positive numbers.
- If something moves up from any place, it is going in the **+** direction. If something moves down, it is going in the **−** direction.

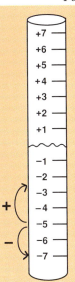

Part 6 Write two complete equations for each item.

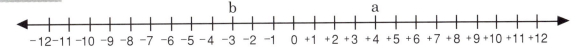

a. ■ − 8 = ■
■ + 8 = ■

b. ■ + 4 = ■
■ − 4 = ■

Part 7 Write the problem and the answer for each item.

a.

b.

c.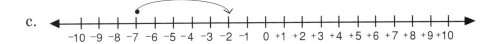

d.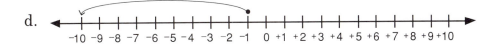

Part 8 Work each item. Rewrite the problem in a column if you need to find the lowest common denominator to work it.

a. $\dfrac{3}{5} \times \dfrac{2}{7} = \blacksquare$ b. $\dfrac{3}{5} + \dfrac{2}{7} = \blacksquare$ c. $\dfrac{5}{9} + \dfrac{2}{3} = \blacksquare$

d. $\dfrac{5}{4} \times \dfrac{7}{9} = \blacksquare$ e. $\dfrac{5}{4} - \dfrac{7}{9} = \blacksquare$

Independent Work

Part 9 Work each item.

a. Rita is 1 year, 35 days older than Tim. Tim is 11 years, 10 days old. How old is Rita?

b. Container F holds 3 gallons, 3 pints. Container G holds 4 gallons, 1 pint. How much more does container G hold than container F holds? What is the total amount the two containers hold together?

c. In January, it snowed 2 feet, 3 inches. Later in the month, it snowed 1 foot, 9 inches. What was the total snowfall for the month? How much more did it snow the first time than the second time?

Part 10 Copy and complete each problem that is not boxed.

a. $\begin{array}{r} 2 \\ \times\ 6 \\ \hline \blacksquare \end{array}$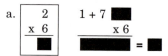

b. $\begin{array}{r} 10 \\ \times\ 2 \\ \hline \blacksquare \end{array}$

c. $\begin{array}{r} 8 \\ \times\ 3 \\ \hline \blacksquare \end{array}$ $\begin{array}{r} 6-2\ \blacksquare \\ \times\ 3 \\ \hline \blacksquare = \blacksquare \end{array}$

Milly told me that I could figure out how much more container G holds by pouring, but all I get is a mess.

Part 11 Work each item.

a. Write $4\frac{1}{2}$ yards as yards and inches.

b. Write $4\frac{1}{2}$ gallons as gallons and quarts.

c. Write $4\frac{1}{2}$ days as days and hours.

d. Write $4\frac{1}{2}$ years as years and weeks.

e. Write $4\frac{1}{2}$ feet as feet and inches.

f. Write $4\frac{1}{2}$ pounds as pounds and ounces.

Part 12 Copy and complete each equation.

a. $.03\,(\blacksquare) = 30$

b. $.03\,(\blacksquare) = 3$

c. $7.614\,(100) = \blacksquare$

d. $.032\,(1000) = \blacksquare$

e. $.08\,(1000) = \blacksquare$

Part 13 Work each item.

a. Mary started out with $250 in her bank account. She took out some money to buy a guitar. Then she put in $80. She now had $200. How much did she take out for the guitar?

b. Start with the mystery number and triple it. Then divide by 2. Then subtract 66. You end up with 3. What's the mystery number?

Part 14 Find the area of the blue figure.

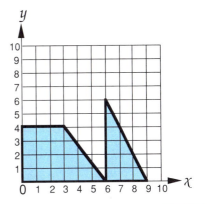

Part J

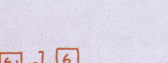

Lesson 65   269

Lesson 66

Part 1

- When you count, you say numbers in this order: 1, 2, 3, 4, 5 . . .
- Here's a rule about how far those numbers are from zero on the number line:

    Numbers that come after other numbers are farther from zero.

    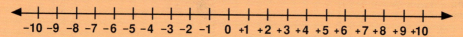

- 6 comes after 5 when you count. So 6 is farther from zero than 5 is.

    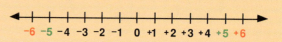

Part 2 For each item, write the value that is farther from zero.

Sample problem
− 4, + 6

a. − 9, − 7
b. − 12, + 11
c. + 6, + 7
d. + 6, − 7
e. − 20, − 21

Part 3 Work each item.

a. Fran starts painting a wall at 10:50 a.m. She works for 5 hours and 30 minutes. At what time does she complete the wall?

b. Dave started roasting a turkey at 9:30 a.m. It roasted for 4 hours and 45 minutes. At what time was the turkey finished?

c. A train started out at 11:30 a.m. It stopped at 3:00 p.m. How long was the trip?

d. A train arrived at 7:25 p.m. It had set out at 6:40 a.m. How long did the trip take?

Part 4 Write a complete equation for each number line.

a.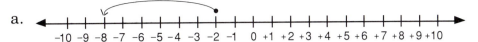

b.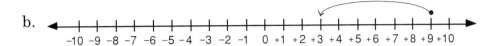

c.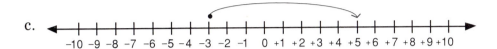

d.

e.

Part 5 Copy and complete each equation.

a. $\dfrac{15.56}{.2} = \dfrac{\blacksquare}{2}$

b. $\dfrac{.320}{.016} = \dfrac{\blacksquare}{16}$

c. $\dfrac{1.05}{.05} = \dfrac{\blacksquare}{5}$

d. $\dfrac{.324}{1.08} = \dfrac{\blacksquare}{108}$

Part 6

- Here's a shortcut you can use for some fractions that are multiplied together:

    Simplify fractions before you do the multiplication.

    - Here's: $\dfrac{5}{12} \times \dfrac{7}{5} = \blacksquare$

- Because the fractions are multiplied you can change the order of the numbers in the numerators or the numbers in the denominators:

$$\dfrac{5}{12} \times \dfrac{7}{5} = \dfrac{7}{12} \times \dfrac{5}{5} = \dfrac{7}{5} \times \dfrac{5}{12} = \dfrac{5}{5} \times \dfrac{7}{12} = \dfrac{7 \times 5}{12 \times 5} = \dfrac{35}{60}$$

- Because the order of the numbers doesn't matter, you can simplify by crossing out part of one fraction and part of another.

- When you cross out both the fives, you cross out $\dfrac{5}{5}$. That's 1. The remaining values are 7 in the numerator and 12 in the denominator. That's just like $\dfrac{7}{12}$. So the answer is $\dfrac{7}{12}$.

    $\dfrac{\cancel{5}}{12} \times \dfrac{7}{\cancel{5}} = \dfrac{7}{12}$

- Remember, if the values are multiplied, you can simplify across fractions. If values are not multiplied, you can't simplify them.

Part 7 Work each item. Simplify first, if you can.

a. $6 \times \dfrac{27}{6} = \blacksquare$

b. $6 + \dfrac{27}{6} = \blacksquare$

c. $\dfrac{2}{3} \times \dfrac{3}{7} = \blacksquare$

d. $\dfrac{25}{80} \times \dfrac{80}{85} = \blacksquare$

e. $\dfrac{4}{3} - \dfrac{3}{5} = \blacksquare$

Part 8 Work each item. Answer the questions.

a. The sale price is 20% less than the regular price. The regular price is $70. What is the sale price? How much would you save if you bought the item on sale?

b. Roger is 140% the height of his baby brother. Roger is 12 inches taller than his brother. How tall is Roger? How tall is his brother?

c. They collected 42% of all the papers. There were 250 papers in all. How many papers were not collected? How many papers were collected?

Independent Work

Remember to complete the items in part 8.

Part 9 For each item, find the area of the orange part. Round your answers to hundredths.

a.

b.

c.

Part 10 Make a complete equation for each item. Box the answer to each question.

There are 32 pounds in each load.

a. How many loads weigh 100 pounds?

b. How many pounds are in 17 loads?

Part 11 Copy and work each item.

a. $\dfrac{5}{8} + \dfrac{1}{12}$

b. $\dfrac{3}{5} + \dfrac{1}{2}$

c. $\dfrac{17}{4} - \dfrac{9}{8}$

Part 12 Work each item.

a. Each container holds 5 pounds, 2 ounces of sulphur. How much sulphur do 8 containers hold?

b. It takes a machine 1 minute and 25 seconds to make each table top. How long does it take the machine to make 3 table tops?

c. The water leaked from the pipe at the rate of 3 gallons and 1 quart every minute. How much water would leak from the pipe in 6 minutes?

Lesson 67

Part 1 For each item, write the value that is farther from zero.

   a. +11, −14
   b. −2, −1
   c. −2, +3
   d. +5, +3
   e. +5, −3
   f. −3, +2

Part 2 Work each item.

a. Each box was 2 feet, 2 inches high. What's the height of a stack of 11 boxes?

b. The pile started out weighing 6 pounds, 11 ounces. 20 ounces were removed from the pile. What was the weight of the remaining pile?

c. Battery A lasts 1 year and 50 weeks. Battery B lasts 7 weeks longer. How long does battery B last?

d. It takes 2 hours, 20 minutes to complete each job. How long does it take to complete 5 jobs?

e. Big Jim could hold his breath for 3 minutes, 3 seconds. Ginger could hold her breath for 1 minute, 10 seconds. How much longer could Big Jim hold his breath than Ginger could?

Part 3

- You've worked with negative numbers on a number line. You can work these problems without using the number line.

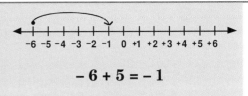

$$-6 + 5 = -1$$

- Here are the rules for finding the number in the answer:
  ✔ If the signs of the numbers shown are the **same, you add.**
  ✔ If the signs in the numbers shown are **different, you subtract.**

- When you subtract, you start with the number that is farther from zero on the number line and subtract the other number.

- Here's a problem:

- The signs are different, so you subtract. The number that's farther from zero is 20.

- You work the problem:

- The number is **11**.

- Here's a problem:

- The signs are different, so you subtract. The number that is farther from zero is 10.

- So you work the problem:

- The number is **8**.

- Here's a problem: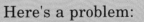

- The signs are the same, so you add:

- The number is **12**.

- Remember, you don't follow the signs that are shown in the problem. You just ask whether the signs are the same or different. Then you say an addition problem if the signs are the same, or a subtraction problem if the signs are different.

Lesson 67

Part 4
For each problem, figure out the missing number.

a. − 6
   − 8
   − ▨

b. + 6
   − 8
   − ▨

c. − 6
   + 8
   + ▨

d. + 6
   + 8
   + ▨

Part 5
Copy and complete each item.

a. + 2
   − 9
   − ▨

b. − 3
   − 4
   − ▨

c. − 8
   + 3
   − ▨

d. − 1
   + 19
   + ▨

e. − 3
   + 11
   + ▨

f. − 4
   − 12
   − ▨

Part 6
Copy and complete each item.

Sample 1
$$\frac{9}{.025} = \frac{\blacksquare}{25}$$

Sample 2
$$\frac{7.2}{.12} = \frac{\blacksquare}{12}$$

a. $\dfrac{5.8}{.004} = \dfrac{\blacksquare}{4}$

b. $\dfrac{8}{.2} = \dfrac{\blacksquare}{2}$

c. $\dfrac{1.8}{1.05} = \dfrac{\blacksquare}{105}$

d. $\dfrac{.6}{.038} = \dfrac{\blacksquare}{38}$

Part 7
Copy and work each problem.

Sample problem
$$5\tfrac{1}{6} + 1\tfrac{3}{4} = \blacksquare$$

a. $3\tfrac{3}{5} + 4\tfrac{2}{7} = \blacksquare$

b. $2\tfrac{3}{4} + 4\tfrac{7}{8} = \blacksquare$

c. $1\tfrac{7}{9} + 3\tfrac{5}{6} = \blacksquare$

Independent Work

Part 8 Make a complete equation for each item. Box the answer to the question.

a. A worker can sew 28 buttons in 3 minutes. How many buttons per minute can the worker sew?

b. Dan can sprint at the rate of 18 feet per second. How far can Dan sprint in $5\frac{1}{2}$ seconds?

Part 9 For each item, combine the values added. Combine the values subtracted. Work the new problem.

a. 0 – 26 – 11 + 91 – 3 + 5 = ■

b. 0 + 13 – 43 – 18 + 10 + 50 = ■

c. 0 – 90 + 56 – 4 + 50 + 1 = ■

Part 10 Work each item.

a. The weight of the go-cart is 140% the weight of the woman. The woman weighs 145 pounds. How much does the go-cart weigh? How much more than the woman does the go-cart weigh?

b. $\frac{3}{7}$ of the eagles haven't produced eggs this year. The rest have. There is a total of 105 eagles. How many eagles have produced eggs? How many eagles haven't produced eggs?

c. A farmer bought sacks of corn and sacks of grass seed. The cost of each sack of grass seed was 3 times the cost of each sack of corn. The farmer paid $5 for each sack of corn. The farmer bought 11 sacks of corn and 10 sacks of grass seed. The sales tax is 5%. How much did the farmer pay for each sack of grass seed? How much did the farmer pay in all?

Part 11 Find the area of the green part.

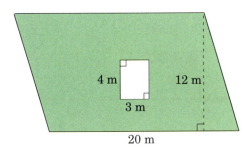

Part 12 Work each item.

a. Jan worked 3 hours and 55 minutes longer than Ted worked. Ted worked 5 hours and 38 minutes. How long did Jan work?

b. The first mail delivery was at 10:35 a.m. The later mail delivery was at 3:15 p.m. How long a period of time was there between mail deliveries?

c. Bonnie started working on a quilt at 7:45 a.m. She worked for 8 hours and 15 minutes. At what time did she finish?

Lesson 67

Lesson 68

Part 1   Copy and complete each problem.

a.   − 4
      − 9
      − ▆

b.   + 3
      − 17
      − ▆

c.   + 2
      + 11
      + ▆

d.   − 15
      + 8
      − ▆

e.   − 7
      + 10
      + ▆

f.   − 11
      − 6
      − ▆

Part 2   Work each item. Simplify first, if you can.

a. $\dfrac{25}{100} \times \dfrac{4}{5} = $

b. $\dfrac{4}{5} + \dfrac{5}{9} = $

c. $\dfrac{75}{3} \times \dfrac{7}{100} = $

d. $\dfrac{25}{50} + \dfrac{14}{100} = $

e. $\dfrac{20}{100} \times 8 = $

f. $\dfrac{7}{10} \times \dfrac{10}{18} = $

Part 3   Work each item the fast way.

a. How many inches are in 50 feet, 7 inches?

b. How many ounces are in 30 pounds, 2 ounces?

c. How many days are in 15 weeks, 3 days?

d. How many seconds are in 8 minutes, 15 seconds?

e. How many inches are in 20 yards, 19 inches?

Part 4   Figure out the green part of each circle.

a.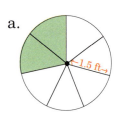

b.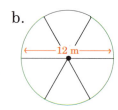

c.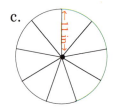

Part 5 Copy and work each item.

a. $3\frac{1}{4}$
$+6\frac{7}{8}$
■

b. $5\frac{1}{6}$
$+2\frac{2}{9}$
■

c. $1\frac{2}{3}$
$+4\frac{5}{7}$
■

Part 6 Copy and complete each equation.

a. $\dfrac{.3}{.07} = \dfrac{■}{7}$

b. $\dfrac{6.28}{.12} = \dfrac{■}{12}$

c. $\dfrac{8}{.125} = \dfrac{■}{125}$

d. $\dfrac{11.06}{.4} = \dfrac{■}{4}$

Independent Work

Part 7 For each item, write the complete equation. Remember the signs.

a.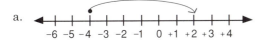

b.

c.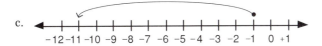

Part 8 Work each item.

a. The winner of the first race took 3 minutes and 18 seconds to complete the course. The winner of the second race took 4 minutes and 4 seconds to complete the course. How much faster was the winner of the first race than the winner of the second race?

b. It takes 3 minutes and 15 seconds to inflate each raft. How long does it take to inflate 6 rafts?

c. Tim could lift 103 pounds and 9 ounces. Jan could lift 109 pounds and 9 ounces. How much weight could the students lift together?

d. Each pair of socks cost $1.03. How much do 20 pairs of socks cost?

Part 9 Find the area of the green part.

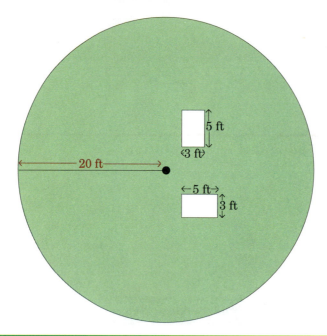

Part 10 Work each item.

a. Start with Jan's age and double it. Then subtract 21. Then multiply by 4. You end up with 100. How old is Jan?

b. Mark started out with some money. He bought gum for 50¢. He paid his sister $3.45 that he owed her. He helped Mr. Brown clean up the yard and he received $5.00 for this work. He ended up with $19.20. How much did he start out with?

Part 11 For each item, write the value that is farther from zero.

a. − 7, − 5   b. − 7, + 6   c. + 2, − 3   d. − 27, + 28

Part 12 Copy and work each problem.

a. M − 82 = 356
M = ▪

b. R = 64 + 12 + 349
R = ▪

c. 17 x 8 = T
T = ▪

d. 15 + B = 53
B = ▪

Lesson 69

Part 1 Copy and work each item.

a. $7\frac{9}{10}$
$-4\frac{3}{5}$

b. $6\frac{2}{5}$
$+1\frac{4}{7}$

c. $2\frac{3}{4}$
$+7\frac{5}{6}$

d. $10\frac{4}{9}$
$-2\frac{1}{3}$

Part 2 Work each item the fast way.

a. How many days are in 2 years, 5 days?
b. How many cups are in 10 gallons, 7 cups?
c. How many weeks are in 7 years, 5 weeks?
d. How many ounces are in 8 pounds, 10 ounces?
e. How many inches are in 6 feet, 8 inches?

Part 3 Work each item.

a. $\frac{2}{5} + \frac{9}{2} = $

b. $\frac{2}{5} \times \frac{9}{2} = $

c. $7 \times \frac{3}{7} = $

d. $7 - \frac{3}{7} = $

e. $\frac{5}{25} + \frac{3}{5} = $

f. $50 \times \frac{11}{100} = $

Part 4 Work each item.

a. $\frac{3}{4}$ of the amount of money that Mary has is in quarters. The rest is not in quarters. She has $2.25 in quarters. How much money does she have in all? How much of her money is not in quarters?

b. $\frac{2}{7}$ of the amount that David has is in nickels. David has $5.60 in all. How much of his money is in nickels? How much is not in nickels?

Part 5   Copy and complete each item.

a.   − 6
     + 20
     + ■

b.   + 4
     − 15
     − ■

c.   − 12
     − 19
     − ■

d.   − 20
     + 8
     − ■

e.   + 5
     + 18
     + ■

f.   − 10
     − 9
     − ■

Part 6   Find the purple part of each circle.

a.

b.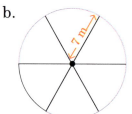

c.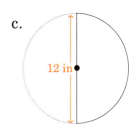

d.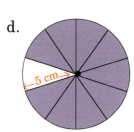

Independent Work

Part 7   Copy and complete each pair of equivalent fractions.

a. $\dfrac{6.84}{.2} = \dfrac{\blacksquare}{2}$

b. $\dfrac{3.2}{.05} = \dfrac{\blacksquare}{5}$

c. $\dfrac{.07}{.009} = \dfrac{\blacksquare}{9}$

d. $\dfrac{.01}{2.64} = \dfrac{\blacksquare}{264}$

Part 8   Work each item.

a. Hilary started climbing the hill at 6:25 a.m. She arrived at the top at 1:05 p.m. How long did the climb take?

b. Hilary started down the hill at 2:15 p.m. It took 2 hours and 30 minutes to reach the bottom. At what time did she reach the bottom?

c. Driving to the ocean takes 45 minutes longer than driving to the canyon. Driving to the canyon takes 3 hours and 15 minutes. How long does it take to drive to the ocean?

Part 9 Copy and work each item.

a. $\dfrac{1}{3} + \dfrac{2}{7} =$

b. $\dfrac{3}{4} - \dfrac{1}{3} =$

c. $\dfrac{5}{8} - \dfrac{1}{4} =$

Part 10 For each item, combine the values added. Combine the values subtracted. Work the new problem.

a. $0 - 3 + 86 + 12 - 50 =$ ■

b. $0 + 3 + 48 - 50 + 12 - 4 =$ ■

Part 11 Answer each question. Round answers to hundredths.

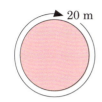

a. What's the diameter?
b. What's the radius?

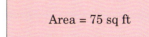

c. What's the height?

d. What's the circumference?
e. What's the area?

Part J

a. $\dfrac{2}{5}\left(\dfrac{2}{2}\right) = \dfrac{4}{10}$

$+ \dfrac{9}{2}\left(\dfrac{5}{5}\right) = + \dfrac{45}{10}$

$\dfrac{49}{10} = \boxed{4\dfrac{9}{10}}$

b. $\dfrac{5}{2} \times \dfrac{9}{7} = \dfrac{9}{5} = \boxed{1\dfrac{4}{5}}$

c. $\dfrac{7}{1} \times \dfrac{3}{7} = \boxed{3}$

d. $7\dfrac{1}{7} \to \dfrac{6}{7}\dfrac{6}{4}$
$- \dfrac{3}{7}$

e. $\dfrac{5}{25}$
$+ \dfrac{3}{5}\left(\dfrac{5}{5}\right) = + \dfrac{15}{25}$
$\dfrac{5}{25} = \boxed{\dfrac{20}{25}}$

f. $50 \times \dfrac{11}{100} = \dfrac{11}{2} = \boxed{5\dfrac{1}{2}}$

Test 7

Part 1 Write the complete equation for the arrow shown. Remember the signs.

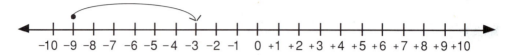

Part 2 Work each item the fast way.

a. How many months are in 5 years, 6 months?

b. How many ounces are in 3 pounds, 4 ounces?

Part 3 For each item, write the value that is farther from zero.

a. $-12, +15$ b. $-9, -8$ c. $+36, -39$

Part 4 Work each item.

a. Each tank holds 7 gallons, 1 quart. How much do 6 tanks hold?

b. Tim solved the first problem in 3 minutes and 12 seconds. He solved the second problem in 1 minute and 49 seconds. How much time did it take for Tim to solve both problems?

c. A can had 3 gallons and 1 pint of milk in it. 1 gallon and 7 pints were removed from the can. How much milk was left in the can?

Part 5 Copy and work each item. Simplify first, if you can.

a. $\dfrac{3}{100} \times \dfrac{50}{5} =$ ▮

b. $\dfrac{15}{2} \times \dfrac{7}{15} =$ ▮

Part 6
Write the regular time for each 24-hour time.

a. 15:16 b. 5:01 c. 22:22 d. 13:55

Part 7
For each item, combine the values added. Combine the values subtracted. Work the new problem.

a. 0 + 23 − 4 − 7 + 8 = ■

b. 0 − 3 + 16 + 30 − 9 − 6 = ■

c. 0 − 12 − 56 + 9 − 1 + 75 = ■

Part 8
Work each item.

a. Jan starts on a bike trip at 10:35 a.m. She completes the trip at 4:05 p.m. How long did the trip take?

b. Frank works for 4 hours and 12 minutes. If he starts at 10:50 a.m., when does he finish work?

Part 9
Copy and complete each item.

a. + 9
   − 15
   − ■

b. − 4
   − 12
   − ■

c. − 26
   + 20
   − ■

d. + 2
   + 18
   + ■

Part 10
Copy and complete each pair of equivalent fractions.

a. $\dfrac{.3}{.012} = \dfrac{■}{12}$

b. $\dfrac{6.14}{.5} = \dfrac{■}{5}$

c. $\dfrac{2.1}{.123} = \dfrac{■}{123}$

Part 11 Copy and work each item.

a. $2\frac{5}{8}$
   $-1\frac{1}{2}$
   ▇

b. $\frac{2}{6}$
   $+\frac{3}{4}$
   ▇

c. $2\frac{5}{6}$
   $+4\frac{4}{5}$
   ▇

Part 12 Figure out the purple part in each item.

a.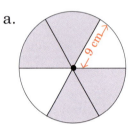

b.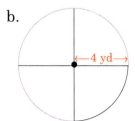

c.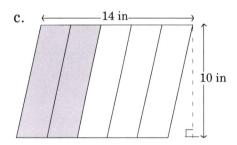

Lesson 71

Part 1

- You can work division problems for fractions that have a decimal denominator. To work those problems, you first write the equivalent fraction that has a whole number in the denominator.

- Here's a fraction: $\frac{.52}{1.4}\left(\ \ \right) = \blacksquare$

- The denominator is not a whole number. You can change it into a whole number that has the same digits. That number is 14.

  $\frac{.52}{1.4}\left(\ \ \right) = \frac{\blacksquare}{14}$

- Now you figure out the fraction that equals 1 and the missing numerator. The fraction that equals 1 is $\frac{10}{10}$. The missing numerator is 5.2.

  $\frac{.52}{1.4}\left(\frac{10}{10}\right) = \frac{5.2}{14}$

- Now you have a division problem that you can work: 5.2 divided by 14.

  $14\overline{)5.2}$

- Remember, change the denominator into a whole number that has the same digits. Then figure out the missing numerator.

Part 2

Copy and complete each equation to show an equivalent fraction with a whole number.

a. $\frac{4}{.08} = \blacksquare$

b. $\frac{11.52}{.6} = \blacksquare$

c. $\frac{6}{.05} = \blacksquare$

d. $\frac{.1075}{.025} = \blacksquare$

Part 3

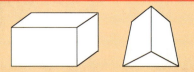

Here are facts about volume:

- The volume of a box is the amount of material the box can hold.
- The material is measured in **cubic units.**
- All cubic units are cubes. Cubes are the shape of sugar cubes.
- A **cubic centimeter** is 1 centimeter wide, 1 centimeter deep, and 1 centimeter high.
- A **cubic inch** is 1 inch wide, 1 inch deep, and 1 inch high.

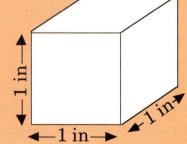

- To find the volume of a box, you use one of these equations:

> **Volume = Area of base x height**

> **Area of base x height = Volume**

- You first find the area of the base. Then you multiply by the height.

- Here is a box:

- The base is red. The base is 8 inches wide and 3 inches deep. So the **area of the base is 24 square inches.**

- The height is 2 inches.

- When you multiply 24 by the height, you get 48. That's the number of **cubic inches** the box holds: **48 cu in.**

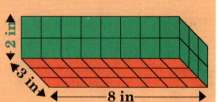

- Remember, figure out the **area of the base,** then **multiply by the height.** The unit name tells about **cubes.**

Part 4 Find the volume of each box.

a.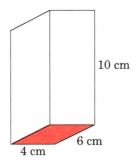

b.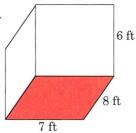

c.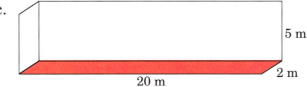

Part 5

- You can change any fraction into a percent. You just figure out what you multiply by to create an equivalent fraction with a denominator of 100.

- Here's: $\frac{5}{4}$

- You can change $\frac{5}{4}$ into hundredths: $\frac{5}{4} = \frac{\blacksquare}{100}$

- The equivalent fraction is $\frac{125}{100}$. That's 125%.

$$\frac{5}{4}\left(\frac{25}{25}\right) = \frac{125}{100} = 125\%$$

Part 6 Copy each fraction. Figure out the percent value it equals.

a. $\frac{2}{5}$ b. $\frac{7}{4}$ c. $\frac{9}{20}$ d. $\frac{12}{25}$

Part 7　Copy and complete each item.

> ✔ Figure out the **number** in the answer.
> ✔ Then figure out the **sign**.
> • The sign in the answer is always the sign of the number that is **farther from zero**.

a. -13
　$+9$

b. -8
　$+17$

c. -20
　-25

d. $+20$
　-32

e. -1
　-14

f. -8
　$+10$

Part 8　For each item, make a fraction number family and ratio table. Answer the questions.

a. $\frac{3}{5}$ of the money is in quarters. There is $6.50 that is not in quarters. What is the amount that is in quarters? What is the total amount?

b. Doris has a total amount of $3.24. $\frac{5}{9}$ of that amount is in dimes. How much of the total is not in dimes? How much is in dimes?

Independent Work

Part 9　Work each item.

a. What's 30% of 80?

b. What's $\frac{3}{8}$ of 800?

c. Bill is $\frac{3}{5}$ of his father's age. His father is 55 years old. How old is Bill?

d. Jane ate $\frac{7}{3}$ the amount of peanuts that Andy ate. Andy ate 150 grams of peanuts. How much did Jane eat?

Part 10　Work each item.

a. $15 - 3 + 17 - 12 - 8 + 27 =$ ■

b. $13 + 50 - 18 - 21 + 5 =$ ■

Part 11 Work each item.

a. $15\frac{7}{8}$
   $- 4\frac{1}{5}$

b. $3\frac{2}{5}$
   $+ 9\frac{1}{2}$

c. $16\frac{3}{10}$
   $- 5\frac{1}{20}$

Part 12 Work each item.

a. Tom left home at 6:50 a.m. He arrived at his cousin's house at 3:25 p.m. How long did the trip take?

b. It takes 3 minutes and 10 seconds to manufacture each plate. How long does it take to make 8 plates?

c. A tank contained 16 gallons and 3 pints of fuel. 5 gallons and 1 pint were removed from the tank. How much fuel remained?

d. It took Jan 1 hour and 13 minutes to go downtown. It took her 1 hour and 48 minutes to return. How much time did the total trip take?

e. Tom's new bike cost $36.20 more than his old bike. His new bike cost $195. How much did his old bike cost?

f. Tina purchases spray paint for $4.90, a loaf of bread for 88¢ and a gallon of milk for $2.19. The sales tax is 6%. Tina gives the clerk $10. What's the total cost of her purchases, including tax? How much change does Tina receive?

Part 13 Work each item.

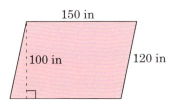
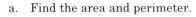

a. Find the area and perimeter.

b. Find the area and circumference.

Part 14 Work each item.

a. $3\frac{2}{5} \times 1\frac{3}{7} =$ ■

b. $5\frac{1}{2} \times 2\frac{3}{4} =$ ■

c. $1\frac{3}{8} \times 1\frac{5}{9} =$ ■

Lesson 72

Part 1 Make the complete table for each item.

a.

%	#
20	■
25	■
40	■
5	4
10	■
total 100	■

b.

%	#
28	■
22	■
50	75
total 100	■

c.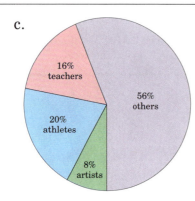

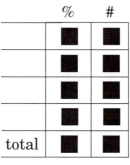

%	#
■	■
■	■
■	■
■	■
total ■	■

There was a total of 350 people at the meeting.

Part 2 Copy each fraction. Figure out the percent value it equals.

a. $\dfrac{3}{2}$ b. $\dfrac{11}{10}$ c. $\dfrac{6}{5}$ d. $\dfrac{8}{25}$

Part 3 Copy and complete each item.

a. + 10
   − 30

b. − 6
   − 12

c. + 4
   − 20

d. + 2
   + 8

e. − 19
   + 5

f. − 15
   − 12

g. − 9
   + 10

Part 4 For each item, write a complete equivalent fraction equation. Then work the division problem for the new fraction.

a. $\dfrac{6.8}{.17} = $ b. $\dfrac{.6}{.003} = $ c. $\dfrac{.42}{.6} = $

Part 5 Find the volume of each box.

a. 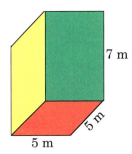   b.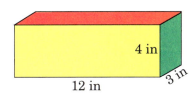

Independent Work

Part 6 For each item, make a ratio table and answer the questions.

a. Tom has coins. $\dfrac{3}{5}$ of the money he has is in quarters. He has $15. How much of that amount is in quarters? How much is not in quarters?

b. Linda has $1.10 in dimes. $\dfrac{2}{5}$ of the amount she has is in dimes. How much does she have in all? How much of the total amount is not in dimes?

c. $\dfrac{2}{7}$ of the tires were new. There were 35 tires that were not new. How many tires were there in all? How many new tires were there?

d. The weight of the mule was $\dfrac{5}{2}$ the weight of the donkey. The donkey weighed 460 pounds. How much more did the mule weigh than the donkey weighed? How much did the mule weigh?

Part 7 For each arrow, make a complete equation. Remember the signs.

a.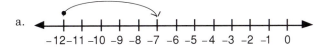

b.

c.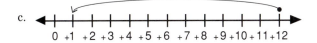

Lesson 72

Part 8

For each item, make a complete equation with names and numbers. Box the answer to the question.

a. How many years are in 45 months?

b. How many ounces are in 13 pounds?

c. How many months are in 11 years?

d. How many days are in 14 weeks?

e. How many hours are in 222 minutes?

f. How many years are in 19 seasons?

Part 9

Work each item.

a. The crew worked 8 hours and 20 minutes. The crew finished at 3:30 p.m. At what time did the crew start work?

b. Doris started doing her homework at 7:11 p.m. She worked for 55 minutes. At what time did she finish?

c. Each box weighs 2 pounds and 5 ounces. How much do 4 boxes weigh?

d. Before the crew started working, the hole in the yard was 3 feet, 4 inches deep. After the crew finished, the hole was 7 feet, 1 inch deep. How much deeper did the crew make the hole?

e. Theresa had 6 hours and 15 minutes of free time. She used 2 hours and 9 minutes of that time to watch TV. How much remaining free time did she have?

Part J

b. $\frac{11}{10} \left(\frac{10}{10} \right) = \frac{110}{100} = \boxed{110\%}$

c. $\frac{5}{5} \left(\frac{20}{20} \right) = \frac{120}{100} = \boxed{120\%}$

d. $\frac{8}{25} \left(\frac{4}{4} \right) = \frac{32}{100} = \boxed{32\%}$

Lesson 73

Part 1

- There's a fast way for figuring out equivalent fractions for fractions that have a decimal value in the denominator. You just move the decimal point in the denominator. Then move the decimal point the same number of places in the numerator.

  - Here's: $\dfrac{3}{1.5}$

- To make the denominator a whole number, you move the decimal point one place. You move the decimal point in the numerator the same number of places.

  $\dfrac{3.}{1.5.} = \dfrac{30}{15}$

- The equivalent fraction is $\dfrac{30}{15}$.

  - Here's: $\dfrac{1.8}{.09}$

- To make the denominator a whole number, you move the decimal point two places. So you move the decimal point in the numerator two places.

  $\dfrac{1.8.}{.0\,9.} = \dfrac{180}{9}$

- The equivalent fraction is $\dfrac{180}{9}$.

- Remember, move the decimal point in the denominator as many places as you need to make a whole number. Then move the decimal point in the numerator the same number of places.

Part 2 Copy and complete each equation to show the equivalent fraction.

a. $\dfrac{.164}{.004} = \blacksquare$

b. $\dfrac{.96}{1.2} = \blacksquare$

c. $\dfrac{1.45}{.029} = \blacksquare$

d. $\dfrac{.02}{.5} = \blacksquare$

e. $\dfrac{1}{.02} = \blacksquare$

Part 3 For each item, write the basic equation: **# x value = amount.** Then answer the question.

	#	x	value of each	= $1.00
quarters	4	x	.25	= 1.00
dimes	10	x	.10	= 1.00
nickels	20	x	.05	= 1.00

a. How many nickels are in $3.45?

b. How many quarters are in $16.50?

c. A person has 46 nickels. How much money does the person have?

d. A person has 30 quarters. How much money does the person have?

e. How many dimes are in $8.20?

Part 4 Copy and work each item.

a. − 142
    − 10

b. + 32
    − 47

c. − 3
    + 15

d. + 41
    + 2
    − 86

You wouldn't believe it, Ann, but I have $8.20 in dimes.

Part 5 Make a complete table for each graph.

a. This graph shows the percentage of a store's income from different sources. Figure the weekly dollar amounts for 1) the cards; 2) the books; and 3) the total.

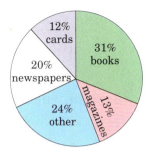

The weekly income for newspapers is $4,000.

b. This graph shows the top three colors sold at a store on a particular day. Figure out the percents for each dollar amount.

Part 6

- You know that there are 360 degrees in a circle. You can use that fact to figure out the degrees in parts of a circle.

- To find the degrees in an angle that is $\frac{3}{8}$ of a circle, you work the problem: $\frac{3}{8} \times 360 =$ ▮

- To find the degrees in an angle that is $\frac{1}{5}$ of a circle, you work the problem: $\frac{1}{5} \times 360 =$ ▮

Lesson 73   297

Part 7

Answer each question. For problems that ask about percent, show the percent as a fraction.

a. An angle is 40% of a circle. How many degrees are in the angle?

b. An angle is $\frac{3}{5}$ of a circle. How many degrees are in the angle?

c. An angle is 25% of a circle. How many degrees are in the angle?

d. An angle is 10% of a circle. How many degrees are in the angle?

Independent Work

Part 8

Work each item.

a. The ratio of quarters to all coins is 5 to 8. If there are 60 quarters, how many coins are there in all? How many coins are not quarters?

b. $\frac{2}{9}$ of the amount of money that Linda has is in nickels. She has $3.60 in all. How much does she have in nickels? How much does she have that is not in nickels?

c. $\frac{7}{8}$ of the papers that Brenda hands in have no mistakes. During last term, she had 6 papers with mistakes. How many papers did not have mistakes? How many papers did she hand in?

Part 9

Find the volume of each box.

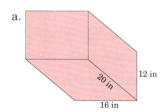

a. 20 in, 12 in, 16 in

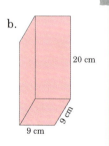

b. 20 cm, 9 cm, 9 cm

Part 10

Work each item the fast way.

a. How many months are in 6 years and 3 months?

b. How many ounces are in 1 pound and 13 ounces?

c. How many days are in 1 year and 26 days?

d. How many seconds are 3 minutes, 4 seconds?

Part 11

Write an equation to show the hundredths fraction and the percent for each item.

a. $\frac{7}{25} = \blacksquare = \blacksquare \%$

b. $\frac{3}{4} = \blacksquare = \blacksquare \%$

c. $\frac{12}{10} = \blacksquare = \blacksquare \%$

d. $\frac{7}{20} = \blacksquare = \blacksquare \%$

Part 12 Make an equation. Box the answer to each question.

> A tractor piled dirt at the rate of 11 tons per hour.

a. If the tractor piled 132 tons, how long did the tractor work?

b. If the tractor worked for 8 hours, how much dirt did it pile?

Part 13 Work each item.

> The diagram shows the area of a deck. The cutout part is for a hot tub.

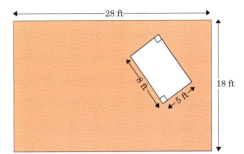

a. What is the area of the part that has decking?

b. What is the area of the part for the hot tub?

c. If the decking costs $3.45 per square foot, what is the cost of the decking?

Part J

a. −142
    − 10
   [−152]

b. +32
   −47
   [−15]

c. −3
   +15
   [+12]

d. +41
   + 2
   −86
   [−43]

Lesson 74

Part 1

- Some problems show repeated multiplication with the same value.
- Here's repeated multiplication with 2s: **2 x 2 x 2**
- Here's repeated multiplication with 7s: **7 x 7 x 7 x 7**
- Here's repeated multiplication with Rs: **R x R**
- The value that is involved in repeated multiplication is called the **base number**.

  - Here's: **4 x 4 x 4 x 4 x 4**
- What's the base number?
- You can rewrite repeated multiplication problems by showing the base number and an **exponent**. The exponent is a LITTLE NUMBER that is written after the base. The exponent indicates the number of times the base is shown.

  - Here's: **5 x 5 x 5 x 5**
- The base is shown **4 times**. The exponent is **4**. So you write: 5^4

  - Here's: **R x R**
- The base is shown **2 times**. So you write: R^2

  - Here's: **3 x 3 x 3 x 3 x 3 x 3**
- The base is shown **6 times**. So you write: 3^6
- Remember, the base is the number that is multiplied. The exponent tells the number of times the base is shown.

Part 2 For each item, write the base and the exponent.

a. 4 x 4 x 4

b. 34 x 34

c. M x M x M x M

d. 9 x 9 x 9

e. 2 x 2 x 2 x 2 x 2

f. B x B x B

Part 3 Make a complete table for the circle graph. Answer each question.

This graph shows the number of trees planted on different streets.

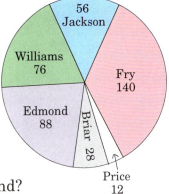

a. What percent of the trees are on Edmond?

b. What percent of the trees are on Briar?

c. What percent of the trees are on Fry?

d. What's the percent for the street that has the largest number of trees?

e. What's the percent for the street that has the fewest number of trees?

Part 4 For each item, write the basic equation: **# x value = amount.** Then answer the question.

a. Mary has $13.70 in nickels. How many nickels does she have?

b. Rob has 22 quarters. How much money does he have?

c. Billy has $10.40 in dimes. How many dimes does he have?

d. Sarah has $5.25 in quarters. How many quarters does she have?

Lesson 74   **301**

Part 5   Answer each question.

a. An angle is $\frac{4}{5}$ of a circle. How many degrees are in the angle?

b. An angle is 15% of a circle. How many degrees are in the angle?

c. An angle is $\frac{1}{8}$ of a circle. How many degrees are in the angle?

d. An angle is $\frac{5}{12}$ of a circle. How many degrees are in the angle?

Part 6   Find the volume of each box.

Area of b x h = V

a.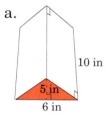
10 in
5 in
6 in

b.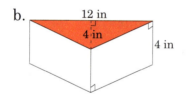
12 in
4 in
4 in

c.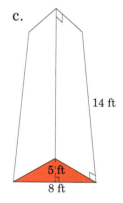
14 ft
5 ft
8 ft

Part 7

- You've worked problems that have decimal denominators. You move the decimal point enough places to make the denominator a whole number.

$$\frac{4}{.25}$$

- Then you do the same thing in the numerator.

$$\frac{4.00}{.25}$$

- You take the same steps when a fraction is written as a division problem:

.2) .68

- The denominator is .2. You move the decimal point one place, and move the other decimal point one place.

.2) .68

- Remember, the number you **divide by** is the **denominator.** You move the decimal point for that number. Then you move the decimal point the same number of places for the other number.

Part 8   Copy and work each problem. Check your answer.

a. .8) 2.56   b. .48) 24   c. .92) 32.2   d. .4) 5.2

Part 9   Figure out the missing numbers in each table.

a.

44	
16	56
	42
28	98
total 100	350

b.

90	30
45	15
	72
108	
total 459	153

Lesson 74   303

Independent Work

Part 10
Work each item.

a. −13
  −11

b. −3
  +36

c. +9
  −36

d. −4
  +7

e. −8
  −14

Part 11
For each item, make a ratio table and answer the questions.

a. The cost of the trailer was $\frac{2}{7}$ the cost of the boat. The difference in cost of the two items was $300. How much did the trailer cost? How much did the boat cost?

b. $\frac{3}{5}$ of Jan's coins were quarters. She had 36 coins that were not quarters. How many coins did she have in all?

c. $\frac{3}{10}$ of the money Clarence has is in quarters. Clarence has $12.25 that is not in quarters. How much does he have in all? How much is in quarters?

Part 12
Figure out the green part of each circle.

a.

b.

Part 13
Write the regular time for each 24-hour time.

a. 23:11

b. 8:32

c. 1:17

d. 14:01

Part 14
Simplify and work each item.

a. $\frac{5}{8} \times \frac{11}{5} = \blacksquare$

b. $\frac{200}{15} \times \frac{4}{100} = \blacksquare$

c. $\frac{7}{10} \times 130 = \blacksquare$

Part 15
Work each item.

a. $25\frac{3}{8}$
  $+12\frac{7}{10}$

b. $28\frac{1}{5}$
  -19

c. $72\frac{1}{2}$
  $-63\frac{3}{8}$

d. $1\frac{2}{3}$
  $+12\frac{1}{4}$

Part 16
For each question, make a complete equation. Box the answer to each question.

a. There were 19 players per team. How many players were there in 8 teams? How many teams could be made up of 95 players?

b. It took a person 6 hours to fill 56 baskets. How many baskets per hour did the person fill?

Lesson 75

Part 1

- You've worked problems by using the equation:

    # x value = amount

- You can figure out either the number of coins or the amount.
- You can make a table so that each row tells about a different coin.
- Here's a table that is completed:

	#	x value	= amount
quarters	15	.25	3.75
dimes	22	.10	2.20
pennies	80	.01	.80
total	117		6.75

- This table is different from a ratio table because you multiply by a different value in each row. That's why you have to show the values you multiply by.

Part 2 Copy and complete each table. Then answer the questions.

	#	x value	= amount
a. quarters	7		
dimes			5.10
nickels			1.45
total			

	#	x value	= amount
b. quarters			2.25
dimes	4		
nickels			1.10
total			

Questions for table b:

1. How many quarters are there?
2. What's the amount for dimes?
3. How many nickels are there?
4. What's the total number of coins?
5. What's the total amount?

Part 3 Find the volume of each figure.

a.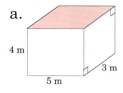
4 m, 5 m, 3 m

b.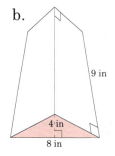
9 in, 4 in, 8 in

c.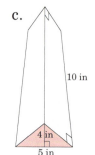
10 in, 4 in, 5 in

d.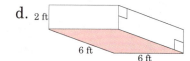
2 ft, 6 ft, 6 ft

Part 4 Make a complete table for the circle graph. Answer each question.

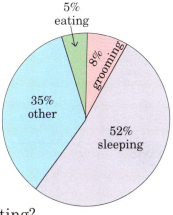

This graph shows the percent of each day that a cat spends in various activities.

a. How many hours does the cat spend eating?

b. How many hours does the cat spend sleeping?

c. How many hours does the cat spend doing things other than sleeping, eating and grooming?

Part 5 Write the complete equation for each item.

a. ■ = 6^3

b. ■ = 1^4

c. f x f x f = ■

d. 5 x 5 = ■

e. ■ = M^5

f. 9 x 9 x 9 = ■

Part 6 Figure out the missing numbers in each table.

a.

16	■
48	24
30	15
72	36
total ■	83

b.

36	27
28	21
■	15
16	12
total 100	■

Lesson 75

Part 7 Copy and work each problem. Check your answer.

a. $1.8 \overline{) 1.44}$ b. $.48 \overline{) 31.2}$ c. $.4 \overline{) 2.824}$ d. $.015 \overline{) .195}$

Independent Work

Part 8 Work each item.

a. Andy filled containers. Each container holds 5 pints, 3 ounces. How much do 7 containers hold?

b. In the morning, a farmer put in a section of fence that was 45 yards and 7 inches long. In the afternoon, the farmer put in a section of fence that was 27 yards and 19 inches long. How much longer was the morning section than the afternoon section? What was the total length of both sections?

c. Tom worked 7 hours and 18 minutes. He started at 10:30 a.m. At what time did he finish?

d. Rita worked 3 hours and 11 minutes longer than Ted. Rita worked for 6 hours and 5 minutes. How long did Ted work?

Part 9 For each item, write an equation to show the hundredths fraction and percent.

a. $\frac{5}{4} = \blacksquare = \blacksquare$

b. $\frac{3}{2} = \blacksquare = \blacksquare$

c. $\frac{4}{5} = \blacksquare = \blacksquare$

d. $\frac{11}{20} = \blacksquare = \blacksquare$

Part 10 Figure out the green part for each item. Answer the questions.

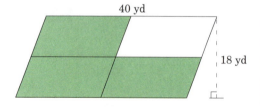

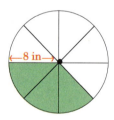

a. This is a diagram of a field. The farmer will plant the green part. The cost of planting this part is 16¢ for each square yard. What's the cost of planting the green section?

b. The green section shows the part of the pizza that was eaten. If each square inch has 20 calories, how many calories are in the part that has been eaten? How many calories are in the part that has not been eaten?

Part 11 Work each item.

a. $+12$ -15
b. -10 -8
c. $+50$ -36
d. -8 -14
e. -72 $+80$

Part 12 Answer the questions.

Jim has a $50 bill. He purchases shoes for $24.50. He purchases a pair of socks for $2.65. He purchases shorts for $8.89. The tax is 8%. How much is the total purchase price, including tax? How much change does Jim receive?

Lesson 76

Part 1 Copy and complete each table.

Steps for finding missing numbers in the first column:
✔ First figure out what to multiply by to go from the first column to the second column.
✔ Put that number in your calculator's memory.
✔ Work the undoing problems.

a.
red	■	42
blue	■	27
green	14	21
brown	■	15
total	■	105

red: [4][2] ÷ [RM] =

b.
40	■
■	56
■	40
20	■
5	8
total ■	200

c.
tan	■	51
blue	40	■
green	■	27
white	16	12
gold	■	9
total	172	■

Part 2 Find the volume of each figure.

a.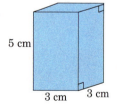

b.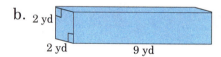

c.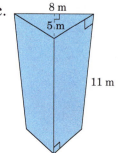

d.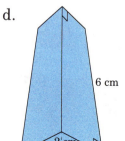

Part 3 Copy and complete each table. Then answer the questions.

a.

	#	x value	= amount
dimes	■	■	2.40
nickels	28	■	■
pennies	100	■	■
total	■		■

1. How many dimes are there?
2. What's the amount for nickels?
3. What the amount for pennies?
4. What's the total amount?
5. What's the total number of coins?

b.

	#	x value	= amount
quarters	■	■	■
dimes	12	■	■
nickels	■	■	1.25
total	48		■

1. How many quarters are there?
2. What's the amount for quarters?
3. What's the amount for dimes?
4. What's the total amount?

c.

	#	x value	= amount
quarters	14	■	3.50
dimes	■	■	1.40
nickels	■	■	■
total	■		6.15

1. How many nickels are there?
2. How many dimes are there?
3. How many total coins are there?

Lesson 76 311

Part 4 Copy and complete each equation.

a. $5 \times 5 \times 5 = \blacksquare$

b. $\blacksquare = 9^4$

c. $\blacksquare = 2^6$

d. $8 \times 8 \times 8 = \blacksquare$

Part 5 Copy and complete the table.

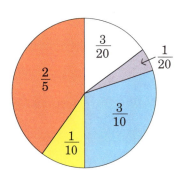

	fraction	degrees
red	■	■
blue	■	■
white	■	■
yellow	■	■
purple	■	■

Independent Work

Part 6 Answer the question.

This diagram shows a piece of land with a section marked out for a barn. The farmer wants to plant the green area with seed. It costs 11¢ per square meter to plant the seed. What is the cost of planting?

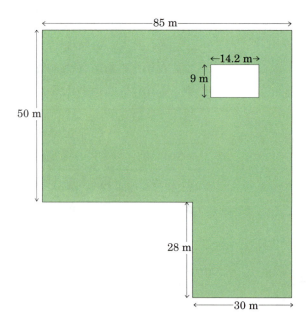

Part 7 Copy and work each problem.

a. + 8
    − 20

b. + 3
    + 14

c. − 25
    − 32

d. − 48
    + 7

Part 8 Change each mixed number into a fraction and multiply.

a. $3\frac{1}{2} \times 5\frac{1}{2}$ =

b. $1\frac{2}{3} \times 5\frac{1}{3}$ =

c. $12\frac{1}{3} \times 1\frac{2}{5}$ =

Part 9 Work each item.

a. Donna began working at 8:15 a.m. She quit at 4:48 p.m. How many hours did she work?

b. Fran worked for 3 hours and 50 minutes. She started work at 11:30 a.m. At what time did she finish?

c. How many hours are in $3\frac{1}{4}$ days?

d. How many hours are in a week?

e. How many hours are in 220 minutes?

f. Each job takes 2 hours and 25 minutes. How long does it take to do 7 jobs?

Part 10 Copy and complete the table.

/100   Decimal

Sample	$\frac{5}{4}$	$\frac{125}{100}$	1.25
a.	$\frac{7}{5}$		
b.	$\frac{9}{20}$		
c.	$\frac{3}{2}$		
d.	$\frac{1}{4}$		

Part 11 Write the missing value for each column.

a.
33	11
21	7
36	12
total 105	35

b.
8	12
	21
12	18
10	15
6	
total 50	75

Part 12 Work the decimal-division problem for each fraction.

a. $\frac{3}{4}$ b. $\frac{1}{5}$ c. $\frac{7}{5}$ d. $\frac{6}{8}$

Part J

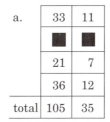

#	× value	= amount
quarters	14	.25	3.50
dimes	14	.10	1.40
nickels	25	.05	1.25
total	53		6.15

Lesson 77

Part 1 Figure out the area of each figure.

a.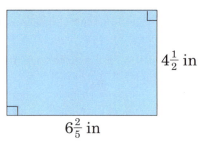

b.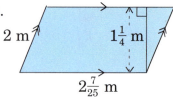

Part 2 Copy and complete each equation. Then use your calculator to figure out the value for each exponent.

a. $7^3 = \rule{2cm}{0.15mm} = \rule{1cm}{0.15mm}$

b. $2^4 = \rule{2cm}{0.15mm} = \rule{1cm}{0.15mm}$

c. $10^4 = \rule{2cm}{0.15mm} = \rule{1cm}{0.15mm}$

d. $8^3 = \rule{2cm}{0.15mm} = \rule{1cm}{0.15mm}$

e. $1^4 = \rule{2cm}{0.15mm} = \rule{1cm}{0.15mm}$

Part 3 For each item, make a complete table. Then answer the questions.

a. **Facts** Brenda has $10.50 in coins. She has 18 nickels. She has $7.50 in quarters. The rest of her money is in dimes.

Questions
1. What's the amount Brenda has in dimes?
2. How many dimes are there?
3. What's the total number of coins?

b. **Facts** Stephen has a total of 45 coins. 18 of those coins are quarters. 60¢ is in dimes. The rest are nickels.

Questions
1. What's the amount Stephen has in quarters?
2. How many nickels does he have?
3. What's the amount in nickels?
4. What's the total amount of money Stephen has?

Part 4
Write the complete equation for each item.

a. 4 lb 63 oz =

b. 2 lb 81 oz =

c. 5 wk 25 d =

d. 8 yr 52 mo =

e. 2 min 138 sec =

Part 5
Make a complete table for the circle. Show fractions in the first column and degrees in the second column.

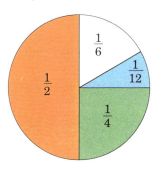

Part 6
For each problem, write the fraction that equals 1. Copy and work each problem.

Sample

.3 5 ⟌.2 4 5

$\frac{100}{100}$ .3 5. ⟌.2 4.5

a. .08 ⟌5.6

b. 1.5 ⟌1.05

c. .11 ⟌.121

d. .003 ⟌.612

e. 2.4 ⟌.048

Part 7
Copy and complete the table.

red		117
yellow		104
blue	32	
green	8	13
total		

Lesson 77

Independent Work

Remember to work the problems in part 6.

Part 8 Work each item.

a. Find the area of the figure.

b. Find the area. Find the perimeter. If the figure is made of copper and copper costs 12¢ a square inch, how much would the figure cost to make?

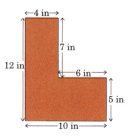

Part 9 Copy and work each item.

a. $\begin{array}{r} -15 \\ +18 \\ \hline \end{array}$
b. $\begin{array}{r} -36 \\ -4 \\ \hline \end{array}$
c. $\begin{array}{r} +84 \\ -85 \\ \hline \end{array}$
d. $\begin{array}{r} -11 \\ +25 \\ \hline \end{array}$
e. $\begin{array}{r} -16 \\ -16 \\ \hline \end{array}$

Part 10 Work each item. Answer the questions.

a. The lunch costs 120% as much as breakfast costs. Breakfast costs $10. How much does lunch cost? How much more does lunch cost than breakfast?

b. The snail moves 3 inches every 5 minutes. How far does the snail move in 13 minutes?

c. .4 of the mushrooms are poisonous mushrooms. There are 160 poisonous mushrooms. How many mushrooms are there in all? How many of the mushrooms are not poisonous?

Part 11 Change each mixed number into a fraction and multiply.

a. $4\frac{3}{5} \times 1\frac{2}{7} = $ ■

b. $2\frac{2}{9} \times 1\frac{4}{5} = $ ■

c. $20\frac{1}{2} \times 3\frac{2}{3} = $ ■

Part 12 Work each item.

a. Walter is $\frac{3}{5}$ as old as his brother. His brother is 15. How old is Walter?

b. What is $\frac{3}{7}$ of 96?

c. The cost of the coat was $\frac{8}{5}$ the cost of the suit. The coat cost $232. How much did the suit cost?

d. What is 35% of 200?

e. How many degrees are in $\frac{4}{9}$ of a circle?

Part J

#	x value	= amount
quarters	18	.25	4.50
dimes	9	.10	.90
nickels	21	.05	1.05
total	45		6.15

Part K

			total
red	72	117	
yellow	64	104	
blue	32	52	
green	8	13	
total	176	286	

Lesson 78

Part 1 For each item, make a complete table. Then answer the questions.

a. Roger has $7.30 in quarters, dimes and nickels. He has $2.60 in dimes. He has 19 nickels.

   1. How many dimes are there?
   2. How much is there in nickels?
   3. How much is there in quarters?
   4. How many coins are there in all?

b. Molly has 220 coins. She has $11.25 in quarters, $1.42 in pennies, and 28 nickels. The rest of her money is in dimes.

   1. What's the amount in nickels?
   2. How many quarters are there?
   3. What's the amount in dimes?
   4. What's the total amount?

Part 2 For each item, write the complete equation.

a. 3 d   75 hr =

b. 2 gal   40 pt =

c. 5 yr   19 seasons =

d. 1 lb   49 oz =

e. 10 yd   23 ft =

Part 3 **Work each item.**

> This graph shows the fraction of time a person spent doing different activities during 3 days.

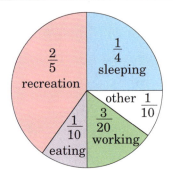

a. How many hours did the person spend sleeping?
b. How much more time did the person spend sleeping than eating?
c. What percent of the time was used for recreation?
d. What percent of the time did the person spend working?
e. How many more hours did the person spend sleeping than working?

Part 4

- To read a base number that has an exponent, you say the base number **to the power of** the exponent.

- For this value, the base is **4**. The exponent is **7**. 4^7
  You read the value as: **4 to the seventh power,** or, **4 to the seventh.**

- For this value, the base is **10** and the exponent is **4**. 10^4
  You read the value as: **10 to the fourth power,** or, **10 to the fourth.**

  - How do you read this value? 5^3

  - How do you read this value? 2^5

Part 5

For each item, show the complete equation. First show the multiplication.

a. 4^5 b. 16^3 c. 32^2 d. 2^6

Part 6

Copy and work each item.

a. 3 − 5 + 8
   　　x 9

b. 7 − 2 − 3
   　　x 5

c. 6 + 1 − 5
   　　x 2

Part 7

Copy and complete the table.

blue		12
red	36	9
brown	44	
green		100
total		

Independent Work

Part 8

Work the decimal-division problem for each fraction.

a. $\frac{10}{4}$ b. $\frac{3}{.5}$ c. $\frac{1}{4}$ d. $\frac{.2}{.8}$

Part 9

Find the volume for each figure.

a.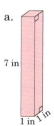

b.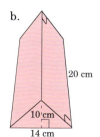

c.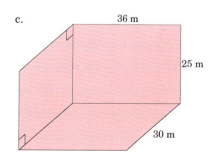

Lesson 78   319

Part 10 Copy and work each item.

a. -20 $+30$
b. -50 -11
c. -50 $+11$
d. $+10$ -70
e. $+60$ -80

Part 11 Work each item.

a. Richard finished work at 7:35 p.m. If he started work at 10:05 a.m., how long did he work?

b. The trip took 8 hours and 25 minutes. If the trip started at 9:13 a.m., at what time was the trip completed?

c. Copying each paper takes 2 minutes and 18 seconds. How long does it take to copy 4 papers?

d. It takes 224 days for Venus to circle Earth. How many weeks does it take for Venus to circle Earth?

e. Each board is 2 feet, 7 inches long. What's the total length of 9 boards?

f. A container holds 3 gallons and 3 pints of fluid. 1 gallon and 7 pints were removed from the container. How much fluid remained in the container?

g. How many inches are in 4 feet, 11 inches?

h. How many yards are in 400 inches?

Part 12 Work each item.

a. Find the length of the blue part.

b. Find the area of the blue part.

Part J

blue	48	12	
red	36	9	
brown	44	11	
green	400	100	
total	528	132	

Lesson 79

Part 1 Work each item.

a. − 20 + 12 − 10 − 8 + 9 = ■

b. + 28 − 10 − 8 + 9 − 42 = ■

c. $3 + 10 − 7 + 1$
    $\underline{\times 3}$

d. $-15 + 8 − 2 + 3$
    $\underline{\times 5}$

e. $5 − 2 − 11$
    $\underline{\times 2}$

f. $-3 − 5$
    $\underline{\times 4}$

Part 2 For each item, make a complete table. Answer each question.

a. Sally has quarters, nickels and pennies. She has $2.40 in nickels, $6.50 in quarters, and 201 pennies.
   1. How much money does Sally have in all?
   2. How many coins does she have in all?

b. Mike has 15 quarters and 24 dimes. He has $.16 in pennies and $.75 in nickels.
   1. How many coins does Mike have?
   2. What is the total amount he has in coins?

Part 3 Work each item.

a. Each block weighs 4 pounds, 8 ounces. How much do 20 blocks weigh?

b. Each shelf is 2 feet, 7 inches long. What's the total length of 15 shelves?

c. Each container holds 3 gallons and 5 pints. How much do 9 containers hold?

d. It takes 2 minutes and 15 seconds to make each invitation. How long does it take to make 11 invitations?

Part 4 Make a complete table for each circle.

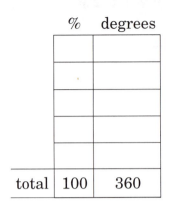

a.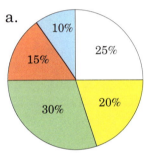

b.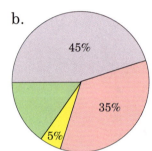

Part 5 Figure out the area of each figure.

a.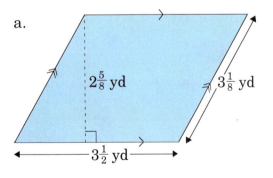

b.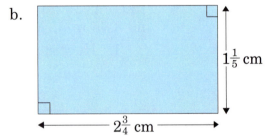

Part 6 Work each item.

This graph shows how a company spent its money. The company spent a total of $80,000.

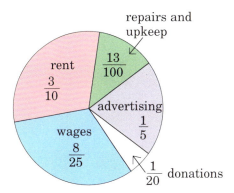

a. What percent of the company's money was spent on wages?
b. How much money was spent on wages?
c. How much more money did the company spend on wages than on donations?
d. What percent of the company's money was spent on rent?

Independent Work

Part 7 Copy and work each item.

a. $.005\overline{).38}$ b. $.2\overline{)2.774}$ c. $.23\overline{).161}$ d. $1.3\overline{)26}$

Part 8 Copy and complete each table.

a.
24	■
■	■
32	8
■	1
12	■
total 100	■

b.
5	18
■	■
10	■
■	90
total ■	360

Part 9 Copy and complete each equation. First show the multiplication. Then show the value it equals.

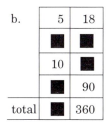

a. $5^4 =$ ■ $=$ ■
b. $10^2 =$ ■ $=$ ■
c. $2^{10} =$ ■ $=$ ■
d. $3^4 =$ ■ $=$ ■

Part 10 Find the volume of each figure.

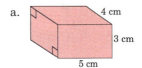
a.

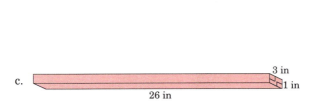
c.

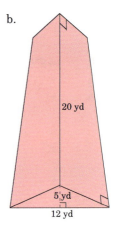
b.

Part 11 Work each item.

a. Mr. Jones will build a deck. The dimensions of the deck will be 36 feet wide and 12 feet long. The material for the deck will cost $2.30 per square foot. The tax on the material is 5%. How much will the material cost?

b. If you double Fran's age, then subtract 20, then multiply by 3, you end up with 12. How old is Fran?

Part 12 Work each item.

a. How many degrees are in $\frac{2}{9}$ of a circle?

b. How many degrees are in $\frac{9}{5}$ of a circle?

c. John had $\frac{8}{3}$ the amount of money Fran had. John had $400. How much did Fran have?

d. Andy had $\frac{4}{5}$ as much money as Donna had. Donna had $300. How much did Andy have?

e. What number is $\frac{8}{5}$ of 90?

f. What percent is $\frac{3}{5}$?

g. What percent is $\frac{8}{10}$?

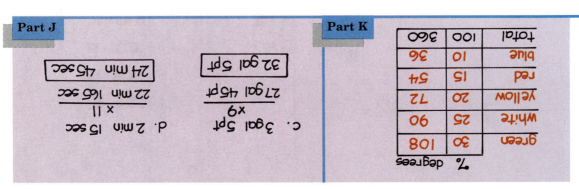

Lesson 80

Part 1

- For some mixed-number problems, you have to borrow.
  - Here's a problem: $5\frac{2}{3}$
    $-2\frac{8}{9}$

- You find the common denominator for the fractions:
  $5\frac{2}{3}\left(\frac{3}{3}\right) = \frac{}{9}$
  $-2\frac{8}{9} = -\frac{}{9}$

- Then you work the new fraction problem:
  $5\frac{2}{3}\left(\frac{3}{3}\right) = \frac{6}{9}$
  $-2\frac{8}{9} = -\frac{8}{9}$

- You can't subtract 8 from 6. So you borrow 1 whole from 5. You change the whole number to 4. The 1 you borrow is $\frac{9}{9}$. You add that to $\frac{6}{9}$. That gives you $\frac{15}{9}$.

  $5\frac{2}{3}\left(\frac{3}{3}\right) = \overset{4}{\cancel{5}}\overset{15}{\cancel{\frac{6}{9}}}$
  $-2\frac{8}{9} = -2\frac{8}{9}$

  $\frac{9}{9} + \frac{6}{9} = \frac{15}{9}$

  $2\frac{7}{9}$

- Now you subtract and end up with $\frac{7}{9}$. The whole answer is $2\frac{7}{9}$.

- Remember the steps you follow after you have a common denominator:

  > ✔ Borrow 1.
  > ✔ Show the new whole number.
  > ✔ Add the 1 you borrow to the top fraction and show the new top fraction.
  > ✔ Then subtract.

Part 2 Copy and work each item.

a. $8\frac{1}{6}$
   $-1\frac{3}{4}$

b. $7\frac{3}{5}$
   $-4\frac{7}{10}$

c. $4\frac{2}{7}$
   $-3\frac{4}{5}$

Part 3 Make a complete table for each circle graph. Answer the questions.

a.

The entire meal weighs 1,250 grams.

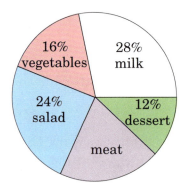

---

b.

	grams	%
milk	600	30
salad	440	■
meat	■	■
vegetables	360	■
dessert	■	10
total	■	■

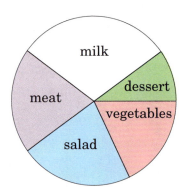

1. What part of the meal accounted for 18% of the weight?

2. What percentage of the meal's weight was accounted for by meat?

3. What percentage of the meal's weight was accounted for by salad?

4. What was the weight of the dessert?

Test 8

Part 1 Copy and work each item.

  a. − 5
      − 11

  b. − 19
      + 12

  c. + 21
      − 18

  d. + 13
      − 18

Part 2 Copy and work each item. Show a sign for each value.

  a. 12 + 5 − 9
      × 4
      ▬ = ▬

  b. − 2 − 9 + 1 − 5
      × 2
      ▬ = ▬

Part 3 Find the volume of each figure.

a.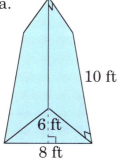

b.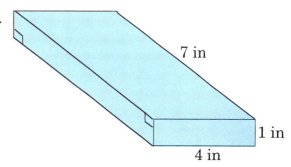

Part 4 Figure out the area of the figure.

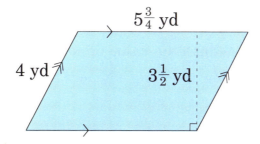

Part 5 Work each item.

a. Each carton weighs 3 pounds, 3 ounces. How much do 15 cartons weigh?

b. It takes 5 minutes and 15 seconds to fill each tank. How long does it take to fill 11 tanks?

Part 6 Answer each question.

a. What percentage of the circle is red?

b. What's the difference in percent between the red and the blue parts?

c. How many degrees are in the yellow slice?

d. What's the total number of degrees for the yellow part and the green part?

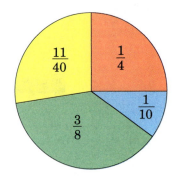

Part 7 Copy and work each item.

a. $.15\overline{).6}$

b. $.004\overline{).0128}$

Part 8 Make a complete table. Answer the questions.

Facts Frieda has $2.50 in quarters. She has 17 nickels. The rest of her money is in dimes. The total number of coins she has is 35.

Questions a. What's the total amount of money that she has?

b. How many dimes does she have?

c. What's the value of her dimes?

d. How much money does she have in nickels?

Part 9 Copy and complete the table.

red	65	5
yellow	13	■
blue	■	6
green	■	■
total	260	■

Part 10 Copy and complete each equation. Then use your calculator to figure out the value for each exponent.

a. $4^3 =$ ■ $=$ ■   b. $3^5 =$ ■ $=$ ■   c. $12^2 =$ ■ $=$ ■

Part J

	%	grams
milk	28	350
salad	24	300
meat	20	250
vegetables	16	200
dessert	12	150
total	100	1250

Test 8   329

Lesson 81

Part 1

- You know that dividing by 4 is the same as multiplying by $\frac{1}{4}$. Dividing by 5 is the same as multiplying by $\frac{1}{5}$.
- This is also true: Dividing by $\frac{3}{5}$ is the same as multiplying by the reciprocal of $\frac{3}{5}$.

$$\div \frac{3}{5}$$
$$\times \frac{5}{3}$$

- Here's the rule:

  Dividing by a value gives the same answer as multiplying by the reciprocal of that value.

  $4 \times 5 = 4 \div \frac{1}{5}$

  or

  $2 \times 4 = 2 \div \frac{1}{4}$

  Multiplying by a value gives the same answer as dividing by the reciprocal of that value.

  $8 \times \frac{3}{5} = 8 \div \frac{5}{3}$

Part 2 Rewrite each item with the opposite sign.

a. 3×4
b. $5 \times \frac{4}{5}$
c. $8 \div 2$
d. $5 \div \frac{1}{2}$
e. $3 \times \frac{5}{3}$
f. $6 \div \frac{2}{3}$

Part 3 Make the complete table and answer each question.

Fact: The angle for the white slice is 36°.

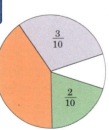

		degrees
red	■	■
purple	3	■
green	■	■
white	■	■
total	■	■

a. What's the fraction for the white part?
b. What's the fraction for the red part?
c. What are the degrees for the red part?

Part 4

- Some math problems involve probability. When you work the calculations, you find **expected numbers.** When you do the probability experiment, the outcomes are not the expected numbers. But the outcomes are close to these numbers.

- Here's a circle with a spinner:
- All the areas are the same size, so each part has the **same probability.**
- If we spin the spinner 4 times, we would expect it to land on each color 1 time. If we spin the spinner 12 times, we would expect it to land on each color 3 times.

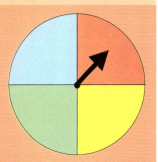

- Here's a different circle with a spinner:
- The probabilities for the different parts are not the same because the areas are not the same size.
- The percents for the parts of the circle show the probabilities. The blue is 45%. So we would **expect** 45% of all spins to land on blue. Yellow is only 10%. So we would expect only 10% of all spins to land on yellow.

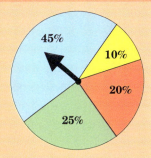

Part 5 Make a complete ratio table for the problem. Answer each question.

A person spins the arrow 50 times.

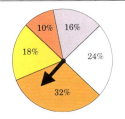

a. On how many trials would you expect the arrow to land on purple?
b. On how many trials would you expect the arrow to land on yellow?
c. On how many trials would you expect the arrow to land on orange?
d. On how many trials would you expect the arrow to land on white?
e. On how many trials would you expect the arrow to land on red?

Part 6 Copy and work each item. Show a sign for each part of the answer.

a. 10 − 4 + 6 − 7
                  x 3

b. − 4 + 6 + 1 − 5
                  x 2

c. 6 − 2 − 8 + 1
                x 4

Part 7

- Some problems ask about the average.

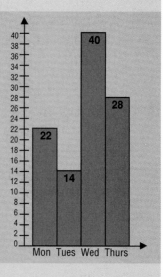

This graph shows the number of bluebirds observed on 4 different days.

- When you find the **average** number of birds, you find the number of birds you would observe on each day if you observed the same number on each day.

- To find the average, you **add** the numbers for the 4 days. Then you **divide** by 4.

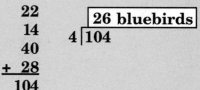

- This graph shows what the average would look like:
- The total red area is the same in both graphs.

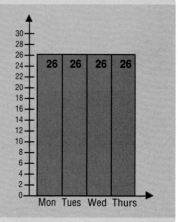

- Remember, to find the average, you find the **total,** then divide by the number of parts.

332   *Lesson 81*

Part 8 Answer each question.

a. What is the average number of cardinals seen each day?

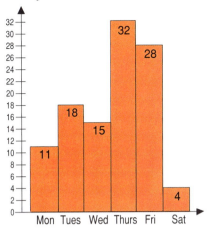

This graph shows the number of cardinals seen on 6 different days.

b. What's the average number of accidents per month?

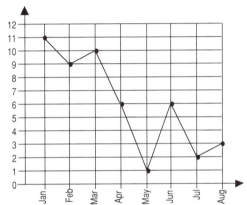

This graph shows the number of auto accidents in Brewtown over an 8-month period.

Part 9 Copy and work each item.

a. $5\frac{1}{3}$
    $-1\frac{5}{6}$

b. $8\frac{3}{4}$
    $-5\frac{2}{5}$

c. $7\frac{3}{8}$
    $-6\frac{1}{4}$

d. $4\frac{2}{7}$
    $-2\frac{4}{5}$

Independent Work

Part 10   Make a complete equation for each item. Box the answer to the question.

a. There were 72 buttons in 8 boxes. How many buttons per box were there?

b. The bus moved at a steady rate of 45 miles per hour. How many miles did the bus travel in 6 hours?

c. A train traveled at the steady rate of 62 miles per hour. How long did it take the train to travel 300 miles?

d. A car traveled at a steady rate. The car traveled 128 miles in 4 hours. How many miles per hour did the car travel?

Part 11   Find the volume of each figure.

a.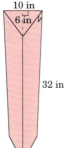

b.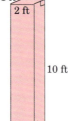

c.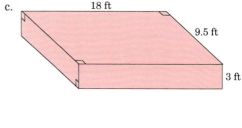

Part 12   Work each item.

a. The regular price of the chair is 145% of the discount price. The discount price is $222. What's the regular price? How much would a person save by purchasing the chair at the discount price?

b. The weight of the iceberg in the spring was 30% more than it was in the fall. If the difference in weight is 450 tons, what was the weight of the iceberg in the fall? What was the weight in the spring?

Part 13   For each item, write the base and the exponent.

a. 2 x 2 x 2 x 2

b. 27 x 27

c. .04 x .04 x .04

d. 10 x 10 x 10 x 10 x 10

Part 14   Work each item.

a. John started out with some money. He gave $2 to his brother. Then he received $11 for doing chores. Then he spent $6 on a book. He ended up with $20. How much did he start out with?

b. Start with Jane's age and triple it. Then subtract 10. Then divide by 2. You end up with 13. What's Jane's age?

Part 15   Copy and work each item.

a. -4
   $+17$

b. -12
   -6

c. -4
   $+9$

d. $+20$
   $+40$

e. -10
   -60

Lesson 82

Part 1
Work each item. First, figure out the top value.

a. $-3 + 8 + 12 - 21$
    $ \times 5$

b. $-19 - 15 + 41$
    $ \times 8$

c. $20 - 18 + 4 - 7$
    $ \times 10$

d. $-25 + 26 + 11$
    $ \times 3$

Part 2
Make a table for both problems. Answer the questions.

Fact The income from sources **other** than agriculture and manufacturing is $628 million.

a. Write the dollar amount for manufacturing.
b. Write the total income for Reed County.
c. Write the fraction for manufacturing.

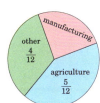

Reed County

Fact The total income is $4,400 million.

d. Write the dollar amount for agriculture.
e. Write the fraction for **other**.
f. Write the dollar amount for manufacturing.

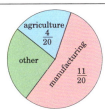

Nixon County

Part 3

- You've learned the rule that dividing by a value is the same as multiplying by the reciprocal of that value.

- You can use that rule to work division problems without using your calculator. You just rewrite division problems as multiplication problems and work them.

  - Here's a division problem: $\dfrac{3}{5} \div \dfrac{1}{10} = \blacksquare$

- You're dividing by $\dfrac{1}{10}$. That's the same as multiplying by the reciprocal of $\dfrac{1}{10}$.

  $\dfrac{3}{5} \times 10 = \dfrac{30}{5} = \boxed{6}$

  - Here's another division problem: $\dfrac{1}{5} \div \dfrac{3}{15} = \blacksquare$

    - You rewrite it as: $\dfrac{1}{5} \times \dfrac{15}{3} = \dfrac{15}{15} = \boxed{1}$

Part 4 Rewrite each problem and work it.

a. $4 \div \frac{2}{5} = \blacksquare$
b. $\frac{3}{2} \div \frac{4}{9} = \blacksquare$
c. $\frac{5}{3} \div \frac{1}{3} = \blacksquare$
d. $\frac{2}{3} \div 4 = \blacksquare$
e. $\frac{2}{9} \div \frac{6}{5} = \blacksquare$

Part 5 Answer each question.

This graph shows the number of times James got 100% on his math papers each month.

This table shows the number of girls in different families.

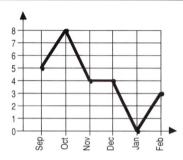

Jones	4
Brown	3
Roberts	0
Gilham	1
Murray	2
Davis	0
Wickman	3
Baker	5
Ryan	1
Cooper	4

a. What is the average number of perfect math papers James handed in each month?

b. What's the average number of girls per family?

Part 6 Make the complete table for each spinner. Answer the questions.

You take 80 trials at spinning the arrow.

You'd expect the spinner to land on red 75 times.

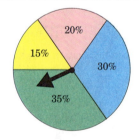

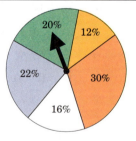

a. How many times would you expect the spinner to land on pink?

b. How many times would you expect the spinner to land on blue?

c. How many times would you expect the spinner to land on yellow?

d. How many times would you expect the spinner to land on green?

e. How many times would you expect the spinner to land on purple?

f. How many times would you expect the spinner to land on white?

g. How many times would you expect the spinner to land on orange?

h. How many times would you expect the spinner to land on green?

Independent Work

Part 7 Work each item.

a. $-10 \atop -3$

b. $+6 \atop -5$

c. $+6 \atop -15$

d. $+2-1-1-1 = \blacksquare$

e. $+2+6-10 = \blacksquare$

Part 8 Copy and complete the table. Figure out the number of degrees in each slice. Show the degrees as whole numbers or decimal values.

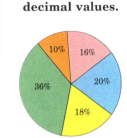
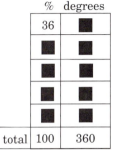

%	degrees
36	■
■	■
■	■
■	■
■	■
total 100	360

Part 9 Work each item.

a. There are 6 bottles in each carton. How many cartons hold 144 bottles?

b. There are 12 cans in each box. How many cans are needed to fill 9 boxes?

c. A runner moves at the rate of 15 feet per second. How long will it take the runner to go 200 feet?

d. There is 500 tons of sand. It is divided into 25 equal-sized piles. How many tons per pile are there?

e. A snail moved 15 centimeters in 40 seconds. How many centimeters per second did the snail move?

Part 10 Find the volume of each figure.

a.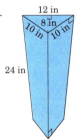

b.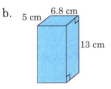

c.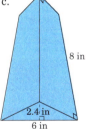

Part 11 Copy and work each item.

a. $7\frac{1}{2} - 3\frac{1}{2} = \blacksquare$

b. $12\frac{1}{8} - 1\frac{3}{8} = \blacksquare$

c. $6 - 2\frac{3}{20} = \blacksquare$

d. $15\frac{3}{8} - 2\frac{1}{2} = \blacksquare$

Part 12 For each item, write the base and exponent.

a. 5 x 5 x 5 x 5 x 5 x 5

b. 7 x 7 x 7

c. M x M x M x M

d. 10 x 10 x 10 x 10 x 10

e. 2 x 2

Lesson 82 **337**

Lesson 83

Part 1

- You've learned how to express repeated multiplication as a base and an exponent.
- Here's a set of tens:

$$10 \times 10 \times 10 \times 10 \times 10 \times 10 = 10^6$$

- Here's the same set of tens in two groups:

$$(10 \times 10 \times 10) \times (10 \times 10 \times 10) = 10^3 \times 10^3$$

- The groups are multiplied together. There are three in the first group and three in the second group. So 10 to the sixth equals 10 to the third times 10 to the third.

- Here's the same set of tens in different groups:

$$(10 \times 10) \times (10 \times 10 \times 10 \times 10) = 10^2 \times 10^4$$

- Remember, if the base number is shown 6 times, the exponents must add up to 6.

Part 2   Copy and complete each boxed equation.

a. $8 \times 8 \times 8 \times 8 \times 8 \times 8$
   $\boxed{8^6 = \blacksquare \times \blacksquare}$

b. $7 \times 7 \times 7 \times 7 \times 7$
   $\boxed{7^5 = \blacksquare \times \blacksquare}$

c. $9 \times 9 \times 9 \times 9 \times 9 \times 9 \times 9$
   $\boxed{9^7 = \blacksquare \times \blacksquare}$

d. $5 \times 5 \times 5 \times 5$
   $\boxed{5^4 = \blacksquare \times \blacksquare}$

e. $10 \times 10 \times 10 \times 10 \times 10 \times 10 \times 10 \times 10$
   $\boxed{10^8 = \blacksquare \times \blacksquare}$

Part 3   Copy and work each item.

a. $3\frac{5}{8} + 1\frac{2}{3}$

b. $4\frac{2}{9} - 2\frac{2}{3}$

c. $5\frac{3}{5} + 8\frac{1}{10}$

d. $7\frac{5}{6} - 6\frac{3}{4}$

e. $2\frac{7}{8} + 3\frac{1}{4}$

f. $5\frac{1}{2} - 4\frac{3}{5}$

Part 4

- When people do experiments with real spinners, the arrow doesn't often land on a color the **expected number** of times. But the number of times it lands on that color is usually closer to the expected number than it is to any of the other expected numbers.

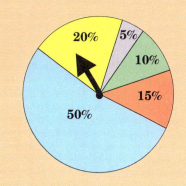

- If a problem shows the number of times the arrow landed on different colors, but doesn't tell which number goes with which color, you can figure out the colors by comparing the expected numbers with the actual numbers.

Total spins: 200
Actual numbers: 26, 50, 8, 92, 24

- Remember, figure out the expected numbers. Compare them to the actual numbers.

	%	expected	actual
blue	50	100	92
yellow	20	40	50
red	15	30	26
green	10	20	24
purple	5	10	8
total	100	200	200

Part 5 Copy and complete the table.

This experiment involves 60 trials.

Facts
1. The spinner landed on this color 14 times.
2. The spinner landed on this color 19 times.
3. The spinner landed on this color 23 times.
4. The spinner land on this color 4 times.

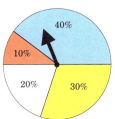

colors	%	expected	actual
■	■	■	■
■	■	■	■
■	■	■	■
■	■	■	■
total	■	60	60

Part 6 Work each item. First, figure out the top value.

a. $15 - 25 + 8 - 5 - 2$
$ \times 8$

b. $16 - 20 + 24$
$ \times 5$

c. $-13 + 2 + 8$
$ \times 3$

d. $+20 - 40 - 2 + 1$
$ \times 2$

Lesson 83   339

Part 7

- You've worked with boxes that have rectangular or triangular bases. You use the equation:

    Area of b x h = V

- You can use that same equation for finding the volume of cylinders.

- Cylinders have a base that is a circle. So you multiply π x r x r to find the area of the base. Then you multiply that value by the height.

    π x r x r = A

    3.14 x 7 x 7 = A

    $\boxed{A = 153.86 \text{ sq in}}$

    Area of b x h = V

    153.86 x 25 = V

    $\boxed{V = 3{,}846.5 \text{ cu in}}$

- Remember, the only difference between figuring out the volume of cylinders and boxes has to do with how you find the area of the base.

Part 8 Find the volume of each cylinder.

a.
    12 cm
    4 cm

b.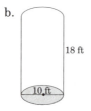
    18 ft
    10 ft

c.
    6 in
    40 in

340   Lesson 83

Part 9   Work each item.

a. $\dfrac{2}{3} \times \dfrac{5}{9} =$ ▮

b. $\dfrac{3}{8} \div 3 =$ ▮

c. $\dfrac{7}{9} \div \dfrac{9}{8} =$ ▮

d. $\dfrac{12}{5} \times 8 =$ ▮

e. $\dfrac{6}{11} \div \dfrac{1}{5} =$ ▮

f. $\dfrac{3}{7} \div \dfrac{11}{9} =$ ▮

Independent Work

Part 10   Work each item. Write answers as mixed numbers.

a. The graph shows the number of cars that were painted at Joe's Paint Shop on 6 days. Find the average number of cars painted per day.

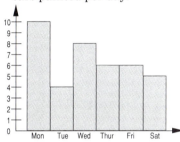

b. The graph shows the number of parked cars on different streets during lunch hour. Figure out the average number of cars per street.

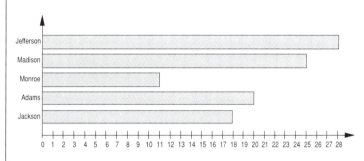

Part 11   Answer each question.

This diagram shows a sidewalk around a circular garden.

a. What is the area of the sidewalk?

b. What's the area of the garden?

c. If it costs 50¢ per square foot to put in the sidewalk, how much does the sidewalk cost?

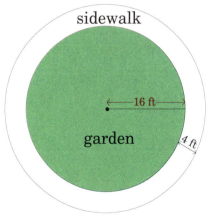

Lesson 83   341

Part 12 Work each item.

a. Jim purchased 3 caps, 4 baseballs and 10 cards. The tax on the sale is 8%. How much did Jim pay?

b. Donna purchased 4 bats and 3 baseballs. How much did she pay, including the 8% sales tax?

Part 13 Work each item.

a. -27
   $+10$

b. $-68 + 90 =$ ■

c. -15
   -28

d. $+8 + 11 =$ ■

e. $+150 + 89 =$ ■

Part 14 Work each item.

a. There were 4 potatoes for every 8 onions. If there were 21 onions, how many potatoes were there?

b. If it costs $4 to make 3 covers, how much does it cost to make 42 covers?

c. 6 pounds of tomatoes cost $5. How many pounds can you buy for $2.75?

Part J

a. $3\frac{5}{8}\left(\frac{3}{3}\right) = 3\frac{15}{24}$
   $+1\frac{2}{3}\left(\frac{8}{8}\right) = +1\frac{16}{24}$
   $4\frac{31}{24} = 5\frac{7}{24}$

b. $4\frac{6}{9}$
   $-2\frac{2}{3}\left(\frac{3}{3}\right) = -2\frac{6}{9}$
   $\overline{} = \frac{1}{5}$
   $3\frac{}{} = \frac{}{}$

c. $5\frac{5}{6}\left(\frac{2}{2}\right) = 5\frac{10}{6}$
   $+8\frac{1}{10} = +8\frac{1}{10}$
   $13\frac{7}{10}$

d. $7\frac{5}{6}\left(\frac{2}{2}\right) = 7\frac{10}{12}$
   $-6\frac{9}{4}\left(\frac{3}{3}\right) = -6\frac{12}{12}$
   $1\frac{1}{12}$

e. $2\frac{7}{8}$
   $+3\frac{1}{4}\left(\frac{2}{2}\right) = +3\frac{2}{8}$
   $5\frac{9}{8} = 6\frac{1}{8}$

f. $5\frac{1}{2}\left(\frac{5}{5}\right) = 5\frac{5}{10}$
   $-4\frac{3}{5}\left(\frac{2}{2}\right) = -4\frac{4}{10}$
   $1\frac{9}{10}$

Part K

a. $\frac{2}{3} \times \frac{5}{9} = \frac{10}{27}$

b. $\frac{1}{8} \times \frac{3}{3} = \frac{3}{24}$

c. $\frac{7}{9} \times \frac{8}{9} = \frac{56}{81}$

d. $\frac{12}{5} \times 8 = \frac{96}{5} = 19\frac{1}{5}$

e. $\frac{11}{6} \times 5 = \frac{30}{11} = 2\frac{8}{11}$

f. $\frac{7}{3} \times \frac{9}{11} = \frac{27}{11}$

342 Lesson 83

Lesson 84

Part 1 Work each item.

a. $\frac{4}{5} \div \frac{1}{10} = \blacksquare$
b. $\frac{1}{2} \times \frac{5}{8} = \blacksquare$
c. $12 \div \frac{3}{9} = \blacksquare$
d. $\frac{3}{5} \times \frac{1}{2} = \blacksquare$

Part 2 Copy and complete each boxed equation.

a. $\underline{4 \times 4 \times 4} \times 4 \times 4 \times 4 \times 4$
$\boxed{4^7 = \blacksquare \times \blacksquare}$

b. $\underline{4 \times 4} \times 4 \times 4 \times 4 \times 4 \times 4$
$\boxed{4^7 = \blacksquare \times \blacksquare}$

c. $\underline{4 \times 4 \times 4 \times 4} \times 4 \times 4 \times 4$
$\boxed{4^7 = \blacksquare \times \blacksquare}$

d. $\underline{8 \times 8 \times 8 \times 8 \times 8} \times 8 \times 8 \times 8$
$\boxed{8^\blacksquare = \blacksquare \times \blacksquare}$

e. $\underline{12 \times 12 \times 12} \times 12$
$\boxed{12^\blacksquare = \blacksquare \times \blacksquare}$

f. $\underline{5 \times 5 \times 5} \times 5 \times 5 \times 5$
$\boxed{5^\blacksquare = \blacksquare \times \blacksquare}$

g. $\underline{7 \times 7} \times 7 \times 7 \times 7 \times 7 \times 7$
$\boxed{7^\blacksquare = \blacksquare \times \blacksquare}$

Part 3 Find the volume of each figure.

a.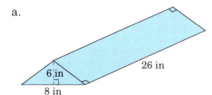

b.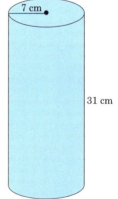

c.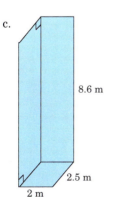

d.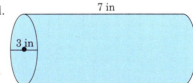

Part 4 Write each item as a division problem. Below, write the corresponding multiplication problem and work it.

a. $\dfrac{\frac{4}{5}}{\frac{3}{8}}$ b. $\dfrac{\frac{9}{5}}{\frac{3}{2}}$ c. $\dfrac{\frac{5}{8}}{\frac{2}{3}}$ d. $\dfrac{\frac{1}{2}}{\frac{9}{8}}$ e. $\dfrac{\frac{6}{7}}{\frac{2}{7}}$

Part 5

- You've worked problems that multiply by a positive value. That's a **+** value. When you work those problems, you just copy the signs in the answer. Then you do the multiplication.

- Some problems multiply by a **−** value, not a **+** value.

- Here are the rules for multiplying by a **−** value:
    ✔ You don't copy the signs for the top numbers.
    ✔ You write the **opposite** sign for each number.
    ✔ If the sign on top is **+**, you write **−** in the answer.
    ✔ If the sign on top is **−**, you write **+** in the answer.

- Here are the same top values multiplied by + 2 and by − 2:

    $$\begin{array}{r} +2 -4 -1 \\ \times\ +2 \\ \hline \end{array} \qquad \begin{array}{r} +2 -4 -1 \\ \times\ -2 \\ \hline \end{array}$$

- When you multiply by + 2, the signs in the answer are the same as the signs above. The first is a +, the rest are − signs.

    $$\begin{array}{r} +2 -4 -1 \\ \times\ +2 \\ \hline +\ \ -\ \ - \end{array}$$

- When you multiply by − 2, the signs are reversed. The first is −. The rest of them are + signs.

    $$\begin{array}{r} +2 -4 -1 \\ \times\ -2 \\ \hline -\ \ +\ \ + \end{array}$$

- Remember, if you multiply by a minus value, you don't copy signs; you write the opposite of each sign.

Part 6
Copy and work each item.

a. $-6 - 5 + 2$ $-6 - 5 + 2$
      $x + 3$ $x - 3$
    ─────────   ─────────
     = ■   = ■

b. $+8 - 5 + 7$ $+8 - 5 + 7$
      $x - 4$ $x + 4$
    ─────────   ─────────
     = ■   = ■

c. $-10 + 2 + 7 - 3$ $-10 + 2 + 7 - 3$
         $x - 6$ $x + 6$
    ──────────────   ──────────────
       = ■   = ■

Part 7
Make a table showing the percents, expected numbers and the actual numbers.

The experiment involves 120 trials. Here are the number of times the spinner landed on different colors: 26, 21, 3, 13, 57.

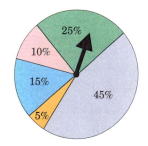

Part 8
For each item, find the average.

a. This graph shows the number of days it rained during each month of the year. What is the average number of days per month that it rained?

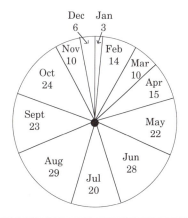

b. This table shows the number of glasses of water Ted drank on different days. On the average, how many glasses per day did he drink?

	glasses
Mon	4
Tue	2
Wed	5
Thur	0
Fri	3
Sat	2
Sun	2

Lesson 84   345

Independent Work

Part 9 For each item, make a complete equation. Box the answer to the question.

a. A plane travels at the rate of 600 yards per second. How many seconds will it take for the plane to travel 45,000 yards?

b. A boat goes 88 miles in 16 hours. How many miles per hour does the boat travel?

c. 51 pounds of gold is divided into piles. If there are 3 pounds per pile, how many piles are there?

d. There are 2.4 ounces of silver per coin. A stack of coins weighs 96 ounces. How many coins are in the stack?

e. Another stack of coins has 120 coins in it. The coins are the same. That pile weighs 40 ounces. How many ounces per coin are there?

Part 10 For each item, write a simple problem and work it.

a. $-3 + 9 + 22 - 17 - 1$

b. $25 + 52 - 16 - 18 - 20$

c. $-50 - 28 + 56 + 11 - 42$

Part 11 Work each item.

a. Bill started walking at 6:40 a.m. He walked 55 minutes. When did he finish walking?

b. Mary started working at 10:30 a.m. She finished work at 3:10 p.m. How long did she work?

Part 12 Copy and work each item.

a. $3\frac{1}{5} + 2\frac{7}{8}$

b. $14\frac{1}{3} - 6\frac{5}{6}$

c. $2\frac{3}{8} - 1$

d. $20 - 9\frac{3}{7}$

Part 13 For each item, write a simple problem and work it.

a. How many feet are in 120 inches?

b. How many inches are in 120 feet?

c. How many inches are in $2\frac{3}{36}$ yards?

d. How many yards are in 200 inches?

e. Write 56 inches as feet and inches.

f. Write 2,330 feet as yards and feet.

Part 14 Copy and complete the table.

	Fraction	Decimal	Percent
a.			620%
b.		.07	
c.	$\frac{120}{100}$		
d.	$\frac{3}{100}$		

Part J

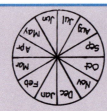

Lesson 85

Part 1

- Some figures come to a point.

- Here's a cone:
  It has a circular base. It comes to a point.

- Here's a pyramid shape with a triangular base:

- Here's a pyramid shape with a rectangular base:

- Here's the rule about the volume of any figure that comes to a point:

  The volume is $\frac{1}{3}$ of the volume that figure would have if its sides were vertical.

- Here are two figures with the same base and height:

  This figure 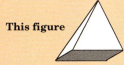 **has $\frac{1}{3}$ the volume of this figure**

- Here's the equation you use to find the volume of figures that come to a point: $\dfrac{\text{Area of b} \times \text{h}}{3} = V$

Part 2   Find the volume for each figure.

a.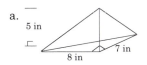
5 in, 8 in, 7 in

b.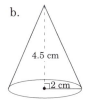
4.5 cm, 2 cm

c.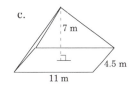
7 m, 4.5 m, 11 m

d.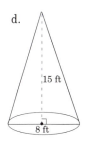
15 ft, 8 ft

Part 3 Copy and complete each boxed equation.

a. (2 x 2 x 2 x 2) x (2 x 2)

   $2^\blacksquare = \blacksquare \times \blacksquare$

b. (10) x (10 x 10 x 10 x 10)

   $10^\blacksquare = \blacksquare \times \blacksquare$

c. (8 x 8 x 8 x 8 x 8) x (8)

   $8^\blacksquare = \blacksquare \times \blacksquare$

d. (7 x 7 x 7) x (7 x 7 x 7 x 7 x 7)

   $7^\blacksquare = \blacksquare \times \blacksquare$

e. (1 x 1) x (1 x 1)

   $1^\blacksquare = \blacksquare \times \blacksquare$

Part 4 Copy and work each item.

a. + 4 + 10 − 6 − 9
    x − 2
    = ■

b. − 8 − 5 + 10
    x + 4
    = ■

c. − 7 − 6 + 20
    x + 3
    = ■

d. − 5 + 9 − 4 − 6
    x − 7
    = ■

Part 5 Work each item.

a. A box contained sand that weighed 64 pounds. The sand was divided into parts that each weighed $\frac{1}{2}$ pound. How many parts were there?

b. Irma has 7 pounds of mercury. She will divide her mercury into parts that each weigh $\frac{7}{20}$ of a pound. How many parts will she have?

c. A piece of silver ribbon was $\frac{16}{5}$ inches long. The ribbon was cut into pieces that were each $\frac{4}{10}$ inch long. How many pieces were there?

d. Fran had 2 pounds of butter. She divided the butter into cubes that were the same weight. Each cube weighed $\frac{1}{4}$ pound. How many cubes did she have?

Part 6 Make a table. Show each percent, expected value, and the corresponding actual value.

Facts about people who work in River City:

- 40% ride in cars to work
- 28% take a bus to work
- 18% take a train to work
- 10% ride bikes to work
- 4% walk to work

You do an experiment. You have information about every worker in the city. Information for each worker is on a small strip of paper. It tells how that worker goes to work.

All the strips are in a large container. You blindfold yourself, reach into the jar and pull out 250 names.

Here are the numbers for the five different ways workers get to work: 14, 88, 32, 38 and 78. The total is 250.

348 *Lesson 85*

Independent Work

Part 7

Work each item.

a. $\frac{4}{5}$ of the children wore white socks. There were 300 children. How many wore white socks?

b. $\frac{3}{8}$ of the animals in the park were squirrels. There were 48 squirrels. How many animals were not squirrels? How many animals were in the park?

c. The tower was 185% the height of the building. The tower was 660 feet tall. How much taller was the tower than the building?

Part 8

Work each item.

a. The graph shows the amount of money Al spent on different days of a week. Figure out the average amount per day that Al spent.

b. The table shows the number of penguins observed on 5 different occasions. Figure out the average number of penguins observed per occasion.

	Penguins
April 5	62
April 30	58
May 8	75
June 15	67
June 30	63

Part 9
Work the problem. Answer each question.

Here's a diagram of a kitchen counter with an area cut out for the sink. Putting tiles on the counters costs $4.20 per square foot. The sales tax on purchases is 5%.

a. How many square feet need tiles?
b. What's the cost of the tiles before tax?
c. What's the total cost including tax?

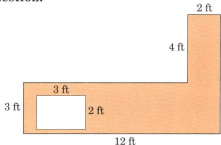

Part 10
Copy and work each item.

a. -20
   $+12$

b. $-6-5+9$

c. $+2-10-4$

d. $+50$
   -45

e. $-26-4$

Lesson 85   349

Part 11 Work each item. Show each answer as a whole number or a proper mixed number with a unit name.

a. Each piece of rope is 3 feet, 4 inches long. How much rope is needed for 27 pieces?

b. A tank had 12 gallons and 2 quarts of gas in it. 3 gallons and 3 quarts were removed from the tank. How much gas remained in the tank?

c. It takes 3 minutes and 13 seconds to print each magazine. How long does it take to print 11 magazines?

Part 12 Copy and work each problem.

a. 2,315 − R = 1,692

   R = ■

b. M + 182 = 560

   M = ■

c. 15 × B = 4

   B = ■

d. 510 ÷ 17 = D

   D = ■

Part J

b. $10^5 = 10^1 \times 10^4$

d. $7^8 = 7^3 \times 7^5$

c. $8^6 = 8^5 \times 8^1$

e. $1^4 = 1^2 \times 1^2$

Lesson 86

Part 1

- Some problems give information about **more than one unit**.
- Here's a problem:

  Find the volume of a sandbox. The sandbox is 12 feet wide, 6 feet long and 8 inches deep.

  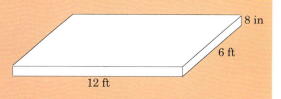

- The problem tells about **feet** and about **inches**.
- Before you work the problem, you must make all the units the same. You'll do that by changing the smaller unit into a fraction.
- The **smaller unit** is **inches**.
- You change inches into a fraction of a foot by dividing by the number of inches in a foot:

  $8 \text{ in} = \frac{8}{12} \text{ ft}$

- Now you can work the problem:

  Area of b x h = V

  $12 \times 6 \times \frac{8}{12} = V$

  $\frac{576}{12} = V$

  $\boxed{V = 48 \text{ cu ft}}$

- Remember, change the smaller unit into a fraction.

Part 2 Figure out the area of each rectangle.

a. 4 yd × 7 ft

b. 5 in × 2 ft

c. 1 m × 48 cm

d. 2 yd × 40 in

Part 3 Work each item.

a. A plot of land is $\frac{8}{5}$ acres. It will be divided into parcels that are each $\frac{2}{5}$ of an acre. How many parcels will there be?

b. A lot is $\frac{3}{4}$ of an acre. It will be divided into parcels that are each $\frac{1}{8}$ of an acre. How many parcels will there be?

c. A piece of gold weighed $\frac{2}{5}$ of a pound. It was divided into piles that each weighed $\frac{2}{15}$ of a pound. How many piles were there?

d. A board was $\frac{3}{2}$ yards long. It was divided into pieces that were each $\frac{1}{18}$ of a yard long. How many pieces were there?

Part 4

- You can write fractions that tell about the probability of something happening.

- Here's a problem:

  > 3 out of every 4 blocks are red. What's the probability of a blindfolded person picking up a red block?

- The answer is $\frac{3}{4}$.
  That means $\frac{3}{4}$ of the blocks are red. So we expect the person to pick up a red block on $\frac{3}{4}$ of the trials.

- New problem:

  > $\frac{2}{5}$ of the people who work in the office wear contact lenses. What's the probability that the first person you meet will be wearing contact lenses?

- The answer is $\frac{2}{5}$.
  If $\frac{2}{5}$ of the people wear contact lenses, $\frac{2}{5}$ of the time the first person you'd meet would be wearing contact lenses.

- Here's how you make the fraction that shows probability:

  The **total number** of possibilities is the **denominator**.
  The possibilities for the **part you're interested in** is the **numerator**.

  $$\frac{\text{part you're interested in}}{\text{total number}}$$

- Remember, the total number is the denominator; the number for the part you're interested in is the numerator.

- You can make fractions from percents or numbers.

Part 5 Write a fraction for each item.

a. In March, the wind blows from the north on 3 out of every 10 days. What's the probability that the wind will blow from the north on any day in March?

b. If you take 15 trials with a spinner, you'd expect it to land on black 4 times. What's the probability of the spinner landing on black?

c. 15% of the circle is blue. One raindrop lands on the circle. What's the probability of the drop landing on a part that is blue?

d. The ratio of girls to all the children is 5 to 9. What's the probability that the first child you'd meet would be a girl?

e. Tim daydreams 1 minute out of every 47 minutes. What's the probability that he is daydreaming right now?

Part 6 Copy and work each item.

a. $-1+12+2-10$
   $\underline{x+2}$

b. $-3+6-10$
   $\underline{x-3}$

c. $+9-2-6-1$
   $\underline{x-6}$

d. $+8-4+10$
   $\underline{x-2}$

Lesson 86 353

Part 7

- You can write the base and exponent for fractions that show repeated multiplication in fractions. You ask yourself two questions:

  ✔ First question: **Is the base shown more times in the numerator or in the denominator?**

  ✔ Second question: **How many more times is the base shown?**

- Here's a fraction with a base of 10: $\dfrac{10 \times 10}{10 \times 10 \times 10 \times 10 \times 10}$

- The base is shown more times in the denominator. So you write the base in the denominator. $\dfrac{10 \times 10}{10 \times 10 \times 10 \times 10 \times 10} = \dfrac{1}{10^{\blacksquare}}$

- Next you ask: How many **more times** does the base appear in the denominator?

- There are 3 more 10s in the denominator than in the numerator. So the exponent is 3. $\dfrac{10 \times 10}{10 \times 10 \times 10 \times 10 \times 10} = \dfrac{1}{10^3}$

- Here's another fraction: $\dfrac{2 \times 2 \times 2 \times 2 \times 2 \times 2 \times 2}{2 \times 2 \times 2}$

- There are more 2s in the numerator than the denominator. So you write the base 2 in the numerator. $\dfrac{2 \times 2 \times 2 \times 2 \times 2 \times 2 \times 2}{2 \times 2 \times 2} = 2^{\blacksquare}$

- The next question is: How many more 2s are in the numerator than the denominator?

- There are 4 more 2s in the numerator. So the exponent is 4. $\dfrac{2 \times 2 \times 2 \times 2 \times 2 \times 2 \times 2}{2 \times 2 \times 2} = 2^4$

- Here's proof that the above equation equals 2 to the fourth power: $\dfrac{\cancel{2} \times \cancel{2} \times \cancel{2} \times 2 \times 2 \times 2 \times 2}{\cancel{2} \times \cancel{2} \times \cancel{2}} = 2^4$

- Remember, if the base is shown more times in the numerator than in the denominator, that's where you write the base and the exponent.

Part 8   Rewrite each fraction with a base and exponent.

a. $\dfrac{5}{5 \times 5 \times 5 \times 5}$ b. $\dfrac{6 \times 6 \times 6}{6 \times 6 \times 6 \times 6 \times 6}$ c. $\dfrac{3 \times 3 \times 3 \times 3 \times 3 \times 3}{3 \times 3}$

d. $\dfrac{2 \times 2 \times 2 \times 2 \times 2 \times 2}{2 \times 2 \times 2 \times 2}$ e. $\dfrac{9 \times 9}{9 \times 9 \times 9 \times 9 \times 9 \times 9 \times 9}$ f. $\dfrac{7 \times 7 \times 7 \times 7 \times 7 \times 7 \times 7 \times 7}{7 \times 7 \times 7 \times 7}$

Part 9   Find the volume of each figure.

a. 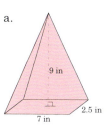   b. 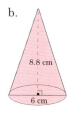   c. 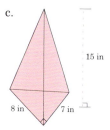   d.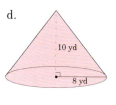

Independent Work

Part 10   Copy and work each item.

a. $-19 \\ +14$ b. $+6 \\ -12$

c. $-4 \\ -11$ d. $-14 \\ +22$

Part 11   Make a table to show the number of times you'd expect the spinner to land on each color.

You spin the spinner a total of 80 times.

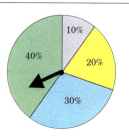

Part 12   Write the complete boxed equation for each item.

a. $(3 \times 3 \times 3 \times 3) \times (3 \times 3)$

    $3^\blacksquare = \blacksquare^\blacksquare \times \blacksquare^\blacksquare$

b. $(12 \times 12) \times (12)$

    $12^\blacksquare = \blacksquare^\blacksquare \times \blacksquare^\blacksquare$

c. $(a \times a) \times (a \times a) \times (a)$

    $a^\blacksquare = \blacksquare^\blacksquare \times \blacksquare^\blacksquare \times \blacksquare^\blacksquare$

Part 13   Work each item.

a. $\dfrac{\frac{3}{8}}{\frac{1}{2}}$ b. $\dfrac{2}{3} \div 5$ c. $\dfrac{3}{5} \div \dfrac{4}{5}$ d. $\dfrac{\frac{2}{7}}{\frac{1}{4}}$

Part 14 Find the volume of each figure.

a.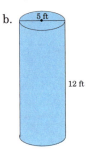

b.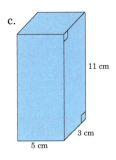

c. (rectangular prism: 11 cm, 5 cm, 3 cm)

Part 15 Copy and work each item.

a. $\begin{array}{r} 5 \\ -\,2\frac{2}{3} \\ \hline \end{array}$

b. $\begin{array}{r} 3\frac{5}{8} \\ +\,1\frac{3}{4} \\ \hline \end{array}$

c. $\begin{array}{r} \frac{7}{5} \\ -\,\frac{9}{7} \\ \hline \end{array}$

d. $\begin{array}{r} 4\frac{1}{3} \\ +\,7\frac{5}{8} \\ \hline \end{array}$

Lesson 87

Part 1 Work each item.

a. $\frac{3}{8}$ of a circle is green. What's the probability of a raindrop landing on the part of the circle that is **not** green?

b. There are 25 children at the picnic. 17 of them are girls. What's the probability that the first child you meet will be a girl? What's the probability that the first child you meet will be a boy?

c. It rains on 2 out of every 7 days at Bakersville. What is the probability of rain on any given day? What's the probability that it will not rain on a given day?

d. A circle is divided into 7 equal-sized parts. One of the parts is green. What's the probability of a blindfolded person touching the green part on the first trial? Three of the parts are blue. What's the probability of the blindfolded person touching a part of the circle that is blue?

Part 2 Copy and work each item.

a. -3
   $\underline{x - 5}$

b. $+4 \text{ x } -8 =$

c. $-6 \,(+2) =$

d. $+8$
   $\underline{x + 7}$

e. $-1 \text{ x } -10 =$

Part 3

- You've worked with the coordinate system.
- Any point on a coordinate system can be described by giving the x value and the y value.

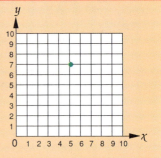

- The x value is the distance from zero this way: ⟶
- Here the x value is 5.

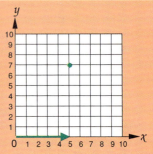

- The y value is the distance from zero this way: ↑
- Here the y value is 7:

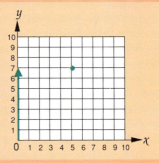

- Here are the coordinates for a point:

  $x = 4, y = 3$

- The point is 4 places in the x direction: ⟶

  and 3 places in the y direction: ↑

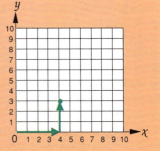

- Here are the x and y values for the point at A: $x = 7, y = 4$.
- To get to point A, you go 7 places in the x direction and then 4 places up for y.

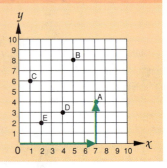

Part 4

Write the base and exponent for each fraction.

a. $\dfrac{9 \times 9 \times 9 \times 9}{9 \times 9 \times 9}$

b. $\dfrac{5 \times 5 \times 5 \times 5 \times 5}{5 \times 5 \times 5 \times 5 \times 5 \times 5}$

c. $\dfrac{7 \times 7 \times 7 \times 7}{7 \times 7 \times 7 \times 7}$

d. $\dfrac{12 \times 12}{12 \times 12}$

e. $\dfrac{6 \times 6 \times 6 \times 6 \times 6 \times 6 \times 6}{6 \times 6}$

f. $\dfrac{3}{3 \times 3 \times 3 \times 3 \times 3}$

g. $\dfrac{10 \times 10 \times 10}{10 \times 10 \times 10 \times 10}$

h. $\dfrac{8}{8}$

Part 5

Find the volume of each figure.

a.
b.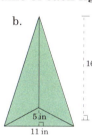
c.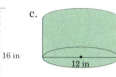
d.
e.

Part 6

Work each item.

a. Tim went on a trip for 3 weeks. Later, he went on a trip for 17 days. How many weeks was he gone in all?

b. A board is 7 feet long. A piece that is 34 inches is cut off. How much of the board remains?

c. Paint costs $10 a gallon. How much would 15 quarts cost?

d. Fred has 3 gallons of water. Milton has 22 pints of water. How much more water does Fred have?

Part 7

Copy and complete the table. Then answer each question.

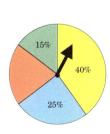

	%	degrees
yellow		
blue		
red		72
green		
total		

a. What's the probability of the spinner landing on green?

b. What's the probability of the spinner landing on yellow?

c. What's the probability of the spinner landing on blue?

d. What's the probability of the spinner landing on red?

Lesson 87

Independent Work

Part 8
Work each item.

a. Jim wants to enlarge a photo. The original has a length of 4 inches and a height of 3 inches. The enlarged photo will have a length of 16 inches. What will the height of that photo be? What will the area of the enlarged photo be?

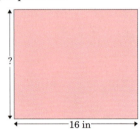

b. Jim wants to make a drawing of a triangle. His drawing will be larger than the original triangle. How long will the horizontal side of Jim's triangle be? How long will the slanted side of Jim's triangle be?

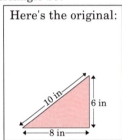
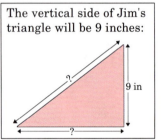

Part 9
Work each item.

a. $3\frac{1}{2} \times 2\frac{1}{3}$

b. $4\frac{1}{2} - \frac{3}{4}$

c. $12\frac{1}{2} + 2\frac{5}{7}$

d. $\frac{3}{8} \times \frac{1}{2}$

Part 10
Write a complete equation for each item. Show the base number and exponent.

a. $12 \times 12 \times 12 = \blacksquare^{\blacksquare}$

b. $(2) \times (2 \times 2) \times (2 \times 2 \times 2)$

$2^{\blacksquare} = \blacksquare^{\blacksquare} \times \blacksquare^{\blacksquare} \times \blacksquare^{\blacksquare}$

c. $3 \times 3 = \blacksquare^{\blacksquare}$

d. $(3) \times (3 \times 3 \times 3)$

$3^{\blacksquare} = \blacksquare^{\blacksquare} \times \blacksquare^{\blacksquare}$

Part 11
Work the item.

The table shows the number of seagulls observed in 5 different places. Find the average number of seagulls per place.

	Seagulls
Place a	34
Place b	56
Place c	19
Place d	20
Place e	31

Part 12 Work each item.

a. $\dfrac{\frac{3}{8}}{\frac{1}{4}}$ b. $\dfrac{3}{5} \times \dfrac{1}{2}$ c. $\dfrac{3}{7} \times 4$ d. $\dfrac{3}{7} \div 4$ e. $\dfrac{1}{2} \div \dfrac{1}{5}$

Part 13 Copy and work each item.

a. $-4 + 7$ b. $-13 - 2$ c. $+4 - 10$ d. $\begin{array}{r}-26\\+14\end{array}$ e. $\begin{array}{r}-11\\+76\end{array}$

Part J

c. Area of b × h = V
$113.04 \times 6 = V$
$V = 678.24$ cu in

d. $V = \dfrac{\text{Area of b} \times h}{3}$
$V = \dfrac{9.45 \times 3.3}{3}$
$V = 10.40$ cu ft

e. $V = \dfrac{\text{Area of b} \times h}{3}$
$V = \dfrac{254.34 \times 28}{3}$
$V = 2373.84$ cu cm

Part K

	?	degrees
yellow	40	144
blue	25	90
red	20	72
green	15	54
total	100	360

Lesson 88

Part 1

- You're going to do work with simple machines. The equation you'll use gives an answer that is close to the answer you'd get in real-life situations, but in real life some of these problems are very, very complicated. You would need very complicated equations to figure out the exact answer.

- A simple machine permits you to use less force to do work.

- Here's a small boy holding the end of a teeter-totter:

- On the other side is a man who weighs 4 times as much as the boy.

- The teeter-totter is a simple machine. If the man is close to the center, the boy can lift the man easily.

- Here's the basic equation for all simple machines:

$$\overset{\text{in}}{\text{force x distance}} = \overset{\text{out}}{\text{force x distance}}$$

- The force **in** is the weight or the push that is put into the machine.

- The force **out** is the weight that the machine moves.

- The equation shows that you can balance a large weight with a very small force. To do that, you have to apply the small force farther from the center than the weight is.

Part 1 continued

- Here's a girl balancing a weight of 300 pounds. The weight is 1 foot from the center. The girl is applying the force 6 feet from the center. So the girl's force is much less than 300 pounds. It is only 50 pounds.

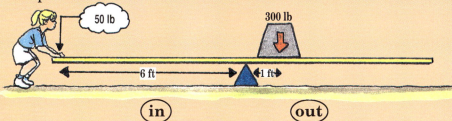

(in) (out)
force x distance = force x distance

50 x 6 = 300 x 1

300 = 300

Part 2 Figure out the missing value in each item.

(in) (out)
f x d = f x d

Part 3 Copy and work each item. First, circle the value you're multiplying by.

a. $^-3 \times ^+4 =$ b. $^+8 \, (^+9) =$ c. $\begin{array}{r} ^-10 \\ \underline{\times \; ^-2} \end{array}$ d. $\begin{array}{r} ^+4 \\ \underline{\times \; ^-6} \end{array}$ e. $^-5 \, (^-7) =$

Lesson 88   363

Part 4

- Any straight line that goes through zero on the coordinate system shows a set of equivalent fractions. So that line can be used to show ratio numbers.

- Here's a fact:

  The ratio of older dogs to puppies is 3 to 2.

  $$\frac{\text{older dogs}}{\text{puppies}} \quad \frac{3}{2}$$

- You make a line that goes through the point: $y = 3$, $x = 2$.

- The line goes through the corner of some squares on the coordinate system. You can make a point at each of those corners. And the points show different numbers for **older dogs** and **puppies.**

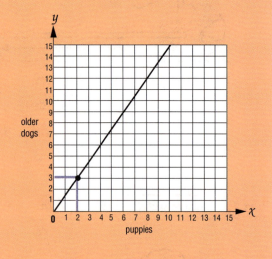

- You can look at the coordinate system and answer questions about older dogs and puppies.

  a. If there are 6 older dogs, how many puppies are there?

  b. If there are 10 puppies, how many older dogs are there?

  c. If there are 6 puppies, how many older dogs are there?

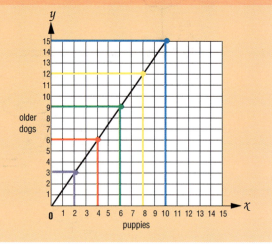

Part 5 Answer each question.

For every brown egg, there were 3 white eggs.

a. How many brown eggs were there for 18 white eggs?

b. If there were 3 brown eggs, how many white eggs were there?

c. If there were 15 white eggs, how many brown eggs were there?

d. How many white eggs were there for every 4 brown eggs?

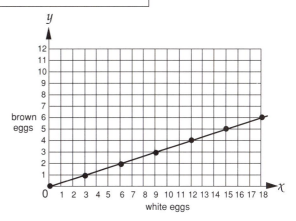

Part 6 For each item, write the fraction with the names. Show the y value as the numerator and the x value as the denominator.

Coordinate System 1

The ratio of green bottles to brown bottles is 4 to 3.

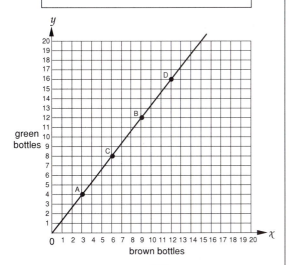

A $\dfrac{\text{green}}{\text{brown}}$ ▇

B

C

D

Coordinate System 2

The ratio of frogs to birds is 3 to 5.

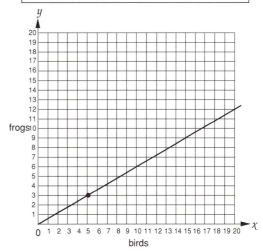

e. What fraction shows the number of frogs if there are 15 birds?

f. What fraction shows the number of birds if there are 6 frogs?

g. What fraction shows the number of birds if there are 12 frogs?

h. What fraction shows the number of frogs if there are 5 birds?

Lesson 88

Part 7 Make a complete table for each item.

a. These facts tell about a circular spinner. $\frac{4}{9}$ of the circle is yellow. $\frac{2}{9}$ of the circle is red. The rest of the circle is pink. The expected number for pink is 51.

b. The probability of the spinner landing on red is $\frac{1}{6}$. The probability for yellow is $\frac{3}{6}$. The probability for blue is $\frac{2}{6}$. The total number of trials is 36.

Part 8

- Here are problems you know how to work: $-4 - 3 = \blacksquare$, $-4 + 3 = \blacksquare$
- When you work these problems, you refer to **plus** and **minus.** You can also think about these problems as combining the values. Some problems that combine values have signs for the values and signs that tell how you'll **combine** these values.
- Here's a problem with a large +: $\qquad ^-4 + {}^-3 =$
- The large + means that you'll combine $^-4$ with the value that is shown after the plus sign. So you just **copy** the sign for $^-3$.
- Here's the problem rewritten: $\qquad -4 - 3 = -7$
- Here's a problem with a large –: $\qquad ^-4 - {}^-3 =$
- The large – tells you to combine the first value with the **opposite** of the value shown after the large minus sign.
- Here's the problem rewritten: $\qquad -4 + 3 = -1$
- Remember, these rules work just like the multiplication rules you've learned.
    - ✔ The large **+** tells you to **copy** the sign of the following value.
    - ✔ The large **–** tells you to write the **opposite** of that sign.

Part 9 Rewrite each problem without the large operational sign and work it.

a. $^-3 + {}^+2 =$

b. $^+5 - {}^+8 =$

c. $^+10 - {}^-5 =$

d. $^+9 + {}^-7 =$

e. $^-3 - {}^+9 =$

Part 10 Work each item.

a. A rectangular field is 240 feet long and 30 yards wide. What is the area of the field in square yards?

b. The first part of the trip took 650 days. The second part of the trip took 2 years. How many years was the entire trip?

c. A cylinder is 2 feet in diameter and 65 inches tall. What is the volume of the cylinder in cubic feet?

d. A poster is 3 feet wide and 88 inches tall. What is the area of the poster in square feet?

Independent Work

Part 11 Work each item.

a. A field is $\frac{9}{5}$ acres. It is divided into parcels that are each $\frac{3}{5}$ acre. How many parcels are there?

b. A pile of sand weighs $\frac{3}{5}$ ton. It is divided into 4 loads that have the same weight. How much does each load weigh?

c. 6 ounces of gold is divided into parts that each weigh $\frac{2}{7}$ of an ounce. How many parts are there?

Part 12 Make a table to show the expected number for each of the four colors and the actual numbers.

Somebody took 180 trials. Here are the results:
The spinner landed on one of the colors 75 times.
The spinner landed on another color 35 times.
The spinner landed on another color 50 times.

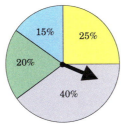

	%	expected #	actual #
total			

Part 13 Rewrite each fraction with a base number and exponent.

a. $\frac{2 \times 2 \times 2}{2 \times 2 \times 2 \times 2}$

b. $\frac{3 \times 3 \times 3 \times 3 \times 3}{3}$

c. $\frac{8 \times 8}{8 \times 8}$

Part 14 Write a fraction for each question.

a. In a park, there are 5 dogs and 2 of them have spots. What's the probability that the first dog you see will have spots? What's the probability that the first dog you see will not have spots?

b. During a 24-hour period, Bill sleeps 8 hours. A bug peeks out of a hole at some time on a 24-hour clock. What's the probability that Bill is asleep at that time? What's the probability that he's awake?

c. A circle is divided into 7 equal-sized parts. 2 of those parts are yellow. What's the probability that the first time you touch the circle with your eyes closed, your finger lands on a part that is yellow?

Part 15 Find the volume of each figure.

a. [cone: 18 ft height, 15 ft radius]

b. [cylinder: 18 ft height, 15 ft radius]

c. [rectangular prism: 9 in, 8 in, 10 in]

d. [pyramid: 9 in, 8 in, 10 in]

Part 16 Copy and complete the table to show the x and y values for each point.

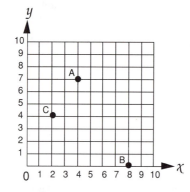

	x	y
A	■	■
B	■	■
C	■	■

Part J

b. $\begin{array}{r}1285 \\ +2 \\ \hline 3\frac{285}{365}\text{ yr}\end{array}$

c. Area of b × h = V
$3.14 \times 65 \times \frac{12}{12} = V$
$V = 1701 \text{ cu ft}$

d. $b \times h = A$
$3 \times \frac{88}{12} = A$
$A = 22 \text{ sq ft}$

368   Lesson 88

Lesson 89

Part 1

- Some equations begin with a value that is alone.
  - Here's: $10 = 40 \times A$
- You want to find out what **A** equals. One way to work the problem is to exchange the values on either side of the equal sign. 40 x A goes on the left side; 10 goes on the right side.

  $10 = 40 \times A$

  $10 = 40 \times A$

  - Here's the new equation: $40 \times A = 10$
- Now you can figure out the missing value: $40 \left(\dfrac{10}{40}\right) = 10$
- It's $\dfrac{10}{40}$.
- Remember, just move the sides the way they are written.
- Here's a different equation: $^-3 = {^-4} + M$

   = ▮

Part 2   **Rewrite each equation.**

a. Area = length x width   b. $30 = M - 6$ c. $\dfrac{5}{8} = R + \dfrac{1}{8}$

d. $14 = R \times 5$ e. $103 = 110 \times J$

Part 3

- Signed-number problems that involve division work just like problems that involve multiplication. You look at the value after the division sign.
- If that value is a **+ value,** you **copy** the sign of the first value in the answer.
- If the value after the division sign is a **– value,** you write the **opposite** sign.

  - Here's: $^-12 \div {}^-6 = \boxed{^+}$

- The value after the division sign is a minus, so the answer has the opposite sign of $^-12$.
- Fractions work the same way. The value you divide by is the denominator.
- If that value is a **+,** you **copy** the sign of the other value.
- If that value is a **–,** you write the **opposite** sign.
- Here are two fractions: $\dfrac{^-8}{^+2}$ $\dfrac{^-8}{^-2}$
- For the first fraction, the value you're dividing by is a **+,** so you **copy** the sign of $^-8$.

  $\dfrac{^-8}{^+2} = \boxed{^-}$

- For the other fraction, the value you're dividing by is **–,** so the sign is the **opposite** of $^-8$.

  $\dfrac{^-8}{^-2} = \boxed{^+}$

Part 4 Copy and work each item.

a. $\dfrac{^-20}{^-4}$ b. $\dfrac{^+15}{^-5}$ c. $^-28 \div {}^+7$ d. $\dfrac{^+100}{^+25}$ e. $^-42 \div {}^-6$

Part 5 Figure out the missing force in each diagram.

a.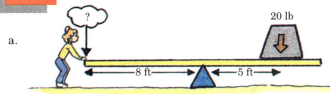

b.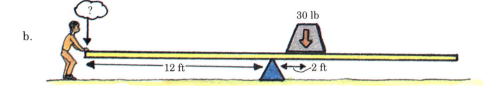

c.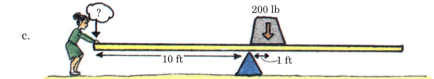

d.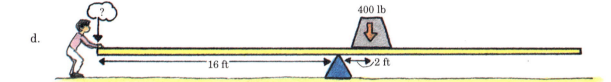

Lesson 89   371

Part 6

- Some figures are similar. That means they have the same shape, but not necessarily the same size.

- Here are two triangles that are similar:

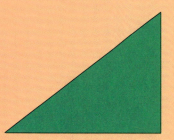

- Here are the same two triangles in a different arrangement:

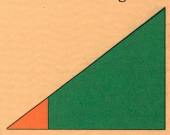

- You can use ratio equations to work with similar triangles.

- This diagram shows the sides for the smaller triangle. It also shows that the horizontal side of the larger triangle is 8 inches long.

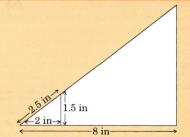

- To find the vertical side of the larger triangle, you can work a ratio problem:

$$\frac{\text{horizontal}}{\text{vertical}} \quad \frac{2}{1.5}\left(\frac{4}{4}\right) = \frac{8}{\blacksquare}$$

- The first fraction shows two dimensions of the smaller triangle: the horizontal side of 2 and the vertical side of 1.5. The horizontal side of the larger triangle is 8. You figure out the vertical side.

$$\frac{\text{horizontal}}{\text{vertical}} \quad \frac{2}{1.5}\left(\frac{4}{4}\right) = \frac{8}{6}$$

6 in

- The smaller triangle has a horizontal side of 2 and a slanted side of 2.5. So the larger triangle has a horizontal side of 8 and a slanted side of 10.

$$\frac{\text{horizontal}}{\text{slanted}} \quad \frac{2}{2.5}\left(\frac{4}{4}\right) = \frac{8}{10}$$

10 in

- Remember, you can use ratio equations to figure out the dimensions of similar triangles.

Part 7 For each item, use ratio equations to find the missing sides of the larger triangle.

a.

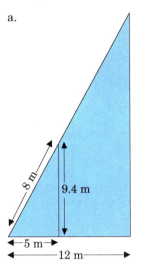

b.

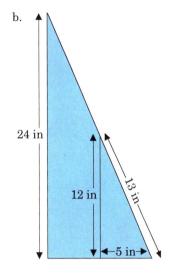

Part 8 Answer each question.

There are 4 toads for every 3 frogs.

a. If there are 12 frogs, how many toads are there?

b. How many frogs are there for 8 toads?

c. If there are 20 toads, how many frogs are there?

d. How many toads are there for 6 frogs?

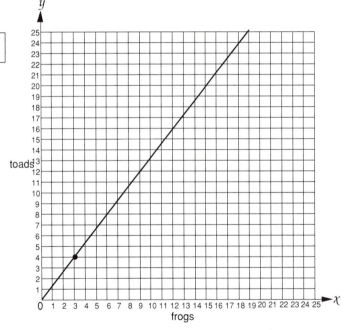

Lesson 89 373

Part 9

- Some equations have four values. If the missing value is on the left side, you work the problem by figuring out the value on the right side, then figure out the missing value.
- Here's a problem: $\quad$ M x 3 = 5 x 6
- You can find the missing value by using the inverse operation 30 ÷ 3. $\quad$ M x 3 = 30

    M = 10

- Some equations with four values have the missing value on the right side of the equal sign. You can work those problems by rewriting the equation so the missing value is on the left side of the equation.
- Here's an equation: $\quad$ 150 = 15 x M
- Here's the equation rewritten so that 15 x M is on the left: $\quad$ 15 x M = 150
- Now you can find the missing number: $\quad$ M = 10

Part 10 Work each item. Rewrite the equation if you need to.

a. R x 8 = 6 x 4 $\qquad$ b. $\frac{2}{3}$ x 7 = M x 2 $\qquad$ c. M ÷ 5 = 7 x 8

d. 15 − 3 = R + 8 $\qquad$ e. 20 − 6 = 7 x T

Part 11 Rewrite each item and work it.

a. $^-4 + {}^+7 =$ $\qquad$ b. $^-4 - {}^+7 =$ $\qquad$ c. $^+8 - {}^+3 =$ $\qquad$ d. $^-1 + {}^-6 =$ $\qquad$ e. $^+9 - {}^-5 =$

Independent Work

Part 12
Copy and work each item.

a. $-10(-3) =$ b. $+4(-1) =$ c. $+8(+2) =$ d. $-8(+2) =$ e. $-4(-5) =$

Part 13
Answer each question.

a. Fran had a photo enlarged. The original photo had a height of 5 inches and a length of 4 inches. The enlarged photo had a length of 12 inches. What's the height of the enlarged photo? What's the area of the enlarged photo?

b. 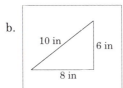 The picture of this triangle will be enlarged. In the larger picture, the slanted side is 14 inches long. What's the length of the vertical side? What's the length of the horizontal side?

Part 14
Work each item.

a. $2\frac{3}{7} \times \frac{1}{2} = \blacksquare$

b. $1\frac{5}{8} \times 10\frac{1}{2} = \blacksquare$

c. $13\frac{1}{3} - 12 = \blacksquare$

d. $5\frac{1}{2} - 2\frac{3}{5} = \blacksquare$

Part 15
Write what each item equals. Show the base number and exponent.

a. $2 \times 2 \times 2 =$

b. $(3 \times 3) \times (3 \times 3) \times (3)$

$\blacksquare^\blacksquare = \blacksquare^\blacksquare \times \blacksquare^\blacksquare \times \blacksquare^\blacksquare$

c. $\dfrac{3}{3 \times 3 \times 3} =$

d. $\dfrac{M \times M \times M \times M}{M \times M} =$

e. $\dfrac{12 \times 12}{12 \times 12} =$

Part 16
Make a table to show two columns. Answer the questions.

Facts
- The expected number for green is 12.
- $\frac{1}{10}$ of the circle is blue.
- $\frac{4}{10}$ of the circle is orange.
- $\frac{3}{10}$ of the circle is green.
- The rest of the circle is brown.

a. How many trials were taken?
b. What's the expected number for orange?
c. What's the expected number for blue?

Part 17
Work the item.

The table tells the number of things lost at the train station on different days. Find the average number of things lost per day.

	things lost
day 1	30
day 2	33
day 3	44
day 4	0
day 5	6
day 6	11

Lesson 89

Part 18 Work each item.

a. Find the volume in cubic yards.

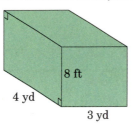

b. Find the area in square feet.

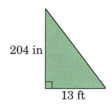

c. Find the area in square inches.

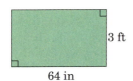

Part J

c. $R + \frac{1}{8} = \frac{5}{8}$

$\boxed{R = \frac{4}{8}}$

d. $R \times 5 = 14$

$\boxed{R = \frac{14}{5}}$

e. $110 \times J = 103$

$\boxed{J = \frac{103}{110}}$

Part K

vertical $\frac{12}{24} \left(\frac{2}{2}\right) = \frac{13}{26}$ slanted

$\boxed{26 \text{ in}}$

$\frac{5}{12} \left(\frac{2}{2}\right) = \frac{10}{24}$ vertical horizontal

$\boxed{10 \text{ in}}$

Part L

c. $M \div 5 = 7 \times 8$
$M \div 5 = 56$
$\boxed{M = 280}$

d. $R + 8 = 15 - 3$
$R + 8 = 12$
$\boxed{R = 4}$

e. $7 \times T = 20 - 6$
$7 \times T = 14$
$\boxed{T = \frac{14}{7}}$ [or $T = 2$]

Lesson 90

Part 1 For each item, write a problem with three signs. Then write the simple problem and work it.

    a. Combine ⁺7 with the opposite of ⁺3.
    b. Combine ⁻3 with the opposite of ⁻6.
    c. Combine ⁻2 with ⁻8.
    d. Combine ⁺7 with ⁻10.
    e. Combine ⁺20 with the opposite of ⁻5.
    f. Combine ⁻1 with the opposite of ⁺20.

Part 2 For each item, find the missing value.

a.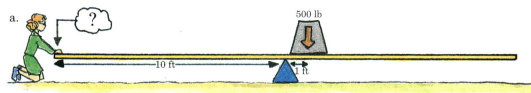

b.

c.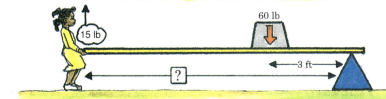

d.

Part 3 Copy and work each item.

    a. ⁺9 ⟌⁻7 2
    b. ⁻4 ⟌⁻3 6
    c. ⁺40 ÷ ⁻10
    d. $\frac{^-15}{^-15}$
    e. ⁺28 ÷ ⁺14

Test 9

Part 1 Work each item.

a. $\dfrac{3}{2} \div \dfrac{3}{4}$

b. $8 \div \dfrac{3}{8}$

c. $\dfrac{4}{5} \div 3$

d. A field is $\dfrac{4}{3}$ acres. It is divided into parcels that are each $\dfrac{1}{9}$ acre. How many parcels are there?

e. A load of sand weighs $\dfrac{7}{5}$ tons. It is divided into piles that each weigh $\dfrac{1}{4}$ ton. How many piles can be made?

Part 2 Rewrite and work each item.

a. $^-2 - {^+4} =$ b. $^+7 - {^-15} =$ c. $^-5 - {^-12} =$ d. $^+7 - {^+4} =$ e. $^-5 + {^+9} =$

Part 3 Make a table. Show the ratio numbers, the expected numbers for trials, and the actual numbers for trials.

The graph shows fractions for the different colors.

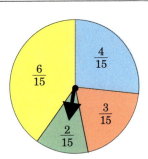

Facts
- The expected number for red is 60.

  A person took trials with a spinner. Here are some of the results:
  - The spinner landed on one color 83 times.
  - The spinner landed on another color 37 times.
  - The spinner landed on another color 128 times.

Questions

a. How many trials did the person take?
b. How many times did the spinner land on red?
c. How many times did the spinner land on green?
d. What's the expected number for green?
e. What color was landed on 128 times?

Part 4 Write the x and y value for each point.

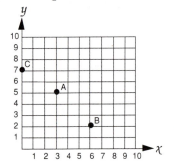

Part 5 Work each item.

a. Find the area of a rectangular field that is 118 feet long and 25 yards wide. Express the answer in square yards.

b. The first part of the job took 29 days. The second part of the job took 3 weeks. How many weeks did the entire job take?

c. A container held 34 gallons of fuel. 13 pints were removed. How many gallons remained in the container?

Part 6 Copy and work each item.

a. $-20(-2) =$

b. $+4(-6) =$

c. $-9(+3) =$

d. $\begin{array}{r} -14 \\ \times \;\; -1 \\ \hline \end{array}$

e. $\begin{array}{r} +3 \\ \times \;\; -4 \\ \hline \end{array}$

Part 7 Answer each question.

a. At a kennel, 3 out of every 4 dogs wear a collar. What's the probability that the first dog you see at the kennel is wearing a collar?

b. In a park, 3 out of every 7 persons is older than 10 years. What's the probability that the first person you see in the park is older than 10 years of age? What's the probability that the first person you see is not older than 10 years of age?

Part 8 Work each item.

a. $\begin{array}{r} 3\frac{1}{5} \\ -\,4\frac{4}{5} \\ \hline \blacksquare \end{array}$

b. $\begin{array}{r} 7\frac{1}{2} \\ +\,9\frac{7}{8} \\ \hline \blacksquare \end{array}$

c. $\begin{array}{r} 2\frac{1}{5} \\ \times \; 7 \\ \hline \blacksquare \end{array}$

d. $\begin{array}{r} 17\frac{1}{2} \\ -\,3\frac{4}{5} \\ \hline \blacksquare \end{array}$

Part 9 Write a complete equation for each item. Show the base number and exponent.

a. $(3 \times 3 \times 3) \times (3 \times 3 \times 3 \times 3)$

b. $(9) \times (9 \times 9) \times (9 \times 9 \times 9 \times 9)$

c. $\dfrac{7 \times 7 \times 7}{7 \times 7 \times 7 \times 7} = \blacksquare$

d. $\dfrac{R \times R \times R \times R}{R \times R \times R \times R} = \blacksquare$

Part 10 Answer each question.

The line shows the ratio of tigers to lions.

a. If there are 4 lions, how many tigers are there?

b. If there are 15 tigers, how many lions are there?

c. If there are 5 tigers, how many lions are there?

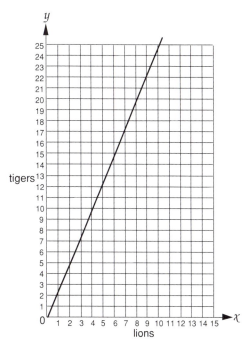

Part 11   Work the item.

The graph shows the price of different items bought in a drug store. Find the average price of the items.

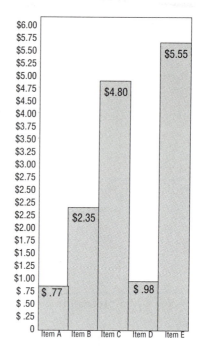

Part 12   Find the volume of each figure.

a.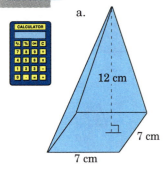

b.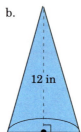

c.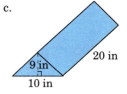

Lesson 91

Part 1 For each item, find the missing distance.

a. How far is the force from the fulcrum?

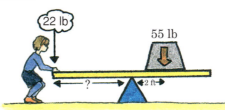

b. How far is the weight from the fulcrum?

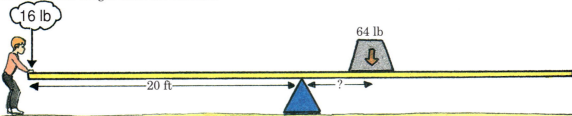

c. How much force is needed to balance the weight?

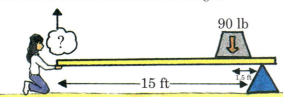

Part 2

- You're going to work on projects during the rest of this program. You'll work in teams and use the things you've learned.
- The project for today involves using what you know about angles.
- The instrument that you use to measure angles is called a **protractor.**

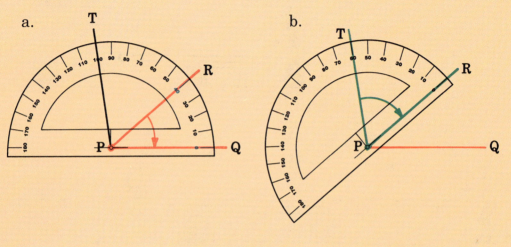

Part 3 Use your protractor to measure each angle.

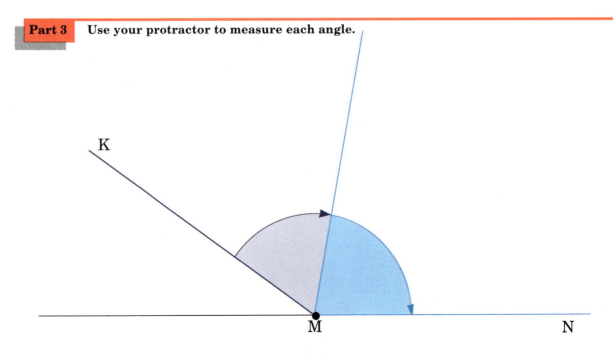

Part 4

- Some complex figures are symmetrical. That means, one side of those figures is exactly the same as the other side, except everything is backwards. It is a mirror image.

- Here are some figures that are symmetrical:

- The broken lines show the two mirror-image halves of each figure.

- Here are figures that are not symmetrical:

Part 5 Make a copy of this graph on Graph A. Complete the graph so it is symmetrical.

Independent Work

Part 6 Copy and complete the table for the circle graph.

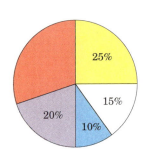

	%	degrees
yellow		
white		
blue		
purple		
red		
total		

Part 7 For each item, find the length of the vertical side of the smaller triangle.

a.

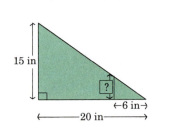

b.

Part 8 Rewrite each equation and solve it.

a. $360 = 48 \times J$

b. $26 \times 4 = 30 \times F$

c. $146 - 12 = P \times 10$

Part 9 Work each item.

a. The first part of the work project took $1\frac{1}{2}$ years. The second part took 28 months. How many years did the entire project take?

b. A poster is 30 inches wide and 2 feet long. What is the area of the poster in square feet?

Part 10 Work each item.

a. $-8 + 7 - 15 =$

b. $^-5(^-10) =$

c. $^-9 + {^-8} =$

d. $\dfrac{^+15}{^-3}$

e. $^-45 \div {^+15} =$

Part 11 Rewrite each problem and work it.

a. $^+6 - {^+4} =$

b. $\dfrac{^-5}{4} - \dfrac{^-12}{4} =$

c. $\dfrac{^+3}{8} \times \dfrac{^-2}{7}$

d. $\dfrac{^+3}{5} + \dfrac{^-12}{5} =$

384   Lesson 91

Lesson 92

Part 1

Figure 1

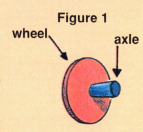

- A wheel and axle works just like a lever. We apply a force to the wheel that turns the axle. The farther the force is from the center of the wheel, the less force we need to turn the axle.

- You use the equation: **f x d = f x d**

Figure 2

- A is 3 feet from the center of the wheel. The force at A is pushing down with 60 pounds.

- B is 1 foot from the center of the wheel. The force at B is 180 pounds. That's the amount of force needed to balance the force at A.

Figure 3

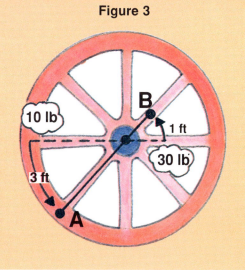

- If the wheel moves, it works just like a lever. The point that is farther from the center moves farther, but it requires less force.

- The wheel moves 3 feet at A. The force is 10 pounds. That balances what happens at B. B moves 1 foot with a force of 30 pounds.

Part 2 Work each item.

a. Somebody is trying to turn a wheel. The person is exerting a force of 40 pounds, 3 feet from the center of the wheel. You're holding the wheel steady by exerting a force. Your force is 16 pounds. How far from the center of the circle is your force?

b. The diagram shows that a force near the center of the wheel moves 6 inches with a force of 80 pounds. The outside of the wheel moves 21 inches. What is the force on the outside of the wheel?

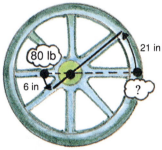

Part 3

Opposite angles created by intersecting lines are equal.

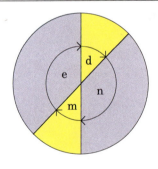

Part 4 Make a copy of this graph on Graph B. Do not use a protractor.

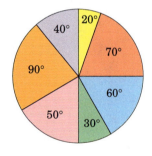

386   *Lesson 92*

Part 5

- For some problems that involve symmetrical figures, you can take a short cut. You can figure out $\frac{1}{2}$ of the figure, then multiply by 2 to find the total.

- Here's a figure that's symmetrical:

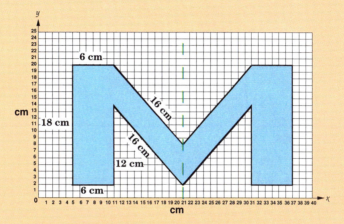

- The perimeter of $\frac{1}{2}$ is **74 cm**.
- So the perimeter of the whole figure is: **2 x 74 = 148 cm**
- The area of $\frac{1}{2}$ of the figure is **168 sq cm**.
- So the area of the whole figure is: **2 x 168 = 336 sq cm**

Part 6 Find the area of each figure.

a.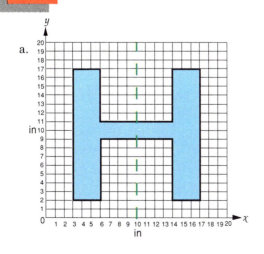

b.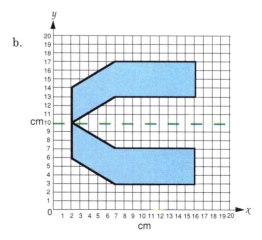

Lesson 92

Independent Work

Part 7 Find the missing letter.

a. 465 = 12 × B
b. 190 + 264 = H × 7
c. 360 = 90 + F
d. 26 × 94 = 18 × K

Part 8 Work each item. Use the equation:

in	out
f × d	= f × d

a. A person moves a lever 3 feet with a force of 45 pounds. This causes a weight of 250 pounds to move. How far does that weight move?

b. A weight of 80 tons is moved by a large lever. The weight is moved up 16 feet. If the other end of the lever moves 78 feet, how much force is used on that end?

c. A worker pushes down on the handle of a shovel with a force of 66 pounds. The handle moves 1 foot. The other end of the shovel moves 3 inches. How much force is on that end of the shovel?

Part 9 Answer each question.

a. The line shows the ratio of pigs to sheep. If there is 1 sheep, how many pigs are there? If there are 10 pigs, how many sheep are there? If there are 4 sheep, how many pigs are there?

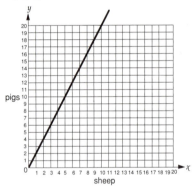

b. The line shows the ratio of dry days to wet days in Rover City. If it is wet 4 days, how many days is it dry? If it is dry 9 days, how many days is it wet? If it is wet 2 more days than it is dry, how many days is it dry?

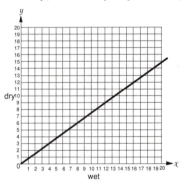

Part 10 Copy and complete the table for the circle graph.

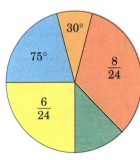

	degrees
yellow	
blue	
orange	
red	
green	
total	

Part 11 Answer each question.

Jane earns $\frac{3}{5}$ as much as her sister earns. If her sister earns $200, how much does Jane earn? If her sister earns $700, how much does Jane earn? If Jane earns $150, how much does her sister earn? How much more does her sister earn than Jane earns?

Lesson 93

Part 1 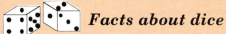 *Facts about dice*

- Each die has 6 faces, and each face has a different number of dots, from 1 through 6.
- The probability of rolling any number with one die is $\frac{1}{6}$. The probability of rolling a 3 is $\frac{1}{6}$. The probability of rolling a 5 is $\frac{1}{6}$.
- When you use two dice, the totals shown on the dice range from 2 to 12.
- The probability of totals for 2 dice depends on how many ways there are to reach the total. There are more ways to get a total of 4 than there are to get a total of 2. There's only one way to get a total of 2. The left die must show 1 and the right die must show 1.

  Here are the **different ways to get** a total of **4**:

	left die	right die
Here's one combination:	1	3
Here's another combination:	3	1
Here's another combination:	2	2

  There are three possible ways to get a 4, so getting a 4 is more likely than getting a 2.

- To figure out the possibilities, you start with 2 dice. You call one of them the left die and one the right die. Then you just list all the combinations for a particular number.

Part 2 Complete Table 1 and the circle graph.

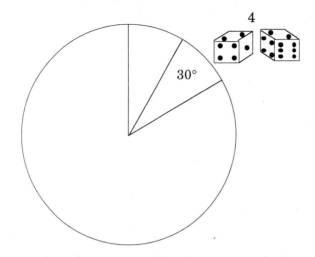

Rules for trials:

1. Put the dice into a container.
2. Shake the container.
3. Dump the dice onto a flat surface.
4. Make a tally mark in the row for the number shown on the dice.

Independent Work

Part 3 For each item, find the length of the horizontal side of the large triangle.

a.
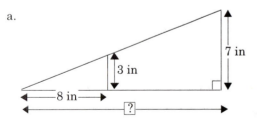

b.
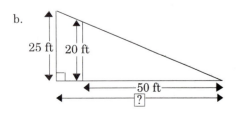

Part 4 Work each item. Use the equation:

$$\begin{array}{cc} \text{in} & \text{out} \\ f \times d = f \times d \end{array}$$

a. A lever lifts a weight of 600 pounds 2 feet. The force on the other end of the lever is 80 pounds. How far does that end of the lever move?

b. A person holds the handles of a wheelbarrow. The person's hands are 4 feet from the fulcrum and the person is exerting a force of 55 pounds. The weight inside the wheelbarrow is 165 pounds. How far from the fulcrum is that weight?

Part 5   Find the volume of each figure.

a.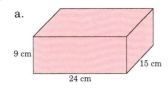

b.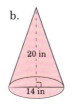

c.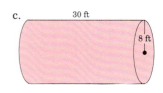

Part 6   Answer each question.

a. Folding each paper takes a machine 3 seconds. How many papers can the machine fold in 6 minutes?

b. A field is 40 yards wide and 650 feet long. What's the area of the field in square yards?

Part 7   Work each item.

a. $\dfrac{-1}{5} \div \dfrac{-1}{8} =$

b. $\dfrac{-1}{4} + \dfrac{+3}{4} =$

c. $\dfrac{+2}{5} - \dfrac{+1}{10} =$

d. $\dfrac{-3}{8} \times \dfrac{+4}{5} =$

e. $\dfrac{+5}{9} - \dfrac{+8}{3} =$

Lesson 94

Part 1

- Some simple-machine problems ask about the amount of work that is done.
- The amount of work is the product of the **force x distance.**

  force x distance = work

- The work done is the same on both sides of the equation.

  work in = work out
  f x d   =   f x d

- The units for the work are very strange because they are products.
- If the problem tells about feet and pounds, the unit of work is **foot-pounds.**
- Here's a problem:

  | A force of 200 pounds moves 4 feet. How much work is done? |

  f x d = w
  200 x 4 = w
  | w = 800 ft-lb |

- The answer is 800 foot-pounds.
- Each side of the equation shows the same amount of work. If you know the number for either side, you know the amount of work.

Part 2   Work each item.

a. A girl moves a lever 3 feet, with a force of 39 pounds. How much work does she do?

b. A girl moves a lever 4 feet. The weight she moves goes up 3 feet. The weight is 50 pounds. How much force did the girl use? How much work did the girl do?

c. The weight of 40 pounds is moved up 3 feet. The force the boy uses is 5 pounds. What is the distance of the force the boy uses? What is the amount of work the boy does?

Part 3   Work the item.

The force moves 18 feet when the weight moves 3 feet. What force must be applied to the outside of the wheel?

Part 4
Each member of the team will make a different letter.

- ✔ Make a point for each pair of x and y values.
- ✔ Connect the first point to the second point by making a straight line.
- ✔ Connect the second point to the third point with another straight line.
- ✔ Continue until all the points are connected.

Letter 1
1. $x = 1, y = 2$
2. $x = 10, y = 30$
3. $x = 16, y = 30$
4. $x = 25, y = 2$
5. $x = 20, y = 2$
6. $x = 17, y = 12$
7. $x = 9, y = 12$
8. $x = 6, y = 2$
9. $x = 1, y = 2$

Letter 2
1. $x = 4, y = 2$
2. $x = 4, y = 30$
3. $x = 9, y = 30$
4. $x = 9, y = 20$
5. $x = 17, y = 20$
6. $x = 17, y = 30$
7. $x = 22, y = 30$
8. $x = 22, y = 2$
9. $x = 17, y = 2$
10. $x = 17, y = 15$
11. $x = 9, y = 15$
12. $x = 9, y = 2$
13. $x = 4, y = 2$

Letter 3
1. $x = 1, y = 2$
2. $x = 5, y = 30$
3. $x = 10, y = 30$
4. $x = 13, y = 25$
5. $x = 16, y = 30$
6. $x = 21, y = 30$
7. $x = 25, y = 2$
8. $x = 20, y = 2$
9. $x = 17, y = 22$
10. $x = 13, y = 14$
11. $x = 9, y = 22$
12. $x = 6, y = 2$
13. $x = 1, y = 2$

Letter 4
1. $x = 10, y = 2$
2. $x = 10, y = 25$
3. $x = 3, y = 25$
4. $x = 3, y = 30$
5. $x = 22, y = 30$
6. $x = 22, y = 25$
7. $x = 15, y = 25$
8. $x = 15, y = 2$
9. $x = 10, y = 2$

Independent Work

Part 5 Work each item.

a. 56 x J = 200 x 7

b. 13 x 15 = A x 10

c. $\frac{3}{2} \div \frac{8}{3} = 4 \times M$

Part 6 Find the volume of each figure.

a.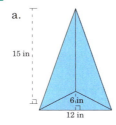

b.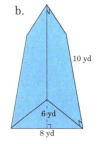

Part 7 Work each item.

a. $\begin{array}{r} {}^+8 \\ \times\ {}^-11 \\ \hline \end{array}$

b. $^-10(^-6) =$

c. $^+17 - {}^-13 =$

d. $\dfrac{^-24}{^-12}$

e. $-5 + 8 - 11 - 4 =$

f. $^-5 + {}^-16 =$

g. $^+5 + {}^+9 =$

Part 8 Answer each question.

a. The entire lot is $\frac{7}{5}$ of an acre. You want it divided into parcels that are $\frac{1}{3}$ acre each. How many of these parcels will you have? What is the area of 3 of these parcels? If you sold 3 of these parcels for $7,000 each, how much would you receive?

b. If a windowpane is $\frac{7}{9}$ square yards, what's the area of $\frac{1}{3}$ of the windowpane?

c. .2 of a gallon of paint costs $3.60. How much do 5 gallons cost?

d. Greg eats $\frac{7}{5}$ the number of calories that Hank eats. If Hank eats 260 calories, how many does Greg eat? If Greg eats 1,400 calories, how many does Hank eat? If Greg eats 100 calories more than Hank eats, how many does Hank eat?

Part 9 Figure out the value for each item.

a. $7^4 =$ ■

b. $\dfrac{7 \times 7}{7 \times 7} =$ ■

c. $\left(\dfrac{4}{3}\right)^4 =$ ■

d. $6^3 =$ ■

e. $\dfrac{3 \times 3}{3 \times 3 \times 3} =$ ■

Lesson 95

Part 1

- An inclined plane works like other simple machines.

- This picture shows a worker lifting a weight of 100 pounds up to a platform that is 4 feet off the ground. The worker does 400 foot-pounds of work.

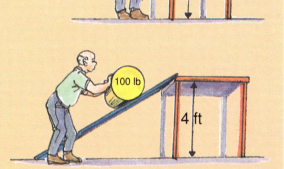

- This picture shows the same worker rolling the weight up to the platform using an inclined plane. Using the inclined plane requires a greater distance, but less force than lifting the weight straight up. The worker still does 400 foot-pounds of work.

Part 2   Work each item.

a. What's the force required to raise the weight 8 feet, using the inclined plane?

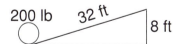

b. If 25 pounds of force is used to move the weight to the end of the inclined plane, how far does the weight move?

Part 3

- You can solve some problems that involve patterns by making the pattern simpler.

- Here's a series of numbers: 14 15 16 17 18 19 20 21

- You can find the sum of these numbers by adding them the regular way.

- The sum is 140.

- You can simplify the problem by making the series symmetrical. The series has 8 numbers. The middle of the series is between 17 and 18. So you just fold the series in half around that middle point. By folding the series, you made it symmetrical.

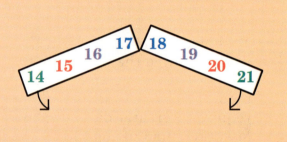

- You have 4 pairs and each pair has the same sum. You can find the total by figuring out how much one of the pairs equals, then multiplying by 4.

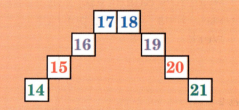

Part 4   Work each item.

a. Find the sum of the numbers from 1 through 22.

b. Find the sum of the numbers from 1 through 40.

c. Find the sum of the **odd** numbers from 1 through 23.

Independent Work

Part 5   Answer each question.

a. A tank had 58 gallons of fuel in it. 88 quarts were removed. How many gallons remained in the tank?

b. A store sold clocks at a discount price. The discount price was 68% of the regular price. If the discount price was $34, what was the regular price of the clocks? How much would a person save by buying a clock at the discount price?

c. Mr. Briggs built a cargo container. The container was 10 feet high, 30 feet long, and 12 feet deep. The container has a top, a bottom and four sides. The average cost of the materials is $4.50 a square yard. How many square yards of material did Mr. Briggs need? What was the total cost of the material? (*Hint:* Figure out the area of each side of the container. Add the areas.)

d. Ginger bought 8 pounds of flour, 2 loaves of bread and 2 pounds of oranges. The flour cost 20¢ a pound, the bread 75¢ a loaf, and the oranges 45¢ a pound. The tax is 8%. How much did the purchase cost, including tax?

Part 6   Work each item.

a. $^-4(^-12) =$

b. $^-3 - {^-8} =$

c. $\begin{array}{r} ^-24 \\ \times\ ^+3 \\ \hline \end{array}$

d. $^-28 + {^+16} =$

Part 7   Figure out the value for each item.

a. $\dfrac{1 \times 1 \times 1 \times 1}{1 \times 1 \times 1 \times 1 \times 1 \times 1} = \blacksquare$

b. $\dfrac{6 \times 6 \times 6 \times 6}{6 \times 6} = \blacksquare$

Part 8   Answer the question.

These are the heights of the players on the Eagles basketball team.

Player	Height
Henry	6 feet 11 inches
James	6 feet 4 inches
Tim	6 feet 6 inches
Ray	6 feet
Harry	6 feet 2 inches

What's the average height of an Eagle player? (*Hint:* You know that the average height will be 6 feet and some inches. You may not have to worry about the 6 feet, just the inches.)

Part 9   Answer each question.

a. A wall is going to be covered with siding. The wall is 10 feet high and 24 feet long. The wall has two windows in it. Each window is 4.5 feet high and 2.3 feet wide. The siding costs 75¢ per square foot. How much siding is needed? How much will the siding cost?

b. Start with Jan's turtle's age and add 30. Then divide by 10. Then subtract 1. You end up with 9. What's the age of Jan's turtle?

Lesson 95

Lesson 96

Part 1 Work each item.

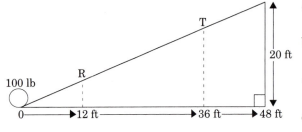

a. What is the vertical distance from the floor to point R?

b. What is the vertical distance from the floor to point T?

c. How much work is required to move the weight to point R?

d. How much work is required to move the weight to point T?

Part 2 Work each item.

Facts: There are 22 numbers from 1 through 22.
There are 38 numbers from 1 through 38.
There are 99 numbers from 1 through 99.

a. What is the rule for working any of these problems?
   1. How many numbers are there from 16 through 100?
   2. How many numbers are there from 5 through 31?
   3. How many numbers are there from 10 through 50?
   4. If a person reads pages 3 through 16 in a book, how many pages did the person read?

Part 3 Figure out the inclined side of each triangle. Then answer each question.

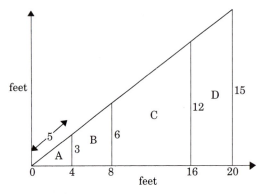

a. How does the force change as the distance increases?

b. What is the fraction you multiply by for any inclined distance to get the corresponding vertical distance?

c. How could you make a table to show the distances?

398 Lesson 96

Part 4

- Sometimes ratio problems are shown with a colon between the numbers.

    3 : 4 means the ratio of 3 to 4

    7 : 5 means the ratio of 7 to 5

- Work this problem: **5 : 6 = 20 : ?**

Independent Work

Part 5 For each item, write a ratio equation.

a. 7 : 5 = ■ : 45

b. 3 : 2 = ■ : 40

c. 2 : 3 = 150 : ■

Part 6 Work each item.

a. 4 of every 9 children had teeth missing. There were 120 children who did not have teeth missing. How many children did have teeth missing? How many children were there in all?

b. It cost $.07 for each 6 inches of molding. How much molding could a person buy for $4.13?

c. If you buy 6 or more shirts of the same kind at X-Mart, the cost of each shirt is reduced by 25%. If Vern buys shirts that cost $14.60 before the discount, how much do 6 of these shirts cost after the discount? (***Hint:*** Figure out how much each shirt costs when its price is reduced.)

Part 7 Work the item.

Here are the distances that Fran ran last week.

Day	Distance
Sunday	4.5 miles
Monday	6.4 miles
Tuesday	5.5 miles
Wednesday	0 miles
Thursday	6.4 miles
Friday	5.5 miles
Saturday	4.5 miles

What is the average distance Fran ran each day?

Part 8 Work each item.

a. $^-56 - 10 + 12 =$

b. $^-22 \times {}^+11 =$

c. $^+9 - {}^+20 =$

d. $\begin{array}{r} -2 + 9 - 14 \\ \times \quad {}^-3 \\ \hline \end{array}$

Part 9 Work each item.

a. A dealer sold all new cars at a discount of 35% less than the regular price. One car had a regular price of $12,000. What was the discount on that car? What was the new price of the car?

b. The ratio of cars to trucks on 6th Street is 7 to 3. On Tuesday, 238 cars went on 6th Street. How many trucks went on the street? How many more cars than trucks went on the street?

c. How many yards are in 16 feet?

d. How many feet are 344 inches?

e. How many inches are 56 feet?

f. Write 12 gallons and 2 quarts as a mixed number and a unit name.

g. 28 inches is ■ and ■ inches.

h. How many ounces are in $\frac{3}{4}$ pound?

i. How many feet are in $\frac{5}{6}$ mile?

Part 10 Work each item.

a. Two termites start eating a stick. One termite is at each end of the stick. The stick is 11 inches long. One termite eats at the rate of 3 inches of stick every hour. The other termite eats at the rate of 2.3 inches of stick every hour. How long will it take the termites to eat the entire stick? (**Hint:** Figure out how much of the stick is eaten each hour.)

b. Two cars start in the same place. They go in the opposite direction at a steady rate. One car travels 45 miles per hour. The other travels at 62 miles an hour. How far apart will the cars be after 1 hour? How far apart will the cars be after 5 hours?

Part 11 Figure out the value for each item.

a. $15^2 = $ ■

b. $\left(\dfrac{1}{2}\right)^3 = $ ■

c. $\left(\dfrac{3}{7}\right)^3 = $ ■

d. $\dfrac{12}{12 \times 12} = $ ■

e. $5 \times 5 \times 5 = $ ■

Part 12 Answer each question.

a. Jan has 384 cubic feet of sand. She plans to fill sandboxes that are 2 feet deep, 8 feet wide and 8 feet long. How many boxes can she fill with the sand she has? If she wants to fill 8 boxes, how much more sand would she have to get?

b. A box is 7 inches long, 3 inches wide and 1 foot high. The box has 6 sides. Jan will paint the box gold. That will cost $.02 per square inch. How many square inches will Jan need to paint? What is the cost of painting the box?

c. After painting the box, she will fill it with sand. How much sand does the box hold?

Part J

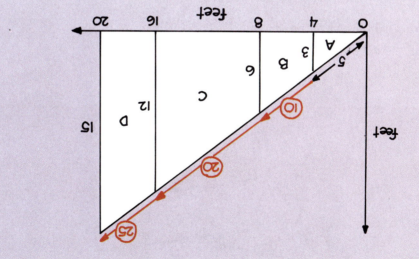

Lesson 97

Part 1

- You've figured out the rule for finding the sum of a series. There's a different rule for finding the sum of even numbers or odd numbers.
- Here are some problems:
  a. How many even numbers are there from 4 through 22?
  b. How many odd numbers are there from 7 through 37?
  c. How many even numbers are there from 2 through 48?
- Here's a hint about working the problems:
  ✔ Figure out how many numbers there are.
  ✔ Then figure out how many even or odd numbers there are.

Part 2 Work each item.

a. Find the sum of the odd numbers between 7 and 37.
b. Find the sum of the even numbers between 2 and 48.
c. Find the sum of the odd numbers between 37 and 71.

Part 3

Part 4 Work each item.

a. How much weight is lifted?

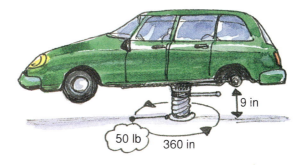

b. The boat weighs 4,600 pounds. It will be lifted up 1 foot. The handle will turn a total of 14 feet. How much force is used to turn the handle?

c. The wrench goes around 10 times. The diameter of the circle is 11 inches. The force is 4 pounds. The bolt moves up 1 inch. With how much force does it move up?

Independent Work

Part 5 Work each item.

a. Each tank holds 4 gallons and 3 pints. How much do 5 tanks hold?

b. The fence is $\frac{5}{3}$ the length of the field. The field is 680 feet long. How long is the fence?

c. The cost of fencing is 20% more than the cost of the posts. If the posts cost $460, how much does the fencing cost? How much more is the fencing than the posts? What is the total cost of the fencing and the posts? (*Hint:* The table will not give you this number.)

Part 6 Work each item.

a. $\frac{4}{5} \div \frac{3}{5} =$ ■

b. $12 \div \frac{3}{4} =$ ■

c. $12 \times \frac{3}{4} =$ ■

d. $\frac{4}{7} \times 8 =$ ■

e. $\frac{3}{4} \times \frac{2}{5} \times \frac{1}{10} =$ ■

f. $2\frac{5}{4} \times 13 =$ ■

g. $6 \times 5\frac{1}{2} =$ ■

h. $\frac{1}{5} \times 3\frac{7}{8} =$ ■

i. $\frac{.76}{3.8}$

j. $9.2\overline{)3.68}$

k. $.006\overline{)4.008}$

l. $\frac{1.8}{.9}$

Lesson 97   403

Part 7 Work each item.

a. Each toy weighs 2 pounds 6 ounces. What do 7 toys weigh?

b. Bill started out at 6:25 a.m. He walked for 1 hour and 45 minutes. When did he return?

c. A shelf will be cut from a board that is 6 feet 7 inches long. The shelf will be 4 feet 9 inches long. How much of the board will be left over?

Part 8 Work the item.

Here are the low temperatures for 5 days in January.

Day	Temperature
Monday	−4°
Tuesday	−6°
Wednesday	−14°
Thursday	+7°
Friday	+19°

What was the average low temperature?

Part 9 Make a complete table to show the expected outcomes for each color. Answer the questions.

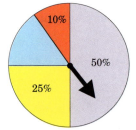

a. If the spinner lands on a color 10 times, which color would that probably be?

b. If the spinner lands on a color 20 times, which color would that probably be?

Part 10 Answer each question.

Tom worked on his vacation home during 4 months. In March, Tom spent 3 weeks working on his vacation home. In April, Tom worked 5 days on the home. In May, Tom worked 4 weeks and 2 days on the home. In June, Tom worked 17 days on the home. How long did Tom work on the home in all? What's the average number of days he worked on his house each month?

Lesson 98

Part 1

- Some symmetrical figures show a repeated pattern. Sometimes you use the pattern to simplify the figure.
- Here's a problem:
- You have to find the colored area.
- You could work this problem the long way, by finding the area of each column.

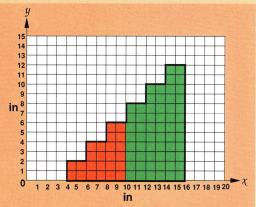

- You could also work this problem the fast way by dividing the figure into two parts and rearranging the two parts – like this:
- Now you have a simple shape to work with. It has the same area as the original shape.

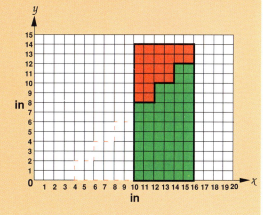

Lesson 98   405

Part 2 Find the area for each colored figure.

a.
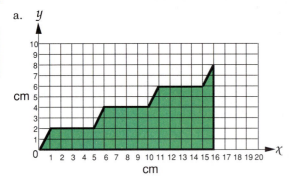

b.
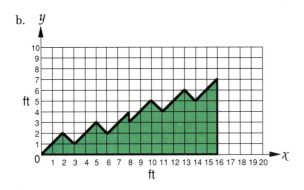

c.
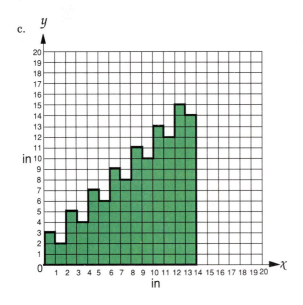

Part 3 Answer each question.

a. If the weight moves up 6 inches, how far does the person raise the end of the string?
b. If the weight is 10 pounds, how much force does the person exert to hold the weight in place?
c. If the person moves the end of the string up 3 feet, how much work does the person do?

Use a string to figure out the relationship between the distance the end of the string moves, and the distance the weight moves up.

Independent Work

Part 4 Answer the question.

Here are the low temperatures for a place near the North Pole during the month of April.

Day	Temperature
Monday	−1°
Tuesday	+5°
Wednesday	+1°
Thursday	−2°
Friday	−2°
Saturday	−1°
Sunday	0°

What's the average low temperature?

Part 5 Answer each question.

a. How many degrees are in half a circle?
b. What is the name of each shape?

    5

c. How many degrees are in a circle?
d. How many degrees are in $\frac{2}{3}$ of a circle?
e. How many degrees are in a triangle?
f. How many degrees are in $\frac{5}{4}$ circles?
g. What's the simple fraction for 50%?
h. What's the simple fraction for 25%?
i. What's the simple fraction for 10%?
j. What's the simple fraction for 80%?

Lesson 98

Part 6 Work each item.

a. Rita started out with some money. She earned $430. She bought 4 chairs. Each chair cost $76. She gave her younger sister $50 for helping her around the house. She ended up with $76. How much did she start out with?

b. A shed has a roof that comes to a point. The shed is 24 feet long and 24 feet wide. The walls are 10 feet high. The roof is the shape of a pyramid. The highest point of the roof is 22 feet above the ground. How many cubic feet of air are inside this building? (**Hint:** Find the volume of the bottom part; find the volume of the roof. Add the volumes.)

c. 5 of every 7 dogs had fleas. There were 36 more dogs that had fleas than dogs without fleas. How many dogs were there in all? (**Hint:** If there are only 7 dogs, there are 3 more dogs that have fleas than dogs without fleas. You want a difference of 36. So you need to multiply the ratio numbers by ⟨?⟩.)

Part 7 Work each item.

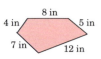 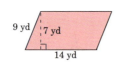

a. What's the perimeter? b. What's the area? c. What's the volume? d. What's the radius?
e. What's the area?

Part 8 Write the complete equation for each item.

a. $\frac{1}{2^4} = \blacksquare$ b. $4^2 = \blacksquare$ c. $2^5 = \blacksquare$

d. $1^8 = \blacksquare$ e. $3^4 = \blacksquare$ f. $\frac{1}{4^4} = \blacksquare$

Part 9 Write the complete statement for each item.

a. 25 quarts are ■ gallons and ■ ■.

b. 2,630 days are ■ years and ■ ■.

c. 240 months are ■ years and ■ ■.

d. 980° are ■ circles.

Lesson 99

Part 1

- Some problems are easier to solve if you make a diagram.

- Here's a problem:

  An ant is trying to climb up a slippery hill. The distance up the hill is 10 inches. The ant slips back 2 inches, and then goes forward 3 inches. Then the ant slides back 2 inches and goes forward 3 inches again. This pattern repeats until the ant reaches the top of the hill. How many total inches will the ant move before reaching the top of the hill?

- Here's a picture of part of the problem:

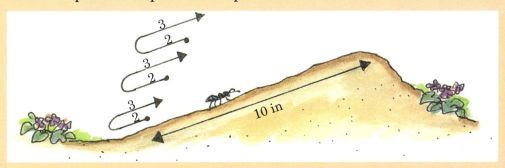

- The up arrows are 3 inches long. The down arrows are 2 inches long. The pattern repeats again and again.

- Here's an easy way to work the problem. First, figure out how much farther up the hill the ant goes each time the pattern repeats itself. Then figure out how many times the pattern would repeat itself before the ant reaches the top of the hill.

- The ant goes up 1 inch farther each time the pattern repeats itself. So the pattern would occur 10 times before the ant reached the top of the hill.

- Now you figure out how many inches the ant moves for each pattern. The ant moves down 2 inches and up 3. That's a total of 5 inches. So you multiply 5 x 10 to find the number of inches the ant would move before reaching the top of the hill.   5 x 10 = 50 in

Part 1 continued

- Remember these steps:
  - ✔ Figure out how many times the pattern must occur.
  - ✔ Figure out how many inches the ant moves each time the pattern occurs.
  - ✔ Figure out the total number of inches.

Part 2 Work each item.

a. An ant wants a supply of 100 seeds. The ant collects seeds and eats some of them. After the ant collects 8 seeds, the ant eats 3 seeds. How many seeds will the ant collect in all before the ant has a supply of 100 seeds?

b. It takes Mr. Wilson 10 minutes to complete each frame. He works for 50 minutes and then has a 10-minute break. He starts work at 7 a.m. If he makes 30 frames, at what time does he finish? If he worked without taking any breaks, when would he finish?

c. A tank has a leak. The water leaks from the tank at the rate of 2 gallons per minute. The tank holds 200 gallons. The tank starts out empty and is filled at the rate of 7 gallons per minute. How much time is required to fill the tank? How many gallons go into the tank before it is filled?

Part 3

- Some word problems that require division ask for whole-number answers. When you work some of these problems, you may get a remainder. You have to convert the answer into a whole number.

- For some problems, the answer is smaller than the mixed number; for others, the answer is larger than the mixed number.

- Here's a problem:

    Each car can hold 5 people. There are 66 people who are going on the trip. How many cars are needed?

- When you work the problem, you get $13\frac{1}{5}$. That's a correct answer, but it means that you would need more than 13 cars. You would need 14 cars.

$$5\overline{)66} = 13\frac{1}{5}$$

14 cars

410   *Lesson 99*

Part 4 Work each item. Figure out the rules for whether the whole-number answer is more or less than the mixed-number answer.

a. You have $4.50. You will buy as many pencils as you can with that money. The pencils cost 12¢ each. How many can you buy?

b. Each bus holds 32 people. There are 400 people who are going on a trip. How many buses are needed?

c. Each carton holds 24 cans. You have 200 cans. How many cartons can you completely fill?

d. Each can of paint covers 56 square feet. You want to paint a wall that is 8 feet by 34 feet. How many cans of paint will you buy?

Part 5

- You've figured out the relationship between how far the end of the string moves up and how far the weight moves up when the string is doubled. The end of the string moves up 2 times as far as the weight moves up. So the force required is $\frac{1}{2}$ the weight of the object being lifted.

- See if your team can figure out how to arrange the string so that you would need a force that is only $\frac{1}{4}$ the amount of the weight. (**Hint:** If the force required to move the weight is only $\frac{1}{4}$ as much as the weight, the distance the end of the string moves must be 4 times the distance the weight moves.)

Independent Work

Part 6 Work each item.

a. 3 lb   7 oz
    x   4

b.   2 hr   30 min
　 + 7 hr   42 min

c. 4 yr   12 wk
    −   25 wk

d. 10 min   25 sec
    x   4

Part 7 Work each item.

a. 3 − 2.75

b. 14.03 + 8 + 10.5

c. 15.5 x .07

d. − 18.2 − 5.10

Part 8 Work the item.

A circle is divided into 6 slices. 3 of the slices are the same size. They are white. Here are facts about the 3 slices that are not the same size: Together, these 3 slices add up to 180°. The largest of these slices is 90°. This slice is orange. The smallest of these slices is 40°. This slice is green. The third slice is yellow. Figure out the degrees for the all the slices and indicate the color.

Part 9 Work each item.

a. ⁻3 (⁻50) =

b. ⁺7 − ⁻42 =

c. − 3 − 8 − 10 − 17
    $\underline{\text{x   − 4}}$

d. − 26
    $\underline{+ 68}$

e. − 382
    $\underline{\text{x   + 2}}$

Part 10 Copy and complete each equation.

a. 3^4 = ■ = ■

b. a x a x a x a = ■■

c. 36^2 = ■ = ■

d. $\dfrac{12 \times 12}{12}$ = ■

e. (5 x 5) x (5 x 5 x 5) = ■■ x ■■ = ■

f. 1 x (1 x 1 x 1 x 1) = ■■ x ■■ = ■

Part 11 Answer each question.

a. A field is 880 feet by 250 feet. The field will be divided into 4 rectangular parcels that are the same size. What is the area of each of those parcels?

b. Each of the 4 parcels has a pair of sides that are each 55 feet long. How long is each of the other pair of sides?

c. The owner of this land will plant trees on 3 of the parcels. There will be 1 tree for every 110 square feet. How many trees will the owner plant on each parcel? How many trees will the owner plant in all?

d. If it takes the owner 2 minutes and 5 seconds to plant each tree, how long will it take the owner to plant all the trees?

e. If the trees cost $1.45 each, how much will the owner pay for the trees?

Part 12 Complete each ratio equation.

a. 6 : 4 = 3 : ■

b. 15 : 20 = ■ : 60

c. 1 : 10 = 7 : ■

d. 8 : 18 = ■ : 9

Lesson 100

Part 1

- You've worked with figures that have holes.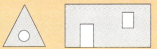
- You can have a space inside figures that have length, width and height.
- Here's a large container with a cube in it:

a.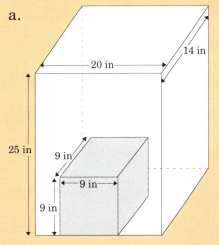

- Work in a team to figure out how much liquid the containers can hold. Explain your solutions.

b.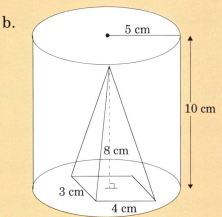

Part 2 Work the item.

There are 8 tourists on one side of the river and 12 tourists on the other side. All the tourists want to go across the river. The boat starts out on the side of the river that has 8 tourists. The boat can hold 5 people including the person who rows the boat. The man who owns the boat rows the people across the river. The river is 350 yards across. How many times will the boat cross the river? How far will the boat travel before all the people are transported across the river?

Independent Work

Part 3 Work the item.

This diagram shows colors and degrees for a circle that is used as a spinner. Make a complete table. Figure out the expected numbers for 72 trials. Then make a column for the actual numbers.

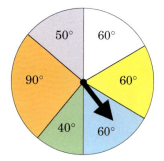

Facts: Of the three slices that are the same size, the spinner landed most often on yellow and least often on white. The actual numbers are: 11, 20, 9, 14, 6 and ?

Answer Key

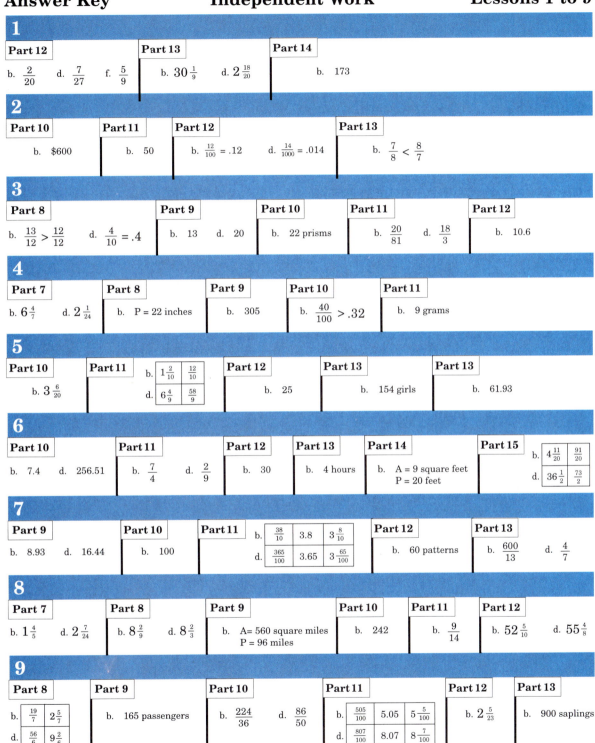

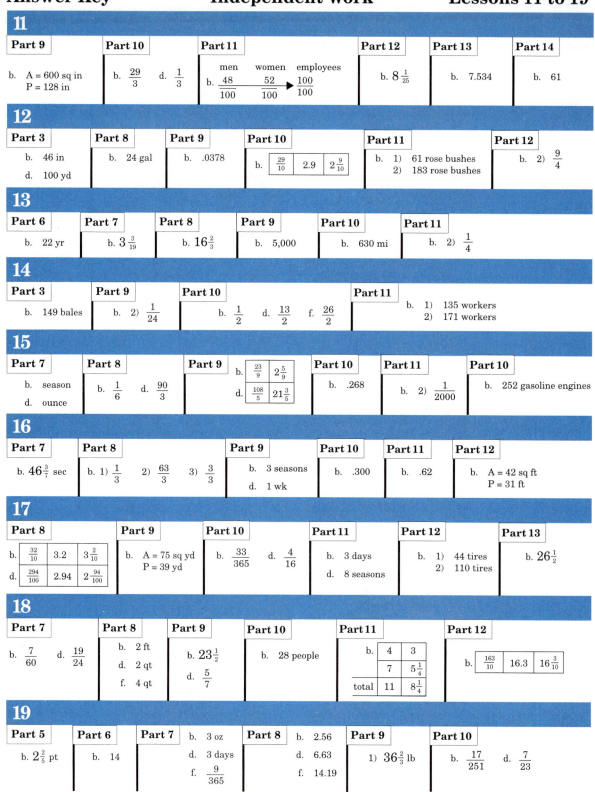

Answer Key Independent Work Lessons 21 to 29

21

Part 6
b. $\boxed{\dfrac{135}{10}}$ 13.5 $13\dfrac{5}{10}$

Part 7
b. 3,300 nails

Part 8
b. 28 hr
d. 9 qt
f. $\dfrac{3}{8}$

Part 9
b. A = 150 sq cm
   P = 59 cm

Part 10
b. 8.540

22

Part 4
b. 108 people

Part 9
b. $\dfrac{11}{16}$
d. 28 pt
f. 3 seasons

Part 10
b. $\dfrac{15}{24}$
d. $\dfrac{2}{7}\left(\dfrac{7}{7}\right)=\dfrac{14}{49}$
f. $9\left(\dfrac{1}{9}\right)=1$

Part 11
b. 2 lb and 4 oz
d. 5 yd and 2 in
f. 2 dollars and 1 quarter

Part 12
c. $2\dfrac{8}{7}=3\dfrac{1}{7}$
g. $4\dfrac{20}{17}=5\dfrac{3}{17}$

Part 13
b. $11

23

Part 3
b. 125 lb

Part 8
b. $15\dfrac{2}{12}$

Part 9
b. 26

Part 10
b. 18 dimes   d. $\dfrac{300}{365}$ f. $\dfrac{25}{60}$

Part 11
b. A = 168 sq cm
   P = 68 cm

24

Part 11
b. $4\dfrac{7}{12}$ yr   d. $3\dfrac{8}{60}$ hr   f. $1\dfrac{9}{24}$ d

Part 12
b. 1) 70 cars
   2) 14 cars
d. 8 gal

Part 13
b. $\boxed{\dfrac{15125}{1000}}$ 15.125 $15\dfrac{125}{1000}$
d. $\boxed{\dfrac{802}{100}}$ 8.02 $8\dfrac{2}{100}$

Part 14
b. 179

25

Part 7
b. 33

Part 8
b. $5\dfrac{4}{5}$ d. $55\dfrac{15}{79}$

Part 9
b. 50 children

Part 10
b. 1.576

Part 11
b. $3\dfrac{3}{16}$ lb   d. $1\dfrac{42}{60}$ hr

26

Part 3
b. 1) 36 perch
   2) 81 fish
d. 36 herons

Part 9
b. $\boxed{2\dfrac{2}{1000}}$ 2.002
d. $\boxed{\dfrac{501}{100}}$ 5.01

Part 10
b. $2\dfrac{1}{4}$ gal
d. $1\dfrac{78}{365}$ yr

Part 11
b. 12
d. $5\dfrac{5}{9}$

Part 12
b. 3.03

Part 13
b. 20

Part 14
b. A = 40 sq yd
   P = 32 yd

27

Part 9
b. $4\dfrac{5}{8}$

Part 10
b. 1) 210 documents
   2) 90 documents

Part 11
b. $\dfrac{1}{2}$ d. $\dfrac{7}{8}$

Part 12
b. 1 ft and 5 in
d. 11 wk and 3 d

Part 13
b. $\dfrac{28}{3}$ d. $\dfrac{9}{5}$

28

Part 3
b. 44 children

Part 8
b. $16\dfrac{1}{5}$ yr   d. 18

Part 9
b. 115 in   d. 19 quarters

Part 10
b. 5

29

Part 8
b. d = 60 in

Part 9
b. $\dfrac{5}{16}$ d. 36 children

Part 10
b. A = 28 sq in
   P = 32 in

Part 11
b. 270 yellow birds

Part 12
b. $2\dfrac{3}{4}$ yr   d. $2\dfrac{3}{24}$ d

Answer Key — Independent Work — Lessons 31 to 38

31

Part 9
b. d = 2.23 in

Part 10
b. $3\frac{17}{43}$

Part 11
b. 3.934

Part 12
b. 455 workers

Part 13
b. $4\left(\frac{37}{4}\right) = 37$
d. $\frac{30}{4}$

Part 14
b. 22 blueberries

Part 15
b. $316.50
d. 60 in
f. 32 years old

32

Part 7
b. 7.77
d. 5.28

Part 8
b. $40.65

Part 9
b. $150

Part 10
b. M = 274
d. V = 483
f. M = 102

Part 11
b. 36 mi

Part 12
e. $13\frac{1}{2}$ h. $1\frac{3}{12}$

33

Part 9
b. 160

Part 10
b. r = 4.14 ft

Part 11
b. 167 cars

Part 12
b. $13\frac{1}{3}$ c

Part 13
b. $\frac{1602}{100}$ | 16.02 | $16\frac{2}{100}$
d. $\frac{10076}{1000}$ | 10.076 | $10\frac{76}{1000}$

Part 14
b. $\frac{15}{40}$

Part 15
b. $\frac{5}{24}$
d. 17 sec

34

Part 7
b. P = 108 yd
A = 234 sq yd

Part 8
b. $40\frac{5}{12}$
d. $2\frac{4}{37}$

Part 9
b. 60

Part 10
b. 175 rabbits

Part 11
b. 8 d
d. 3 oz

35

Part 8
b. C = 75.36 yd
d. d = 56 ft

Part 9
b. 16
d. $17\left(\frac{2}{17}\right) = 2$
f. $1\frac{2}{8}$

Part 10
b. $\frac{1060}{100}$ | 10.60 | $10\frac{60}{100}$
d. $\frac{705}{100}$ | 7.05 | $7\frac{5}{100}$

Part 11
b. 1) 54 people
2) 189 people

Part 12
  dif   pole   building
b. $\frac{3}{2}$ $\frac{2}{2}$ → $\frac{5}{2}$
Picture 1

Part 13
b. $671.60

36

Part 9
b. 45 birds
d. 270 birds

Part 10
b. 18 oz
d. 30 hr

Part 11
b. A = 452.16 sq in
C = 75.36 in

Part 12
b. $36\left(\frac{1}{36}\right) = 1$ d. $\frac{11}{2}(2) = 11$

Part 13
b. 22.439

37

Part 7
b. A = 468 sq ft
P = 88 ft

Part 8
b. 156 lights

Part 9
b. r = 7.64 mi
d. A = 3.14 sq yd

Part 10
b. 1 hr and 12 min
d. 4 yd and 10 in

Part 11
b. 9
d. 7

Part 12
  dif   A   B
b. $\frac{6}{11}$ $\frac{5}{11}$ → $\frac{11}{11}$
Picture 3

38

Part 5
e. $40

Part 7
b. $\frac{20}{100}$ x w
d. 12 years old

Part 8
b. $6\frac{7}{16}$ lb
d. 8 minutes and 11 seconds

Part 9
b. $\frac{7}{100}$ | .07 | 7%
d. $\frac{236}{100}$ | 2.36 | 236%
f. $\frac{502}{100}$ | 5.02 | 502%

Part 10
b. $20.92
d. 30 gal

Answer Key — Independent Work — Lessons 39 to 47

39

Part 6
b. 27 years old
d. $85\frac{2}{4}$ mi

Part 7
b. popcorn maker

Part 8
b. A = 3,936 sq ft
d. A = 892.5 sq cm

Part 9
b.
dif	pole	tree
$\frac{5}{8}$	$\frac{3}{8}$	$\frac{8}{8}$

Picture 2

Part 10
b. 200
d. $\frac{3}{2}$
f. $\frac{9}{5}$

41

Part 8
b. 60 boxes
d. 189 players

Part 9
b. 1) 108 foxes
2) 120 foxes

Part 10
b. 35

Part 11
b. C = 18.84 m
A = 28.26 sq m

Part 12
b. 18.73

Part 13
b. $3\frac{5}{7}$ weeks
d. 10 dollars and 15 cents

Part 14
b. 42 sq units

42

Part 7
b. 72 in
d. 42 models

Part 8
b. 24.876
d. 14.448

Part 9
b. hours = $\frac{\text{miles}}{41 \text{ miles per hour}}$
d. minutes = $\frac{\text{flowers}}{4 \text{ flowers per minute}}$

Part 10
b. 80

Part 11
b. $\frac{14}{6}$

43

Part 8
b. $\frac{1}{2}$
d. $\frac{1}{10}$

Part 9
b. 2 hours and 30 minutes
d. $5\frac{6}{36}$ yards

Part 10
b. A = 21 sq units

Part 11
b. $\frac{9}{7}$
d. 29
f. 27

Part 12
b. A = 1,017.36 sq ft
d. d = 16 m

Part 13
b. 24 bowls
d. 1,700 books

44

Part 9
b. 1) $50
2) $69

Part 10
b. cans = $\frac{\text{dollars}}{14 \text{ dollars per can}}$
d. cartons = $\frac{\text{jars}}{14 \text{ jars per carton}}$

Part 11
b. P = 126 ft
d. P = 80 ft

Part 12
b. 72 hours
d. 120 seconds

Part 13
b.
dif	girls	boys
$\frac{50}{100}$	$\frac{100}{100}$	$\frac{150}{100}$

d.
dif	sale price	regular price
$\frac{60}{100}$	$\frac{100}{100}$	$\frac{160}{100}$

Part 14
b. 63

Part 15
b. $118.72

45

Part 8
b. $42.70
d. $2,294.90

Part 9
b. 9
d. 63

Part 10
b. $\frac{17}{10}$, 1.7 , $1\frac{7}{10}$
d. $\frac{468}{10}$, 46.8 , $46\frac{8}{10}$

Part 11
b. $105\frac{3}{8}$ min
d. $600

Part 12
b. $\frac{1}{2}$
d. $\frac{3}{5}$
f. 10%

Part 13
b. $8\overline{)26}$ with quotient $3\frac{2}{8}$

46

Part 8
b. $\frac{1}{22}$
d. 40 acres

Part 9
b. $7\frac{1}{2}$
d. 84
f. 1

Part 10
48 sq units

Part 11
b. $211.68

Part 12
b. $2\frac{3}{12}$ years
d. 180 minutes

47

Part 9
b. 1) 27 ft
2) 63 ft
d. $466\frac{2}{3}$ sec
f. 1) 115 cats
2) 138 dogs

Part 10
b. 1.50
d. 12.33

Part 11
b. 70
d. $5\frac{5}{8}$
f. $\frac{3}{16}$
h. 1

Part 12
b. 3 hours
d. 48 ounces

Part 13
18 sq units

K 5

Answer Key — Independent Work — Lessons 48 to 57

48

Part 9
b. 19.06
d. .38

Part 10
b. $\frac{1}{8}$
d. $\frac{1}{16}$
f. 26 students

Part 11
b. 30 inches
d. 4 feet

Part 12
b. A = 38 sq yd
   P = 42 yd

Part 13
b. 60 years old
d. 250 gal

49

Part 7
b. 1) $16
   2) $96

Part 8
b. 2.68
d. 8.8

Part 9
b. 54 months
d. 28 quarters

Part 10
b. A = 200 sq in
d. d = 63.69 in

Part 11
b. 0

Part 12
b. 20% = $\frac{1}{5}$
d. 40% = $\frac{2}{5}$

51

Part 8
b. $415.80

Part 9
b. 108
d. $11\frac{3}{5}$

Part 10
b. $21\frac{2}{3}$ miles per hour

Part 11
b. $\frac{5}{6}$
d. $14\frac{3}{60}$
f. $13\frac{1}{2}$

Part 12
b. 272 fish
d. 1) 200 bass
   2) 500 perch

52

Part 7
b. 84 hr

Part 8
b. $50\frac{1}{2}$ sq ft

Part 9
b. $5\frac{5}{7}$ weeks
d. $1\frac{4}{6}$ minutes

Part 10
b. 8
d. $\frac{6}{7}$
f. $12\frac{4}{5}$

Part 11
b. $4,500

53

Part 6
b. $149.89

Part 7
b. $\frac{50}{16}$
d. $\frac{5}{16}$

Part 8
b. $12\frac{4}{7}$ weeks
d. $8\frac{3}{12}$ feet

Part 9
b. $\frac{12}{39}$
d. 13

Part 10
b. 70 children

Part 11
b. A = 153.86 sq cm
   C = 43.96 cm

54

Part 8
2. $22.11

Part 9
b. $5\frac{10}{16}$ days
d. $7\frac{3}{6}$ cards per minute

Part 10
A = 72 sq units

Part 11
b. 36

55

Part 8
b. 8

Part 9
b. 1) 60 hr
   2) 48 hr

Part 10
b. A = 113.04 sq m
d. $197.82

Part 11
b. 408 inches
d. 25 quarts

Part 12
b. 90°
d. $\frac{3}{4}$

56

Part 8
b. 1) 540 lb
   2) 960 lb

Part 9
b. A = 300 sq in

Part 10
b. $\frac{15}{2}$
d. $\frac{91}{8}$

Part 11
b. 5 yr and 7 d
d. 8 hr and 56 min

Part 12
b. 1) 210 bottle tops
   2) 360 bottle tops

Part 13
b. 291.62
d. 42.86

57

Part 7
b. 6.5
d. 7.3

Part 8
b. 12 gal 2 qt
d. 20 min 8 sec

Part 9
b. 62.80

Part 10
b. $9\frac{9}{26}$

Part 11
b. A = 97,600 sq yd

Part 12
b. $\frac{3}{10}$
d. $\frac{1}{5}$

Part 13
b. 180°
d. 4 sides
f. 5 sides
h. $\frac{1}{28}$

Part 14
b. $\frac{7}{5}\left(\frac{5}{7}\right) = \frac{35}{35} = 1$

Answer Key — Independent Work — Lessons 58 to 66

58

Part 7
b. 1) 30 in
2) 72 in

Part 9
b. $4\frac{26}{60}$ hr   d. $1\frac{12}{24}$ d   f. 14 qt

Part 10
b. $3,240

Part 11
b. T is 259% of V.
T is 159% more than V.

Part 12
38.13 sq in

Part 13
b. $43

59

Part 7
b. 1) $25
2) $5

Part 8
b. $1\frac{3}{4}$ gallons = $\frac{7 \text{ quarts}}{4 \text{ quarts per gallon}}$ d. 7 years = $\frac{84 \text{ months}}{12 \text{ months per year}}$

Part 9
b. 18 people

Part 10
b. .33
d. 8.57

Part 11
b. $29.16

Part 12
b. 4 gal 5 pt

Part 13
b. $9\frac{1}{21}$ cabinets   d. $21\frac{8}{50}$ l

61

Part 10
b. 16

Part 11
b. $8.19

Part 12
b. T is 48% of M.
T is 52% more than M.

Part 13
b. 2 lb 10 oz
d. 6 gal

Part 14
b. 99 sq yd

Part 15
b. 2 gal 3 pt
d. 1 d 16 hr

62

Part 10
b. 12 yr

Part 11
b. 9.7

Part 12
b. 55.20

Part 13
b. 19 yr 210 d   d. 1 yr 225 d

Part 14
b. 1) 389 sq ft
2) $836.35

Part 15
b. 1) 10,800 ft
2) $13\frac{6}{18}$ min

63

Part 8
b. 81 ft
d. 1,095 d

Part 9
b. Q is 215% of V.
Q is 115% more than V.

Part 10
b. 30

Part 11
b. 8 gal 3 pt
d. 7 gal

Part 12
b. .019
d. .087

Part 13
b. 196 cows

64

Part 8
b. $1\frac{48}{52}$ yr   d. $1\frac{5}{7}$ wk   f. $1\frac{28}{60}$ hr

Part 9
b. 55.5 sq in

Part 10
b. 14 ft 10 in

Part 11
b. 4 shirts per min   d. 8,800 gal

65

Part 9
b. 1) 6 pt
2) 7 gal 4 pt

Part 10
b. 20

Part 11
b. 4 gal 2 qt
d. 4 yr 26 wk
f. 4 lb 8 oz

Part 12
b. .03(100) = 3
d. .032(1000) = 32

Part 13
b. 46

Part 14
b. 27 sq units

66

Part 8
b. 1) 42 in
2) 30 in

Part 9
b. 253.29 sq ft

Part 10
b. 544 lb

Part 11
b. $1\frac{1}{10}$

Part 12
b. 4 min 15 sec

Answer Key   Independent Work   Lessons 67 to 75

67

Part 8
b. 99 ft

Part 9
b. 12

Part 10
b. 1) 60 eagles
2) 45 eagles

Part 11
228 sq m

Part 12
b. 4 hr 40 min

68

Part 7
b. $+5 - 8 = -3$

Part 8
b. 19 min 30 sec   d. $20.60

Part 9
b. 1,226 sq ft

Part 10
b. $18.15

Part 11
b. -7 d. $+28$

Part 12
b. 425

69

Part 7
b. 320   d. 1

Part 8
b. 4:45 p.m.

Part 9
b. $\frac{5}{12}$

Part 10
b. 9

Part 11
b. 3.19 m   d. 18.84 in

71

Part 9
b. 300
d. 350 g

Part 10
b. $+29$

Part 11
b. $12\frac{9}{10}$

Part 12
b. 25 min 20 sec
d. 3 hr 1 min
f. 1) $8.45
2) $1.55

Part 13
b. A = 2,826 sq in
C = 188.4 in

Part 14
b. $15\frac{1}{8}$

72

Part 6
b. 1) $2.75
2) $1.65
d. 1) 690 lb
2) 1,150 lb

Part 7
b. $+3 - 8 = -5$

Part 8
b. 208 ounces
d. 98 days
f. $4\frac{3}{4}$ years

Part 9
b. 8:06 p.m.
d. 3 ft 9 in

73

Part 8
b. 1) $.80
2) $2.80

Part 9
b. V = 1,620 cu cm

Part 10
b. 29 oz
d. 184 sec

Part 11
b. $\frac{3}{4}\left(\frac{25}{25}\right) = \frac{75}{100} = 75\%$
d. $\frac{7}{20}\left(\frac{5}{5}\right) = \frac{35}{100} = 35\%$

Part 12
b. 88 t

Part 13
b. 40 sq ft

74

Part 10
b. $+33$
d. $+3$

Part 11
b. 90 coins

Part 12
b. 36.63 cm

Part 13
b. 8:32 a.m.
d. 2:01 p.m.

Part 14
b. $\frac{8}{15}$

Part 15
b. $9\frac{1}{5}$
d. $13\frac{11}{12}$

Part 16
b. $9\frac{2}{6}$ baskets per hour

75

Part 8
b. 1) 17 yd 24 in
2) 72 yd 26 in
d. 2 hr 54 min

Part 9
b. $\frac{3}{2}\left(\frac{50}{50}\right) = \frac{150}{100} = 150\%$
d. $\frac{11}{20}\left(\frac{5}{5}\right) = \frac{55}{100} = 55\%$

Part 10
b. 1) 1,507.2 calories
2) 2,512 calories

Part 11
b. -18
d. -22

Part 12
1) $38.92
2) $11.08

Answer Key — Independent Work — Lessons 76 to 83

76

Part 6
b. $545.84

Part 7
b. +17
d. −41

Part 8
b. $8\frac{8}{9}$

Part 9
b. 3:20 p.m.
d. 168 hr
f. 16 hr 55 min

Part 10
b. $\frac{9}{20}$ $\frac{45}{100}$ .45
d. $\frac{1}{4}$ $\frac{25}{100}$ .25

Part 11

b.
8	12
14	21
12	18
10	15
6	9
total 50	75

Part 12
b. .2
d. .75

77

Part 6
b. .7
d. 204

Part 8
b. 1) 78 sq in
2) 44 in
3) $9.36

Part 9
b. −40
d. +14

Part 10
b. $7\frac{4}{5}$ in

Part 11
b. 4

Part 12
b. $41\frac{1}{7}$
d. 70

78

Part 8
b. 6
d. .25

Part 9
b. V = 1,400 cu cm

Part 10
b. −61
d. −60

Part 11
b. 5:38 p.m.
d. 32 wk
f. 1 gal 4 pt
h. $11\frac{4}{36}$ yd

Part 12
b. 360.61 sq in

79

Part 7
b. 13.87
d. 20

Part 8
b.
5	18
60	216
10	36
25	90
total 100	360

Part 9
b. $10^2 = 10 \times 10 = 100$
d. $3^4 = 3 \times 3 \times 3 \times 3 = 81$

Part 10
b. V = 600 cu cm

Part 11
b. $1,043.28

Part 12
b. 648°
d. $240
f. 60%

81

Part 10
b. 270 miles
d. 32 miles per hour

Part 11
b. V = 20 cu ft

Part 12
b. 1) 1,500 t
2) 1,950 t

Part 13
b. 27^2
d. 10^5

Part 14
b. 12 years

Part 15
b. −18
d. +60

82

Part 7
b. +1
d. −1

Part 8

	%	degrees
green	36	129.6
yellow	18	64.8
orange	10	36
total	100	360

Part 9
b. 108 cans
d. 20 tons per pile

Part 10
b. V = 442 cu cm

Part 11
b. $10\frac{6}{8}$
d. $12\frac{7}{8}$

Part 12
b. 7^3
d. 10^5

83

Part 10
b. $20\frac{2}{5}$ cars

Part 11
b. 803.84 sq ft

Part 12
b. $67.45

Part 13
b. +22
d. +19

Part 14
b. $56

Answer Key — Independent Work — Lessons 84 to 91

84

Part 9
b. 5.5 miles per hour
d. 40 coins

Part 10
b. +23

Part 11
b. 4 hr 40 min

Part 12
b. $7\frac{3}{6}$
d. $10\frac{4}{7}$

Part 13
b. 1,440 in
d. $5\frac{20}{36}$ yd
f. 776 yd 2 ft

Part 14

b.
| $\frac{7}{100}$ | .07 | 7% |

d.
| $\frac{3}{100}$ | .03 | 3% |

85

Part 7
b. 1) 80 animals
2) 128 animals

Part 8
b. 65 penguins

Part 9
b. $159.60

Part 10
b. −2
d. +5

Part 11
b. $8\frac{3}{4}$ gal

Part 12
b. M = 378
d. D = 30

86

Part 10
b. −6
d. +8

Part 11

green	40	32
yellow	20	16
total	100	80

Part 12
b. $12^3 = 12^2 \times 12^1$

Part 13
b. $\frac{2}{15}$
d. $1\frac{1}{7}$

Part 14
b. 235.56 cu ft

Part 15
b. $5\frac{3}{8}$
d. $11\frac{23}{24}$

87

Part 8
b. 1) 12 in
2) 15 in

Part 9
b. $3\frac{3}{4}$
d. $\frac{3}{16}$

Part 10
b. $2^6 = 2^1 \times 2^2 \times 2^3$
d. $3^4 = 3^1 \times 3^3$

Part 11
32 seagulls

Part 12
b. $\frac{3}{10}$ d. $\frac{3}{28}$

Part 13
b. −15
d. −12

88

Part 11
b. $\frac{3}{20}$ t

Part 12

purple	40	72	75
green	20	36	35
total	100	180	180

Part 13
b. 3^4

Part 14
b. 1) $\frac{8}{24}$
2) $\frac{16}{24}$

Part 15
b. 3,179.34 cu ft
d. 240 cu in

Part 16

| B | 8 | 0 |

89

Part 12
b. −4
d. −16

Part 13
b. 1) $8\frac{4}{10}$ in
2) $11\frac{2}{10}$ in

Part 14
b. $17\frac{1}{16}$
d. $2\frac{9}{10}$

Part 15
b. $3^5 = 3^2 \times 3^2 \times 3^1$
d. M^2

Part 16
b. 16

Part 17
b. $20\frac{4}{6}$ things

Part 18
b. $110\frac{1}{2}$ sq ft

91

Part 6

white	15	54
purple	20	72
total	100	360

Part 7
b. $3\frac{6}{14}$ in

Part 8
b. $3\frac{14}{30}$

Part 9
b. 5 sq ft

Part 10
b. +50
d. −5

Part 11
b. $\frac{-5}{4} + \frac{12}{4} = \frac{+7}{4}$
d. $\frac{+3}{5} - \frac{12}{5} = \frac{-9}{5}$

Answer Key — Independent Work — Lessons 92 to 98

92

Part 7
b. $64\frac{6}{7}$
d. $135\frac{14}{18}$

Part 8
b. $16\frac{32}{78}$ lb

Part 9
b. 1) 3 d
   2) 12 d
   3) 6 d

Part 10

blue	5	75
red	8	120
total	24	360

Part 11
2) $420
4) $100

93

Part 3
b. $62\frac{10}{20}$ ft

Part 4
$1\frac{55}{165}$ ft

Part 5
1,025.73 cu in

Part 6
$8,666\frac{2}{3}$ sq yd

Part 7
b. $^{+}\frac{2}{4}$
d. $^{-}\frac{12}{40}$

94

Part 5
b. $19\frac{5}{10}$

Part 6
b. 240 cu yd

Part 7
b. $^{+}60$ d. $^{+}2$ f. $^{-}21$

Part 8
b. $\frac{7}{27}$ sq yd
d. 1) 364 cal
   2) 1,000 cal
   3) 250 cal

Part 9
b. 1
d. 216

95

Part 5
b. 1) $50
   2) $16
d. $4.32

Part 6
b. $^{+}5$
d. $^{-}12$

Part 7
b. 36

Part 8
6 ft $4\frac{3}{5}$ in

Part 9
b. 70

96

Part 5
b. $\frac{3}{2}\left(\frac{20}{20}\right) = \frac{60}{40}$

Part 6
b. 354 in

Part 7
b. 4.69 mi

Part 8
b. $^{-}242$
d. $^{+}21$

Part 9
b. 1) 102 trucks
   2) 136 cars
d. $28\frac{8}{12}$ ft
f. $12\frac{2}{4}$ gal
h. 12 oz

Part 10
b. 1) 107 mi
   2) 535 mi

Part 11
b. $\frac{1}{8}$
d. $\frac{1}{12}$

Part 12
b. 1) 282 sq in
   2) $5.64

97

Part 5
b. $1,133\frac{1}{3}$ ft

Part 6
b. 16
d. $4\frac{4}{7}$
f. $42\frac{1}{4}$

Part 7
h. $\frac{31}{40}$
j. .4
l. 2

Part 8
b. 8:10 a.m.

Part 9
$^{+}.4°$

Part 10
b. yellow

2) $18\frac{1}{4}$ d

98

Part 4
0°

Part 5
b. 1) hexagon
   3) rectangle
   5) pentagon
d. 240°
f. 450°
h. $\frac{1}{4}$
j. $\frac{8}{10}$

Part 6
b. 8,064 cu ft

Part 7
b. 98 sq yd
d. 97.45 ft

Part 8
b. $4^2 = 4 \times 4 = 16$
d. $1^8 = 1 \times 1 \times 1 \times 1 \times 1 \times 1 \times 1 \times 1 = 1$
f. $\frac{1}{4^4} = \frac{1}{4 \times 4 \times 4 \times 4} = \frac{1}{256}$

Part 9
b. 7 years and 75 days
d. $2\frac{26}{36}$ circles

Answer Key — Independent Work — Lessons 99 to 100

99

Part 6
b. 10 hr 12 min
d. 41 min 40 sec

Part 7
b. 32.53
d. −23.30

Part 8

orange	90
white	60
yellow	50

Part 9
b. +49
d. +42

Part 10
b. $a \times a \times a \times a = a^4$
d. $\dfrac{12 \times 12}{12} = 12^1 = 12$
f. $1 \times (1 \times 1 \times 1 \times 1) = 1^1 \times 1^4 = 1^5 = 1$

Part 11
b. 1,000 ft
d. 52 hr 5 min

Part 12
b. 15:20 = 45:60
d. 8:18 = 4:9

100

Part 3

yellow	60	12	14
white	60	12	11
green	40	8	6

K 12

FACTS

POLYGONS

POLYGONS are closed figures that have straight sides.

A **triangle** has 3 sides:

A **QUADRILATERAL** has 4 sides:

A **rectangle** is a type of quadrilateral:

A **parallelogram** is a type of quadrilateral:

A **pentagon** has 5 sides:

A **hexagon** has 6 sides:

An **octagon** has 8 sides:

ANGLES

There are **90°** in a corner:

There are **180°** in a triangle: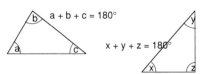

There are **180°** in a half circle:

There are **360°** in a full circle:

SIMPLE FRACTIONS FOR PERCENTS

$50\% = \frac{1}{2}$ $25\% = \frac{1}{4}$ $75\% = \frac{3}{4}$

$20\% = \frac{1}{5}$ $40\% = \frac{2}{5}$ $60\% = \frac{3}{5}$ $80\% = \frac{4}{5}$

$10\% = \frac{1}{10}$ $30\% = \frac{3}{10}$ $70\% = \frac{7}{10}$ $90\% = \frac{9}{10}$

EQUATIONS

Geometry

A = area   **b** = base   **C** = circumference   **d** = diameter
h = height   **P** = perimeter   **π** = pi (3.14)   **r** = radius   **V** = volume

  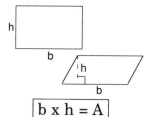 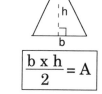

$\pi \times d = C$ $\pi \times r \times r = A$ $b \times h = A$ $\frac{b \times h}{2} = A$

Area of b × h = V $\frac{\text{Area of } b \times h}{3} = V$

Simple machines

d = distance   **f** = force   **ft-lb** = foot-pounds   **w** = work

$f \times d = f \times d$ (in = out) $f \times d = w$

ABBREVIATIONS

U.S. SYSTEM   **METRIC SYSTEM**

CAPACITY

teaspoons = tsp   milliliters = ml
tablespoons = tbsp   centiliters = cl
cups = c   liters = l
pints = pt   kiloliter = kl
quarts = qt
gallons = gal

LENGTH

inches = in   centimeters = cm
feet = ft   meters = m
yards = yd   kilometers = km
miles = mi

WEIGHT

ounces = oz   milligrams = mg
pounds = lb   grams = g
tons = t   kilograms = kg

RATE | TIME | SYMBOLS

miles per hour = mph   seconds = sec   weeks = wk   percent = %
                         minutes = min   months = mo   degrees = °
                         hours = hr   years = yr   number = #
                         days = d   pi = π

MONEY | AREA | VOLUME

dollars = $ square inches = sq in   cubic feet = cu ft
cents = ¢   square centimeters = sq cm   cubic meters = cu m